Henry Irwin Jenkinson

Jenkinson's Practical Guide to Carlisle, Gilsland, Roman Wall, and Neighbourhood

Henry Irwin Jenkinson

Jenkinson's Practical Guide to Carlisle, Gilsland, Roman Wall, and Neighbourhood

ISBN/EAN: 9783744692335

Printed in Europe, USA, Canada, Australia, Japan

Cover: Foto ©Thomas Meinert / pixelio.de

More available books at **www.hansebooks.com**

JENKINSON'S

PRACTICAL GUIDE

TO

,E, GILSLAND, ROMAN WALL, ND NEIGHBOURHOOD.

BY

ENRY IRWIN JENKINSON,
ROYAL GEOGRAPHICAL AND ROYAL HISTORICAL SOCIETIES, AND
'ICAL GUIDE TO THE ENGLISH LAKE DISTRICT;' 'PRACTICAL GUIDE
ISLE OF MAN;' AND 'EPITOME OF LOCKHART'S LIFE OF
SIR WALTER SCOTT.'

VITH MAP AND FRONTISPIECE.

LONDON:
ΓANFORD, 55, CHARING CROSS, S.W.
—
1875.

PREFACE.

The author hopes that this little book, though treating of a district comparatively unknown beyond the border counties, will prove a not unworthy companion of his Guides to the Lake District, and the Isle of Man, which have been so favourably received by the public. He has striven to make it useful, entertaining, and instructive; and it has been his constant endeavour to be concise and accurate. The historical facts have been gleaned from various sources, and the guiding matter is the result of a personal visit to every place mentioned.

A chapter describing a walk along the whole length of the Roman Wall, from the west to the east coast, will, no doubt, be considered a welcome addition; for it will not only enable the reader to gain a knowledge of the geography of the district, and the situation of the principal places of interest on the route, but it will also give him a tolerably accurate idea of the remains of that great work, which has been denominated "the noblest monument of Roman power in Europe."

Many tourists upon visiting a new district miss many of the pleasures that might be derived from a knowledge of its topography and associations, and return to their homes with the uncomfortable feeling that they are almost as ignorant of the neighbourhood as they were before visiting it. With this book in his possession the traveller will, we hope, be enabled to visit the many places of interest around Carlisle and Gilsland without asking a single question, and to feel as though he had obtained the companionship of a friend thoroughly conversant with the neighbourhood.

The author takes this opportunity of thanking the numerous gentlemen who have rendered him assistance, and especially the Reverend Adam Wright, Vicar of Gilsland; Richard S. Ferguson, Esq., M.A., Carlisle; Charles J. Ferguson, Esq., Carlisle; and John Clark, Esq., Haltwhistle.

Being anxious to make the book as nearly perfect as possible, the author desires the co-operation of his readers, and will be glad of any suggestions. All letters to be addressed to Henry Irwin Jenkinson, Keswick, Cumberland.

CONTENTS.

	PAGE
Introduction	vii

CARLISLE SECTION.

Carlisle	1
Carlisle Cathedral	20
Carlisle Castle	25
Rose Castle, and the See of Carlisle	29
The Abbey of Holme Cultram	33
Gretna Green	40
Netherby	43
Corby Castle, and Wetheral Priory	46
The Nunnery	51
Brampton	52
Talkin Tarn	54
The River Gelt, and the Written Crag	56

GILSLAND SECTION.

Gilsland	59
Gilsland Church	63
The Sulphur Well	65
The Popping Stone	68
The Chalybeate Well	70
The Cramel Linn Waterfall	72
Temple Heap	74
Mumps Hall, and Upper Denton Church	75
The Roman Wall between the Poltross and the Irthing	79
Birdoswald and Coome Crags	80
Gilsland to Lanercost Priory and Naworth, *via* Birdoswald and Coome Crags; and back by Upper Denton Church	86
Gilsland to Triermain Castle, Askerton Castle, and Bewcastle	104
Ascent of Tindale Fell	116

CONTENTS.

	PAGE
A Walk to Thirlwall Castle..	117
Gilsland to Carvoran	118
Gilsland to Haltwhistle, and thence to Bellister, Featherstone, Blenkinsop, and Thirlwall Castles	119
Glen Dhu	132
Gilsland to the Northumberland Lakes, and to Housesteads	133
A Walk along the Roman Wall, over the Nine Nicks of Thirlwall	136
Gilsland to Bardon Mill, and thence to Chesterholm and Housesteads..	138
Willimontswyke Castle, the birthplace of Bishop Ridley, the Martyr	141
Haydon Bridge, the birthplace of John Martin, the Artist	145
Langley Castle	151
Alston, and Allendale Town..	152
Staward-le-Peel, and the River Allen	160
Hexham	161
Dilston Castle ..	167

ROMAN WALL SECTION.

A Walk along the Roman Wall, from Coast to Coast .. 172

Local Names	213
Geology	225
Mineralogy	241
Botany	264
Wild Flowers	270
Ferns	281
Grasses	285
Mosses	286
Fungi	295
Butterflies	297
Birds	299
INDEX	301

INTRODUCTION.

The district traversed by the Newcastle and Carlisle section of the North-Eastern Railway is little known, and generally considered bleak and barren border land; but it contains many places of great historical interest, and many lovely bits of scenery.

It is full of romantic associations, and was a favourite haunt of Sir Walter Scott in those happy days between youth and manhood, when he was preparing himself, though perhaps unconsciously, for the production of his imperishable works of poetry and romance. Having written 'Waverley,' and there described the scenes of his boyish ramblings in Scotland, and founded the story on tales which had been related to him by old people to please his youthful fancy and love of wonder; he, in his next work, 'Guy Mannering,' turned to the days of his youth, and to the border country where he had rambled so often, and where, at Gilsland, he at last in one of his excursions met and wooed Miss Carpenter, to whom six months afterwards he was married at Carlisle.

The ancient Romans, too, have greatly added to the interest of this district, by building across from sea to sea that immense wall, many traces of which are still to be met with, and will be examined with wonder and curiosity, not only by the antiquary, but by all who take an interest in Roman and British history.

Full of interest, too, was this district during the Middle Ages, of which the modern traveller is constantly reminded as he comes upon the picturesque ruins of abbeys, castles, and other strongholds reared during those lawless and unsettled times. These ruins present, it is scarcely necessary to say, special objects of attraction for the ordinary tourist, as well as for the artist and the antiquary.

PRACTICAL GUIDE
TO
CARLISLE, GILSLAND, ROMAN WALL,
AND NEIGHBOURHOOD.

CARLISLE SECTION.

CARLISLE.

THE traveller will be liable to disappointment who visits Carlisle, expecting to find an antique border city, where, as in some towns, every street and almost every house and stone bespeak a history. Instead of dirty alleys, darkened by picturesque overhanging gables of wood, clay, and laths, there are now clean wide streets, with modern buildings of stone and brick, and hardly the vestige of an edifice interesting to the historian and the antiquary. Of course we except the Castle, which still proudly overlooks the city; and the Cathedral, now but little more than half its original size, and only of the third rank, but well worth a visit for its Gothic and Norman architecture, and containing a window said to be unequalled for elegance by any other in Great Britain.

The city walls—of which the whole of the west side still remains, though concealed in many places by houses—were probably commenced in the reign of William Rufus, about the end of the eleventh century, and were 1¼ miles in extent, enclosing a triangular space, and containing three gates, leading respectively to the south, west, and north, and in consequence denominated the English, Irish, and Scotch gates. A sallyport also existed in the west wall; it was closed about fifty years ago, but the arch can be seen from the yard of the city police station. The English gate was also sometimes called Botchergate, from one of the first inhabitants, a Fleming, called Bocharda Fleming, who had a grange hard by for pro-

B

visioning his house at Carlisle; and the road or street leading to the grange went by the name of Botchergate. The Flemings afterwards left, and went to Anglesey, but the grange or village was called Bocherby, and the name was given to a family who resided there. In like manner the Scotch gate was called Richardgate, because it guarded the road so called leading towards the grange or village of Rickerby, originally the property of one Richard. The Irish gate was likewise known as the Caldewgate, as it led to the river Caldew. The English gate, the main entrance to the city, was connected with a fortress called the Citadel, which was protected by a strong tower at each side, with guns mounted in several tiers, placed so as effectually to sweep every approach from the London road, and another battery pointed directly up English Street to overawe the citizens. Henry VIII. is said to have built the Citadel with material taken from the Abbey and Cathedral, after the dissolution of monasteries; but it would appear to have been erected before his reign, for it was in a dilapidated condition and required repairing in Queen Elizabeth's time, which could hardly have been the case had Henry built it. On the site of the Citadel have been erected the courts of justice for the county; and the English gate, which stood west of the Citadel, is now covered by the gaol; an Act of Parliament having been obtained in 1807 enabling the king to grant the city walls to the magistrates for that purpose.

Until the middle of the last century Carlisle had kept up the appearance of a formidable place; sentries were stationed at each of the gates, at the commanding officer's house, the Castle, &c.; and the gates were shut and locked every night with much military parade; morning and evening guns were fired as a signal when to open and shut the garrison gates, and pieces of ordnance were placed upon the turrets situated in different parts of the fortification. Seldom in ancient days were the gates without the adornment of heads of rebels. At one time, we are told, one of the heads was that of a comely youth with yellow hair, to look at which there came every morning at sunrise, and every evening at sunset, a young and beautiful lady. It is said that on a Highland regiment passing southward, after the rebellion of 1745, they avoided entering the city by the Scotch gate, on which the grim and ghastly heads were exhibited.

The city does not appear to have been large, for in 1685 it contained a population of only 2000; in 1763, 4158; in 1780, 6299; in 1787, 7677; in 1796, 8516; in 1801, 10,221; and in 1871 these numbers had increased to 33,881.

Though standing on the south bank of the river Eden, between the two smaller streams, Caldew and Petteril, and only a short distance from where the three united waters enter the Solway Firth, it is yet too far away from the sea, and the estuary is too full of shifting sandbanks to allow of the city being approached by ships of even the smallest burden. In consequence of its having had no shipping and manufactures, and merely deriving its importance from being a fortress on the borders between England and Scotland, and on the highway between the two countries, its rate of progression was extremely slow. In the middle of the last century there were only four private carriages kept in the city, certainly not many for a place that gave the title to an earl, that claimed to be the capital of Cumberland, and the seat of a bishopric.

The rebellion of 1745 having finally brought to a close centuries of wars and reprisals between the two countries, Carlisle was dismantled and lost its warlike appearance; but it soon began to enter on a more prosperous future. For the first time in its existence it became possible for wheeled conveyances to travel, by the new military road, to Newcastle, during the whole of the year. Richard Ferguson availed himself of this to start a business in cotton in the rooms under the Town Hall. Some Hamburgh merchants arrived, and established a woollen manufactory, and soon other similar works for linen and cotton, and for calico printing, were in progress; and the place also became noted for the manufacture of hats, whips, and fish-hooks. At the present time there are six, and there will shortly be seven, lines of railway concentrating at Carlisle, and with increasing means of communication the trade of the city has rapidly increased. Strangers should visit the far-famed biscuit manufactories of Messrs. Carr, in Caldewgate; an order for admission being obtained at their establishment near the railway station. Carlisle ales are largely exported to Australia by Messrs. Iredale, and by the Old Brewery Company. There are several cotton manufactories, such as those of Messrs. Slater, and Peter Dixon and Son (Limited). At Cummersdale, 3 miles from Carlisle, the Daltons have a large cotton mill, and Messrs. Lowthian, Fairlie and Co., large dye works, as well as an establishment at Carlisle. Messrs. MacAlpin have large print works there and nearer the city. At Holm Head, on the Caldew, are the extensive bleaching works of Messrs. Ferguson; the senior partner of the firm represents Carlisle in Parliament. There are several foundries in Carlisle, and its ancient fame for fish-hooks still survives. Messrs. Carrick's manufactory for hats is well worth a visit; also the extensive nursery grounds of Little and Ballantyne, the Queen's seedsmen, situated at Knowefield, near Stanwix, one mile from Carlisle. These grounds occupy above 100 acres under nursery and seed crops, and are beautifully laid out and kept in first-rate order by the present proprietors, Messrs. Smith and Watt, who purchased the business some years ago, and which they still carry on under the name of the old firm. These nurseries are well known, not only in this country, but on the Continent, and in America and Canada, where they have a business connection for the supply of young forest trees, shrubs, fruit trees, &c., which are grown in large quantities for this, as well as their large home trade. The soil of these nurseries is remarkably well suited for the growth of roses and fruit trees, and during the summer months when there are many thousand roses in bloom, it is difficult to conceive a more beautiful sight.

Carlisle has received many royal grants, and been invested with great privileges by different monarchs, but nearly all the original charters have been consumed by the fires that have so frequently devastated the city. It is not known when the first incorporation of the burgesses took place, or what was the original constitution; but it is on record that a charter granted by Henry II. was burnt by the Scots and recited and confirmed by Henry III. Great part of the city having again suffered by an accidental fire, the records were a second time destroyed; and again copied verbatim from the enrollment in Chancery, and confirmed by Edward I. A grant by Edward III. recites special privileges, owing to the city being on the frontiers of Scotland, well situated for refuge and defence, subject to the incursions of the Scots, and in commiseration of the late plague and devastations of the enemy; and from it we learn that from time immemorial the city had been governed by a mayor, bailiffs, and coroners. Charters of confirmation were granted by almost every king, until the reign of Charles I., when slight alterations were made as to the manner of electing the different officers; it being decided that the body corporate should consist of a mayor, eleven aldermen, two bailiffs, two coroners, and twenty-four capital citizens or common council. The guilds of Carlisle have played an important part in its municipal history. Those who wish to understand their connection with the corporation must study Luders on Election Cases, and Merewether and Coleridge on Corporations.

The city sends two members to Parliament, and was first represented in 1295, in the reign of Edward I. At one time the electors were confined to the freemen of the city, and on a dispute in the House of Commons in 1711, it was declared that the sons of burgesses born after their fathers' freedom, and persons serving seven years' apprenticeship within the city, have a right to be made free. The exciting history of the Carlisle elections, and the fights between the "Blues" and the "Yellows," has been told by Mr. R. S. Ferguson, in his book called 'The Cumberland and Westmorland M.P.'s from the Restoration to the Reform Bill.'

The assizes for the county are held in the city, in the castellated tower-like buildings situated opposite the railway station, and on the site of the ancient Citadel. The eastern tower is the Nisi Prius or Civil Court; and the western, the Crown or Criminal Court. A subterranean passage leads direct from the prisoners' dock to the gaol, which is said to occupy the site of a house of Dominican Friars, and where many Roman remains have been discovered. The embattled wall of the prison fronts the street. In 1436, in the reign of Henry VI., an Act of Parliament was passed which enacts as follows : "Whereas by a statute made in the time of King Richard II. it was ordained that the justices assigned or to be assigned to take assizes and deliver gaols shall hold their sessions in the principal and chief town of every county, that is to say, where the shire courts of the counties heretofore were and hereafter shall be holden ; our lord the king willing the same statute to be observed and kept in the county of Cumberland, considering that the city of Carlisle is the principal and chief city and town of the said county, and in which the shire court of the same county hath been holden before this time, hath granted and ordained by the authority of the same parliament, that the session of the justices to take assizes and to deliver gaols in the county of Cumberland, be holden in time of peace and truce in the said city of Carlisle, and in none other place within the same county, as it hath been used and accustomed of old time."

Carlisle formerly consisted of only two parishes, namely, St. Mary's and St. Cuthbert's, each of which extended far without the city walls, and was thus divided into St. Mary Within, St. Mary Without, St. Cuthbert Within, and St. Cuthbert Without. The parish church of St. Mary's was formerly in the nave of the Cathedral, open to the rest of the building, and service was held at 9 A.M. to avoid clashing with the Cathedral service at 11 A.M. About the beginning of the century the nave was walled off from the Cathedral. Recently the nave has been thrown into the Cathedral, and a new church erected close by for the parish of St. Mary. Many strangers visit the church to see the entry in the register of the marriage of Miss Carpenter and Walter Scott. St. Cuthbert's Church was built about 100 years ago, and occupies the site of an old church which replaced one still older. It contains a monument (bust) to the Rev. John Fawcett, who was for more than half a century incumbent of the parish, and an eminent Low Church leader; a fine painted window by Ward and Hughes, presented by Joseph Ferguson, Esq., and representing scenes from the life of St. Paul; monuments to the great Oriental scholar Joseph Dacre Carlyle, to the Admiral Mounsey who captured the 'Bon Accord' sloop of war, and to many local families. Christ and Trinity churches were erected some forty years ago, and St. James', St. John's, St. Stephen's, and St. Paul's, within the last few years. St. Stephen's was built at the expense of Baroness Burdett-Coutts during the episcopate of Bishop Waldegrave.

The Society of Friends have always, since the time of George Fox's visit to Carlisle and imprisonment there in 1653, had a meeting-house in Carlisle; it is in Fisher Street, and at the bottom of that street is their disused burial-ground, a grass plot without any monuments. Here sleeps William Penn's friend Thomas Story, of Justice Town, near Carlisle, Keeper of the Great Seal and Master of the Rolls of Pennsylvania. The history of the Society of Friends in Cumberland is very interesting, and will be found in a little book called 'Early Cumberland and Westmorland Friends,' by R. S. Ferguson, and published by Thurnam and Co., of Carlisle. The Catholic Church of SS. Mary and Joseph is in Chapel Street, near Lowther Street. It was opened in 1824 by the exertions of the Rev. Joseph Marshall, who laboured in Carlisle from 1800 to 1850. The Presbyterian Church (Scotch) in connection with the Church of Scotland is also in Chapel Street. The United Presbyterian Church is in Fisher Street; this congregation has existed since at least 1707. The Wesleyan Chapel is also in Fisher Street, and a Wesleyan congregation has existed in Carlisle since 1767. The Congregational Church, Lowther Street, was built in 1843, and the one in Charlotte Street in 1860. The Primitive Methodist and the Evangelical Union chapels are in Cecil Street.

Carlisle possesses few public buildings, and its Town Hall is poor and uninteresting; near it, in the Green Market, stands an old timbered overhanging building; this is the Guildhall, known also as Redness Hall, where on certain days the guilds do meet and hold high festival. In Abbey Street is Tullie House, built by the Tullies circa 1688; and in Fisher Street is Stanwix House, more famous in electioneering records as Mushroom Hall, built by the Stanwixes. Both these Carlisle families, the Tullies and the Stanwixes, the first rich in Church dignitaries, the second in famed generals, are now extinct. The house in English Street, partly occupied by the Clydesdale Bank, was the residence of the Earls of Egremont, and lodged Prince Charlie in 1745. Cromwell put up at a house in English Street, now destroyed to make way for Todd's drug shop. In the King's Arms Lane, between Scotch Street and Lowther Street, is an old Edwardian house, where Judge Jeffries once lodged; it is now a bacon store. The old cockpit still stands up a court in Lowther Street, just north of the end of Bank Street. In 1874, the Victoria Hall was built by a limited liability company. It is a very large handsome room, situated in Lowther Street, and used as a theatre and for lectures and other public meetings.

The open space, now the Market-place,* was once all

* The corporation have recently purchased a considerable property in Fisher Street from Lord Lonsdale, with the view of erecting a new Corn Exchange and Market Hall, &c., the want of which has been long felt, and which will do away with the old-fashioned method of having the grain exposed for sale in sample bags ranged along English Street.

covered with buildings : wooden shambles, a pillory, and the main guard of the city, afterwards made into a fish market, and since demolished. The Convent of the Grey Friars occupied all the space east of English Street, now cut through by Devonshire Street. The Black Friars occupied some of the ground upon which stands the gaol, and the whole or part of their buildings formed the old gaol that made way for the present one.

On the west walls is the Cathedral or Grammar School, situate in ground given to the Priory of Carlisle by Thomas de Eglesfield, the founder of Queen's College, Oxford. Near the Grammar School is a very curious old building, the Tithe Barn of the Priory of Carlisle, erected by Prior Gondibour some 400 years ago; his initials are on a shield on its west end. The roof is remarkable for the immense amount of oak timber it contains ; the building is internally and externally disfigured in every way, but its restoration is contemplated. On the north side it was formerly open to the Priory grounds.

No visitor to Carlisle should omit to walk down Scotch Street and Rickergate, and see " the Bridges," as the noble bridge which crosses the Eden to Stanwix is called, in memory of the day when Eden ran in two channels. A charming variety of country paths here incite to a stroll. The visitor can, on the south side of the river, cross the Weavers' Bank and wend his way under the Castle on a walk called the Castle Banks, both made fifty years ago by the distressed weavers of the city, who were found employment in making walks around Carlisle. The holme through which the Weavers' Bank passes was once the Battail Holme, or fertile holme, and beyond it, bounded by the railway and the river, are the Sauceries (Salieceta, willow beds), where the Carlisle children roll their Easter eggs. Still south of the river, but east of the bridge, a bank conducts the visitor to the Swifts, or Carlisle racecourse. If he care to cross the river to its north bank, he can wander eastward into the Rickerby Holmes and Rickerby Park, the residence of G. H. Head, Esq., which forms a conspicuous object in the view. If he turn westward through the iron wicket at the end of the bridge, a broad path will conduct him past the cricket field and Hyssop Well, between the path and the river, where the Roman wall crossed the Eden, to Etterby Scars and the picturesque villa of Ann's Hill.

CARLISLE. 9

The large building visible on the high ground past the Castle is the Cumberland Infirmary, a magnificent building, making up 100 beds for in-patients, and relieving also annually many hundred out-patients. It has recently been enlarged from the designs of Messrs. Cory and Ferguson, of Carlisle, and is replete with every contrivance known to modern science. The road to it is by Abbey Street and Caldewgate.

Harraby Hill, the Gallows Hill so often mentioned in border story, is an eminence just on the south of Carlisle, through which the London road is cut. The gallows stood on its north side; a workhouse now occupies the top. The whole of this vicinity is thought to have been one great Roman burial-ground, through which the great Roman road to York ran. Criminals were also hung near the river Eden, and Corporation Road runs through the Hangman's Close. When hung they were buried in the north-east corner of the Cathedral burial-ground, a spot noticeable for its lack of tombstones.

Carlisle is well provided with hotels. The principal are the County, close to the Citadel Station; the Bush, in English Street; the Crown and Mitre, near the Marketplace. There are also the Red Lion, Caledonian, City Temperance, and numerous other very good houses.

The two curious figures of soldiers in the County Hotel represent soldiers of the 2nd or Queen's Foot. They were a Tangiers regiment, famous as "Kirk's lambs." See the lamb on their caps. The figures are relics of 1745.

Carlisle is generally thought to have been the Roman station of Luguvallium; but although it is highly probable that it was the site of a station, we think antiquaries are wrong in considering it as Luguvallium, for that name is not mentioned in the Notitia as one of the stations on the line of the wall, and any station here would clearly be on the line of the wall, for that barrier crossed the river Eden close to the present castle, but now no portion of it exists in the neighbourhood.* Dr. Todd in his MS. history of Carlisle, written in 1685, says: "Whether in ancient times the city was seated in

* We are aware that against this opinion we have arrayed many of the learned in antiquarian lore; but after considering all that they advance, we still believe that there would be a garrisoned station at Carlisle, and that it would be mentioned in the Notitia.

the same place as it is at this day is a question amongst geographers, some being of opinion that Luguvallium, its old name, was placed about 8 miles westward in the way to Cockermouth, where are now visible the ruins of a large town or city, built of stones, which the country people call 'Old Carlisle' to this day." When digging amongst the foundations of the city of Carlisle, Roman remains have at various times been found. Malmesbury, Leland, and others mention a spacious hall with arched stonework, which was in a good state of preservation when discovered in the time of William Rufus, but now not a vestige of the work remains, and even its site is totally forgotten. It is said to have had on its front the words Marii Victoriæ, and is thought to have been erected in honour of a Roman general or British prince of the name of Marius. Others have thought the inscription must have been Marti Victori, and that the building was dedicated to Mars, the God of War. Camden mentions two Roman inscribed stones he found in the city. In 1743 a Roman *fibula* and a medal of the reign of Trajan, and a few years later two altars, were discovered. Stukeley, writing in 1725, says: "Fragments of squared stones appear in every quarter of the city, and several square wells of Roman workmanship. At the present day, whenever an excavation is made, articles of Roman make are turned up." Dr. Bruce tells us that in 1854, during the formation of the city sewers, Samian ware, coins, and various bronze articles were found in great quantities. Also, in 1860, a valuable collection of coins and a masonic gold chain, &c., were found by the men making a new railway, near the spot where the Roman wall rose from the river Eden.

We have no certain history of Carlisle until the time of the Norman Conquest. Bede, however, tells us that in 685, Egfrid, King of Northumberland, who then held sway over Cumberland and most of England north of the Humber, granted the city of Carlisle, then called Luol or Caerluel, with land 15 miles about it, to St. Cuthbert, Bishop of Lindisfarn, to be held by him and his successors as part of their Episcopal possessions. St. Cuthbert visited the place, and "was carried by the townspeople to see their walls, and a fountain or well, of admirable workmanship, constructed by the Romans." Several writers tell us that St. Cuthbert founded here a convent of monks, a school, and an abbey of nuns; but from Bede's life of that holy man it seems as if the monastery had been in existence before he arrived. Whilst St. Cuthbert was at Carlisle, Egfrid, the King of Northumberland, was defeated and slain in battle by the Picts, and the Saint at the time the battle was fought declared to those about him the unfortunate event. Bede relates that St. Cuthbert foretold the tragical end of Egfrid the year before it happened, to the King's sister, Elfled, who was abbess of the convent at Carlisle, and had come to visit Cuthbert; who, attended by some of the brethren at Lindisfarn, met her in the Isle of Coquet, which was also at that time a residence of monks. It is highly probable that a religious house did in reality exist at Carlisle during the dark unsettled period of the Saxon occupation, and that it would be a prey to the Norsemen and Vikings who infested our coast during the ninth and tenth centuries. Tradition tells us that here was a city in which resided some kings of Cumberland, and that it was burnt by the Danes, and then remained for 200 years utterly overthrown and desolate until King William II., surnamed Rufus, when returning this route from Alnwick in Northumberland, where he had concluded a treaty of peace with the King of Scotland, observed the ruins, and being pleased with the situation, decided to build a castle and city as a barrier against the Scots on the western frontier, in the same manner as he had done at Newcastle on the eastern coast. One Walter, a Norman, had charge of the undertaking, and he was assisted by Flemish artificers, a colony of whom were settled here by Rufus, but were removed soon afterwards to North Wales and the Isle of Anglesey. The place was then colonized by south country people from the New Forest, who were directed to cultivate the neighbouring lands, and to teach the natives the art of rendering the fertility of the soil conducive to their subsistence.

There has been much dispute amongst the learned as to the original name of the city. Old historians give the spelling in many different ways, such as Carlol, Carliol, Carlovil, Kaarluil, Kaarlion, Kaarluol, Karloil, and Carlisle, which last came to be regularly adopted after it appeared in the patent of the Earl of Carlisle in 1660. It appears to us that the most probable origin of the name is very simple and requires little research. In the

Cathedral is a stone, bearing the following Runic inscription:

"Tolfinn hraita at Ulfhara this stain";

i. e.:

"Tolfin" (or Dolfin) "inscribed this stone in memory of Ulfhar" (or Ulf).

Now Ulf, or Lyulph, appears to have been the name of more than one person of distinction in these northern parts of England in Saxon times. We find one granting lands to the cathedral at York in token of which he left a drinking horn that is still preserved. Ullswater (Ulfswater), a lake in Cumberland, must have been in possession of one named Ulf. If, as appears from the Runic stone, a Lyulph lived in Carlisle, it is not at all unlikely that the very individual this commemorated was a person of distinction, and gave his name to the place; and Caer being the British word for city, we have Caer Lyulph or Lyulph's city, which, by an easy transition, has in modern times been changed into Carlisle.

After the death of William Rufus, his brother, King Henry I., proceeded with the building of the city, and when all was completed, including the abbey and cathedral, Walter, who had superintended the work, became the first prior of the monastery, and a bishopric was also established.

In Stephen's reign, David, King of Scotland, favouring the cause of Matilda and her son Henry, entered England and took possession of Carlisle; and Stephen then bought him over to his side by the cession of the city and the whole county of Cumberland. In 1138, war being again renewed, the Scotch king made the city his place of retreat after his defeat at the *battle of the Standard*, and here he received the Pope's legate, by whose influence all the women who had been taken captive were set at liberty. The war just concluded having been conducted with savage barbarity, the legate got the Scotch leaders to give a solemn promise that in future incursions they would spare the churches, and withhold their swords from the aged, from women and infants. David made the city his home for some time, holding great state; and the English Prince Henry paid him a visit in order to receive from him the honour of knighthood, according to the custom of those times; and here, in 1153, the Scotch king breathed his last.

Soon after the death of Stephen, Henry II. demanded the restitution of Cumberland from David's son Malcolm, and in 1158 he had an interview with the Scotch monarch in this city. The demand was reluctantly acceded to, and Carlisle reverted to the English crown. In the year 1173, William, the successor of Malcolm to the throne of Scotland, made a fruitless attack on Carlisle, and in the next year he returned and commenced a regular siege with an army of 80,000 men. The garrison, under the command of Robert de Vaux, was reduced to great distress, and would probably have surrendered, had the operations continued; but William, having been made prisoner at Alnwick, and the Scots affairs rendered desperate by other disastrous events, the war terminated.

In the year 1200, William, King of Scotland, demanded of King John of England the county of Cumberland as his hereditary patrimony; and coming with an army, besieged Carlisle and took it, but could not reduce the castle. The city was soon afterwards re-possessed by the English, and underwent another siege with the like success in the year 1216.

Edward I., in consequence of his Scotch expeditions, resided frequently in Carlisle, and more than once he summoned his parliament to meet him there. In 1296 a Scotch army again burnt the suburbs and attempted to storm the city, but were frustrated in their enterprise by the bravery of the inhabitants. Even the fair sex, on this occasion, exerted an uncommon degree of spirit; pouring boiling water from the walls on the heads of their assailants, and otherwise distinguishing themselves by fearless and intrepid conduct. Seven years after this event the city was accidentally set on fire, and half of it became a prey to the flames. The year 1307 will be ever memorable in the annals of the city, from the parliament that met here on the 20th of January, and continued sitting till the Palm Sunday following, during which period several important acts were passed and laws made to promote the expedition which the king was meditating against the Scots. Edward remained at Carlisle till the 28th of June, and then proceeded to his army which was encamped a few miles distant, on Burgh Marsh. He there succumbed to a long illness, and died in his camp, July 7th, thus terminating a most active and brilliant reign.

In 1316, the ninth year of the reign of Edward II., and

two years after the battle of Bannockburn, Carlisle was besieged by Robert Bruce, King of Scotland, who carried on the assaults for ten days, and erected warlike engines, but found his whole force insufficient to take the city, and was at length obliged to make a precipitate retreat, being hotly pursued by the English, who made some of the Scottish leaders prisoners.

In the year 1322, Andrew de Harcla, governor and first Earl of Carlisle, and Lord Warden of the Western Marches, was accused of treason. He was eminently brave, and had rendered great service to his country, but owing to the weakness of the English monarch, or from some other cause, he had become dissatisfied, and entered into a secret truce with Robert Bruce. Edward at once sent Anthony, Lord Lucy, to arrest him. Having dispersed his party in the city to prevent suspicion, Lord Lucy, with a few attendants, entered the castle as if on general business. His principal associates in the enterprise were Sir Hugh de Louther, Sir Richard de Denton, and Sir Hugh de Moriceby, with four esquires in arms, and a small party of attendants to whom the design had been communicated. A few men having been left, as though carelessly loitering, near each gate, the four chiefs proceeded to the innermost parts of the fortress, and reached the Earl's apartment unmolested. They found the Earl seated, and wholly unsuspicious of attack, till Lord Lucy informed him that he must either surrender or instantly defend himself. A cry of treason immediately echoed through the castle, and the keeper of the inner gate prepared to shut it, but was instantly slain by Sir Richard Denton. The watchword being given, the parties formed into bodies, took possession of the gates and avenues, and the Earl, with the whole garrison, surrendered without further bloodshed. The King being informed of this while at Knaresborough, appointed five commissioners, having the Earl of Kent at their head, to repair to Carlisle, and there to degrade, and give sentence against Harcla for his crimes. The King sent them a schedule which directed the judgment they were to give, and in which it is affirmed that Harcla had gone to Robert Bruce, and bound himself by oath and writing, to maintain to him and his heirs, the kingdom of Scotland against all men. It had been agreed between them that Bruce should name six men, and Harcla the like number, who were to settle all the great affairs of Scotland and England; and to maintain this alliance, Harcla had

traitorously caused Edward's subjects to swear. After
degradation from his earldom and knighthood, by being
ungirt of his sword, and having his golden spurs cut off
from his heels, he was to be drawn and hanged; his heart
and entrails to be torn out, burnt, the ashes cast to the
wind, and the body beheaded and quartered; the head
to be set upon London Bridge, and the quarters in the
most conspicuous places of Carlisle, Newcastle, York, and
Salop. It is related that Harcla aspired to marry a sister
of Robert Bruce. He suffered in the ordinary place of
execution at Carlisle with great fortitude, affirming to the
end that in his transactions with the King of Scotland he
had meant no hurt to his own king or country. Immediately he was seized some of the family repaired with all
speed to Highhead Castle, to acquaint his brother John,
who immediately fled into Scotland, and with him Sir
William Blount and many others. After Harcla's degradation the title of Earl of Carlisle does not appear to have
been revived for many centuries. There was one Hay, Earl
of Carlisle, in the time of Charles I. On the restoration
of King Charles II., Charles Howard, son of Sir William
Howard, was created Lord Dacre of Gilsland, Viscount
Howard of Morpeth, and Earl of Carlisle, in reward for his
having been highly instrumental in forwarding the cause
of the restoration.

During the reign of Edward III. Carlisle was frequently
besieged by the Scots. In 1338 the suburbs were burnt,
but the city held out. Four years after this, an army
under the command of Sir William Douglas made another
incursion and burnt Carlisle, and also the town of Penrith
and other places, but were afterwards pursued and overcome by the English under Lord Lucy. Again Cumberland suffered like devastation in 1380, when Richard II.
was on the throne of England. The country was laid
waste as far as Penrith, which place was attacked on a
market day, and the Scots returned with large booty and
4000 head of cattle, or, as some historians say, 40,000.
They had designed to attack Carlisle, but finding it well
manned they durst not make the attempt, and some of the
citizens then sallied out and killed many of the stragglers.

A quaint historian tells us that "about four years afterwards, as soon as they had eaten their stolen provisions,
the Scots again invaded Cumberland, burnt part of
Penrith, lay siege to Carlisle, and threw fire into it, which
consumed to ashes one whole street, and they had in all

probability taken the city, but that they were frightened away in the following miraculous manner. When they had put the citizens to great consternation, and were ready to make an assault, there appeared a woman to them, and told them that the King of England, with a puissant army, was coming upon them; they looking about, saw the English banner and a vast army advancing towards them, as they supposed, whereupon they left their ladders and engines at the wall, and took to their heels for security, never looking behind them till they came into their own country. This woman was then supposed to be the Blessed Virgin Mary, the Patroness of the city, who upon other occasions had often appeared to the citizens and inhabitants: and such religious esteem has been towards the Blessed Virgin Mary by the citizens in old times, that her impress, with our Saviour in her arms, is the public seal of the Corporation to this day A.D. 1397."

The wealth of the city was so much reduced by these repeated outrages, that Edward IV. remitted to the inhabitants one-half of the ancient annual rent of eighty pounds paid to the Crown, and also granted them the lordship of the royal fisheries at Carlisle.

During Aske's rebellion in the reign of Henry VIII. the city was besieged by 8000 of the insurgents, under the command of Musgrave and Tilby; but they were repulsed by the garrison, and had their retreat more fatally intercepted by the Duke of Norfolk, who ordered all the leaders, with about seventy other persons, to immediate execution; their bodies were afterwards hung on Carlisle walls.

In the reign of Elizabeth, Cumberland was greatly afflicted by a plague, and 1196 of the inhabitants of the city of Carlisle fell victims to its ravages; this number is supposed to have included nearly one-third of all the persons residing within the walls.

During the year 1568, Mary, Queen of Scots, spent two months in the castle at Carlisle. Having fled from her kingdom she landed on the west coast of Cumberland, and after staying some time at Workington Hall, was escorted through Cockermouth to Carlisle, by Mr. (afterwards Sir Richard) Lowther. Here, by orders from Elizabeth, she was treated with due respect; but we also learn from the following graphic letter, written by Sir Francis Knollys to Secretary Cecil, that her movements were closely watched, and that in reality she was looked upon as a prisoner. He says:

"Yesterday, hyr grace went owte at a posterne to walke

on a playing greene toward' Skotland, and we with 24 halberders of mast^r Read's band wth divers gentlemen and other servants waited upon hyr. Where about 20 of her retinue played at footeball before hyr the space of two howers very stronglye, nymbylly, and skilfullye, without any fowle playe offered, the smaleness of theyr balls occasyoning theyr fayr playe. And before yesterdaye since our comyng she went but twyce owt of the towne, once to the like playe at footeball in the same place, and once roode owte a huntyng the hare, she gallopyng so fast uppon everye occasyon, and hyr hool retinue beyng so well horsyd, that we uppon experyence thereoff, dowtyng that uppon a sett cowrse some of hyr frendes owt of Skotland myght invade and assaulte us uppon the sodayne to reskue and take hyr from us, we mean hereafter yff any Scotche ryding pastymes be reqwyred that waye, so motche to feare the indangering of hyr parson by some sodayne invayson of hyr enemyes, that she must hold us excused in that behalfe." Instead of being restored to her kingdom, Mary, as all our readers know, was taken from Carlisle, first to Bolton Castle and then to Fotheringay, and, after spending eighteen years in captivity, was destined to lose her head on the block.

In 1596 Carlisle was the scene of a daring exploit which has been celebrated in Border song, and greatly resembled in character the story already related of the gallant capture of Harcla by Lord Lucy. A noted Scotch freebooter, William Armstrong, whose sobriquet was "*Kinmont Willie,*" having been captured and placed in irons in Carlisle Castle, William Scott, "Lord of Buccleuch," determined to effect his release, and with that object had the castle reconnoitred and scaling ladders prepared. Having assembled 200 horse, Buccleuch crossed the Esk and then the Eden during the night, and drew up his gallant band in a field below the castle. He then led eighty men forward with scaling ladders, which, however, were found to be too short. He, therefore, gave orders to force the postern gates with instruments which had been kept in reserve. A breach was made, the gate secured, and the sentries were seized. The Scots then made their way to the cell of Kinmont, led him forth, and sounded a trumpet as a signal to those without that all was well. Willie saluted the warden and his deputy with a "good night!" The alarm soon

c

spread, drums beat, the bells were set ringing, and a watch-fire blazed from the castle keep. Buccleuch gathered together his men, recrossed the Eden, and once more entered Scotland, two hours before sunrise. Sir Walter Scott relates that a cottage on the roadside between Longtown and Langholm was, in his time, pointed out as the residence of the smith who was employed to knock off Kinmont Willie's irons, after his escape. "Tradition preserves the account of the smith's daughter, then a child, how there was a sair (great) clatter at the door about daybreak, and loud crying for the smith; but her father not being on the alert, Buccleuch himself thrust his lance through the window, which effectually bestirred him. On looking out (the woman continued) she saw in the grey of the morning more gentlemen than she had ever before seen in one place, all on horseback, in armour, and dripping wet; and that Kinmont Willie, who sat woman fashion behind one of them, was the biggest carle she ever saw—and there was much merriment in the company."

The contentions between Charles I. and his Parliament once more involved this city in the horrors of a siege, and the general distress was increased by the calamities of famine. The blockade commenced on the 9th of October, 1644, and continued till the ensuing June, when the place surrendered for the Parliament. During the intermediate time, the wants of the garrison and inhabitants were so great, that not only horses, but even dogs and rats, were eaten; and hemp seed was substituted for bread, till that also was consumed; the city was then given up on honourable terms. A silver coinage of three-shilling pieces, sixpences, and groats took place in the castle during the siege, from the plate of the inhabitants, sent in for that purpose.

After this severe ordeal Carlisle enjoyed a century of repose, and then came the rebellion of 1745, which finally brought to a close the chequered history of the city as a border fortress. Prince Charles Edward, the young Pretender, arrived before its walls on the 9th of November, with an army of 8000 or 9000 men, when on his way from Scotland to the south. The city shut its gates and refused to surrender, although it was defended by only a hundred invalid soldiers, a few militia, and about 400 able-bodied citizens. The Prince left a few regiments to carry on the siege, and marched with his army to Brampton, expecting to give battle to General Wade, who was thought to be on his way from Newcastle to the relief of Carlisle. A message having been received stating that Wade could not come, the city was surrendered on the 15th instant, and the Mayor and Corporation proceeded to Brampton, and on bended knees presented the keys to the young Chevalier. On the 18th the Prince made a triumphant entry into the city, preceded by a hundred pipers, and four days afterwards he left at the head of his army, and marched southwards. After passing Lancaster, Preston, and Manchester, he reached Derby without a check. A council of war was then called, and as two armies were being rapidly formed by Government, it was decided to commence a retreat, and then came disgrace and ruin. On the 18th December, in the depth of winter, the dispirited army crossed the bleak fells of Shap, and were there overtaken by the vanguard of the Government forces, under the command of the Duke of Cumberland. A slight skirmish took place at Clifton, a few miles south of Penrith, and the rebels made good their retreat to Carlisle. Charles left 400 men to defend the castle, and then entered Scotland by crossing the Eden and the Esk, the latter stream being forded breast deep, there being at one time "two thousand of them in the river, and nothing of them to be seen but their heads and shoulders. Holding one another by the neck of the coat, they stemmed the force of the stream, and lost not a man in the passage. The moment they reached the opposite side, the pipes struck up, and they danced reels till they were dry again." The Duke of Cumberland invested the city, and on the 27th opened a six-gun battery of 18-pounders against the castle. Two days afterwards, the rebels displayed a flag of truce, and on the 30th surrendered on terms offered to their acceptance by the Duke, and conceived in these words: "All the terms his Royal Highness will, or can, grant to the rebel garrison of Carlisle, are, that they shall not be put to the sword, but be reserved for the King's pleasure." Scores of the prisoners were tried and executed in Carlisle and elsewhere, and hundreds suffered transportation. Prince Charles was pursued in Scotland, and after wandering about for a time in disguise, he effected his escape to France.

Carlisle Cathedral.

Carlisle Cathedral was begun in the time of William Rufus, and completed in the reign of Henry I. The only portions now remaining of the original building are the lower half of the piers supporting the tower, the principal part of the south transept, and the two eastern bays of the nave. These two bays are the only parts of the nave yet standing, and were used as the parish church until within the last few years. The nave is said to have been eight bays in length, and about 141 feet long, west of the tower: originally the choir was probably much shorter than now, and circular or apsidal at the east window. Mr. Purday, the clerk of the works during the restoration of the cathedral, estimated the choir at about 80 feet long, the tower at 35 feet square, making, with the nave, the total length of the Norman cathedral 256 feet.

Both the interior and exterior of these portions of the original building present the usual characteristics of Norman architecture— the billet, chevron, and zigzag ornaments, the flat buttresses running into the cornice, and large circular pillars carrying plain round arches; the whole having, notwithstanding its stern simplicity, a grand and imposing effect. As is often the case in Norman buildings, the foundations appear to have been bad, a fact which is attested by the shattered walls and broken arches of the central tower, and also by the leaning walls of the nave and transept.

Whatever might be the cause, the edifice failed to give satisfaction, and in 1246 Bishop Silvester de Everdon commenced to rebuild the whole on an enlarged scale, and in accordance with the new and fashionable style of architecture. The work was continued patiently for years. The choir was enlarged both in width and length, the north side being extended twelve feet farther into the churchyard; thus the central lines of the choir and nave do not coincide, and consequently the cathedral has ever since had an unsymmetrical and twisted appearance both within and without. There are various indications that the original intention was to rebuild the nave as well as the choir on this extended plan. One such proof is found in the pillar at the west end of the north aisle which has been rebuilt. It is supposed that by 1292 the choir was finished and roofed, and preparations made for rebuilding the north transept. A most disastrous fire now broke out and destroyed the conventual buildings, part of the north transept, and all the new choir except the side aisle walls. The portions that escaped destruction are fine specimens of early English. "The beautiful but scanty remains," says Mr. Purday, "left us by the fire, are the outside walls of the north and south aisles (with the exception of the eastern bay), the whole of St. Catherine's Chapel, which is in the angle between the south aisle and south transept, and now used as a vestry; and the arch of the west end of the north aisle opening into the transept. The cinquefoil arcade supported by detached pillars under the aisle windows is very beautiful; above the window heads in each bay is a sunk quatrefoil. The central capitals of the windows are carved in extremely beautiful designs, the stone groining is supported on clustered shafts running up the wall with carved capitals in the north aisle."

Soon after the fire the work of restoration was commenced. The domestic buildings and the north transept being most required were first completed, and then the choir and its east end were again rebuilt, or rather the rebuilding was begun, for Mr. Purday thinks that after the whole of the walls, arches, and piers were raised to about the cill of the triforium, want of funds compelled a cessation, until the work was resumed by Bishops Welton and Appleby, who finished the rest of the choir before the death of Edward III. To these bishops are due the glorious east end, the triforium, clerestory, and the roof and ceiling.

Some of the carving appears to have been left unfinished, and completed at a later date, and in parts of the works the old materials seem to have been employed a second time.

A fire in 1392 destroyed the north transept, which was rebuilt almost from the foundation by Bishop Strickland. who came to the see in 1401. Funds must have been lacking, for the utmost economy was used in the building by the employment of old material as far as it would go. The curious carvings of the nave piers were now executed. All idea of completing the cathedral on the scale and plan of the choir was abandoned; Bishop Strickland rebuilt the upper part of the tower and finished it with a lead and wooden spire. The tower being on the old Norman piers was, of course, only the width of the Norman nave, and narrower than the new choir. This difficulty was most cleverly got over by the introduction of a turret on the north side, where the choir overlapped the tower: the turret rises only part of the height of the tower, which has an angle turret on its top. Bishop Strickland also fitted up the stalls, the entrance through which from the nave is very fine.

In 1646 the greater part of the nave and the chapter house were destroyed, and the materials employed in the construction of guardhouses in the town; and much mischief was done by the idle soldiery of the day. After the civil wars the fragment of the nave was fitted up as a parish church, and so used until a very recent period. In 1764 a general repair was effected in the prevalent taste of the day, lath and plaster being freely used, and a lath and plaster ceiling being placed under the fine oak one. About fifteen years ago a general restoration was effected under Mr. Christian, and but recently the fragment of the nave has been thrown open to the cathedral.

On week days there is service in the cathedral at 10 A.M. and 4 P.M., and on Sundays at 11 A.M. and 3 P.M. The great door of the cathedral in the south transept is almost constantly open, and strangers can enter the cathedral close either from the wicket in Castle Street or by the gateway from Abbey Street. The great door and the south transept are new. The conventual buildings were attached to the cathedral at this point, and formed round the cloister garth a square of about 75 feet, of which one side only, the refectory or fratery, now remains, besides that side formed by the cathedral nave. The chapter house, a tall octagonal building, and some dormitories, formed the east side of the square, and continued along the east end of the fratery. The west side was probably formed by other dormitories, all as well as the fratery raised on crypts or vaults. The building now called the fratery or refectory formed the south side of the square, and was the great hall of the priory: it is now divided into two or three rooms, and used as a chapter house and library. South again of the fratery was the infirmary. The guest house was probably to the eastward. The prior's lodge still exists, and is the present deanery. It was built by Prior Senhouse in 1507, and the modern additions by Bishop Smith (1671-84). The abbey gatehouse was built by Prior Slee, and over the arch is the legend "Orate pro anima Christopher Slee." The burial-ground of the priory was south of the choir, and east of the cloister garth square. The town burial-ground was on the other side, the north side, of the cathedral.

If the visitor now enters the cathedral, he will at once be struck with the massive proportions of the Norman nave, and with the shattered and distorted arches which support the tower. St. Catherine's Chapel, now a vestry, is on his right, and he should here, as elsewhere in the cathedral, examine the beautiful carving of the woodwork, mostly of the time of Prior Gondibour, 1490. Direct in front, in the north transept, is the Consistory Court of the Chancellor of Carlisle, under a fine stained glass window to the memory of five children of the Archbishop of Canterbury, who all died within a few days, when he was Dean of Carlisle. Close to the Consistory Court stands the altar tomb of Prior Senhouse, on which the tenants of the abbey used formerly to pay down their rents. Opposite to St. Catherine's Chapel on the west side of the north transept is a glass covering the Runic inscription mentioned at page 12.

In the transept are monuments to persons of more than local celebrity; Anderson, the Cumberland bard; Smirke, the architect; Blamire, the M.P. and tithe commissioner; Musgrave Watson, the sculptor; and the officers and men of the 34th Cumberland regiment who fell in the Crimea. Two stand of laurel-wreathed colours of the same gallant regiment hang high in the nave. The empty casement of a once magnificent brass is close to the west wall of the nave.

Entering the choir the visitor should note the stalls, forty-six, erected in the time of Henry V. by Bishop Strickland, and the tabernacle arch over them added by Prior Haithwaite after 1433. The fine brass of Bishop Bell should be noticed: he is in full eucharistic vestments, viz. alb with orphreys, stole, tunic, dalmatic, chasuble, amice, maniple, pastoral staff with vexillum, gloves, and the mitra preciosa. This brass is remarkable as showing very clearly the distinction between tunic and dalmatic: its date is 1494. The pulpit and bishop's throne are modern, unworthy of the church, and will probably soon disappear. Behind the pulpit is a fine cinquecento screen by Lancelot Salkeld, last prior and first dean. The reredos and the pavement within the altar rails are both new, from the designs of Mr. Street. The very curious carvings of the capitals of the pillars should be noticed; they represent the occupations of the various months, and commence with a three-headed and much-imbibing Janus on the second pillar at east end of south aisle : Pocula Janus amat; Februus algeo clamat; a husbandman warming his feet at a fire. The carvings at the sides and backs of these pillars are most grotesque, and are said to be masonic in their mysticism. The organ by Willis was new in 1858. The great east window is the glory of the building, the finest window in all England of the Decorated style, for elegance of composition and easy flow of its lines. Mr. Mackenzie Walcott, in his Memorials of Carlisle, states that it contains forty-five trefoils and quatrefoils, and that the tracery consists of eighty-six pieces struck from 263 centres. The upper part of the glass is of the time of Richard II., and represents the last Resurrection and the Judgment. The glass in the lower part is modern.

The colouring of the roof is from the designs of Owen Jones, and the angels on the hammer beams are supposed to have supported magnificent lamps at ends of long chains.

The beautiful aisles now require attention. We have already noticed some of their architectural features. In the south aisle, the wood carving of the screen, cutting off St. Catherine's Chapel, should be noticed, and the monument of Bishop Welton, d. 1362, in eucharistic vestments. Opposite are some curious monkish paintings, long whitewashed over, and due to Prior Gondibour. Similar pictures are in the north aisle. They represent the legends of SS. Cuthbert, Anthony, and Augustus, and of the Apostles. Near the reredos are the casements of some lost brasses; and in the east end is a walled up door, supposed to have been used for bringing in building materials. At the east end of each aisle will be noticed fragments of groining ribs, part of an abandoned design. In the north aisle is the monument of Bishop Halton, once jewelled on breast and mitre; and two niches for effigies, one of which is supposed to have been prepared for Bishop Everdon. A very curious brass to Bishop Robinson is screwed to the wall; he died 1616. He was provost of Queen's College, Oxford, and that building as well as his cathedral are drawn on the brass.

Carlisle Castle.*

Few visitors to Carlisle will leave the city without having a peep at the castle. It stands on a slight headland, near the south bank of the river Eden, and not far from the right bank of the river Caldew. The keep is supposed to have been planned by William II. in 1092, and is a tolerably perfect specimen of Norman work, though in more recent times much disfigured to make it carry artillery, and obscured by its conversion into prisons and store-rooms. In all probability it stands on the site of a Roman station; the great Roman wall having skirted it on the north-west side, and the Vallum on the south-east.

The first entry we find about the castle in the early records is in 1168, during the reign of Henry II., when a bill was paid for removing one of the gates. About the same period the inner and outer wards were probably made, and the castle connected with the city walls. During the reigns of Henry II., Richard I., and John, it was often besieged and consequently undergoing repair. In fact, we are told that "its whole history is one of decay and ruin, and it so constantly required an outlay that it can scarcely be said to have been at any time in a sound state."

Edward I., being often in these parts during his wars with Scotland, resided much in the castle, as well as at Rose, Linstock, and Lanercost, and here he assembled three of his parliaments, viz. those which met in 1299, 1300, and 1307; from the second of which he set out for the famous siege of Caerlaverock Castle, while the third passed the statute, known as the Statute of Carlisle, which was directed against papal encroachments. The room in which the parliaments met was a large hall that was pulled down about forty years ago. It occupied the site of the present magazine.

On the death of Edward I. on Burgh Marsh, his son Edward II. was at once summoned to the north, and he received the homage of his nobles and prelates in the castle of Carlisle.

* We have taken most of these facts, by kind permission, from a paper entitled "Carlisle Castle," by R. S. Ferguson, Esq., read before the Cumberland and Westmorland Antiquarian and Archæological Society.

During the reign of Edward III. the repairs of the castle were very extensive; and for one or two centuries afterwards the Scots frequently harassed and besieged the place, but nothing of great mark happened to harm the castle, though the city and the suburbs suffered severely.

In the latter part of the reign of Edward IV., Richard, Duke of Gloucester (afterwards Richard III.), was governor of Carlisle and Penrith castles, and sheriff of the county. He made extensive repairs, and it is supposed that the great gateway is part of his work.

In 1522 we first hear of Carlisle Castle in connection with artillery: in that year the Duke of Albany was deterred from attacking it by the news that it mounted forty-five pieces of cannon. These would probably be the small guns we hear of in Elizabeth's reign. Henry VIII. made extensive alterations in the building so as to adapt it to carry artillery. The work was probably done in haste, for in 1563 the whole was in great decay, as appears from a survey made by the order of Queen Elizabeth. Three sides of the keep were in a dangerous state. The captain's tower wanted parapets, as did much of the inner curtain, and all the glass of the great hall and great chamber was decayed. In the outer ward was an open breach, 70 feet long, where the wall had fallen in 1557. Apparently this breach was at the south-west angle of the outer ward. The result of this survey was the building of a chapel and barrack, and no doubt the reparation of the wall and keep. The report (printed in all the county histories) is curious as showing the transitional state of warfare: the ordnance, artillery, and munitions include sagars, falcons, pot-guns, demibombarders, half-hags, serpentines, fowlers, murderers, bowes, arrowes, and arquebusses, as well as picks, hammers, chisels, spades, and shovels; the powder was all kept in the town, as no house of ordnance existed in the castle.

Mary, Queen of Scots, resided in the castle for two months during 1568, between her landing at Workington and removal to the south. The tower in which she lodged was in the south-east corner, and was pulled down in 1835. She was the occasion of much anxiety to her keepers, who feared her being rescued from Scotland, and were highly glad when she consented to move southwards. When Nathaniel Hawthorne, the well-known American writer, visited Carlisle Castle, the soldier who showed him round told him a most romantic story of a daughter of Lord Scrope, the governor of the castle, who attempted to aid Queen Mary to escape. She was shot dead by a sentinel, and the very spot where she fell was pointed out to Hawthorne, who says "the story would be very interesting were there a word of truth in it."

James I., on his accession to the throne of England, reduced the garrison of Carlisle, but in 1639 it consisted of 500 men: it was then raised to 1500 on account of troubles in Scotland, but the garrison was, by a treaty with Scotland, disbanded in 1641, and the arms and stores laid up.

In 1644 the castle and city were besieged by the Parliamentary forces under General Leslie. On the surrender of the place, the garrison, according to the terms of the capitulation, marched out under arms, colours flying, drums beating, matches lighted at both ends, bullets in their mouths, with all their bag and baggage, and twelve charges of powder apiece. A garrison of Scots was placed in charge, and there remained until Parliament dismissed them in 1646. Sir Philip Musgrave and Sir Thomas Glenham in 1648 seized the castle by surprise, but it had shortly to surrender to Cromwell, who altered the keep so as to adapt its roof for the service of artillery. For some time after this, the garrison kept at Carlisle was large, so large as to be able to detach flying columns into Scotland of 1000 and 2000 men. On the restoration, Sir Philip Musgrave became the governor, and took great care to select his officers from the veterans of the Tangiers regiments. James II. garrisoned the castle with Irish papists, whose officers celebrated the prospect of an heir to James II. by dancing drunk and naked round a bonfire in the market-place, but who sneaked off by night on hearing of Dutch William's arrival, and the bold stroke made by the two Lowthers on his behalf.

In 1715 the tide of war rolled away from Carlisle Castle; true, the militia were called up, and the horse militia, under Brigadier Stanwix, patrolled to Longtown, only to find that the expected enemy had moved south by way of Brampton. When all was over, and the Highlanders had surrendered at Preston, their arms, mostly broadswords, were sent to Carlisle Castle and stored there.

On the advance of the Highlanders in 1745 the castle was found utterly unprepared to stand a siege. From the records of the court-martial held afterwards upon Colonel Durand for surrendering the place, it appears that the garrison consisted of two companies of invalids, some eighty in number, all old and infirm men, four gunners, two of whom were townsmen, and two old soldiers, but one of them a very old and infirm man; that the militia were disaffected, and in all probability only deterred from supporting Charles Edward by their national hatred for his Scotch supporters; that the castle and city walls were in a ruinous condition and utterly defenceless, the castle having but twenty guns, all 6-pounders, while ten only were available for the city walls, ranging in calibre from 2 to 4-pounders. The consequence was the town and castle quickly surrendered, and the Prince entered in triumph, and then proceeded southwards. A short time saw his fortunes change. In December he was again in Carlisle, and at a council of war Lord George Murray advised that Carlisle should be evacuated, the castle blown into the air, and the stores pitched into the Eden. In a military point of view this advice was sound, but it was rejected. The Prince left a garrison behind, and in the course of a few hours the place was completely invested by the Duke of Cumberland, who drew a cordon of troops around the town, at a distance of half a mile. A week's delay was occasioned by the bringing of six 18-pounders from Whitehaven, which were placed in a trench on the site of the present Infirmary, and at once opened on the 3-gun angle battery of the castle, and on the 4-gun battery, which having only earthen parapets were soon silenced. This was on a Saturday, on which day also the Dutch troops shelled the castle from Stanwix. By Monday the Duke had three more 18-pounders in a new position, whereat the garrison surrendered, the castle walls being breached both at the angle and at the sallyport. The Government now crowded Carlisle with the most famous regiments in the army, and the consequence was that for six months they died off at the rate of a man daily. Henceforth the history of the castle is little more than a record of its destruction. At the beginning of the present century the Government pulled down the Elizabethan barracks; the long hall where Edward I.'s parliaments met; changed the great chamber and chapel into quarters for officers; pulled down Queen Mary's Tower level to the ground; destroyed some trees she had planted; and at one time it was in contemplation to have let the castle for a manufactory. A more healthy public opinion has recently been stimulated on the subject, partly through the exertions of Mr. R. S. Ferguson, and the members of the Cumberland and Westmorland Archæological Society, and partly through the efforts made by some members of the corporation of Carlisle, who have warmly taken up the matter. Thanks to these exertions, some of the old buildings which now hide the castle will soon be pulled down, and any necessary alterations made in the castle itself will be in harmony with its older features.

Rose Castle, and the See of Carlisle.

Rose Castle, the palace of the bishops of Carlisle, stands 6 miles to the south-west of the city, and 2½ miles from the Dalston railway station. Its situation is extremely pleasant, on gentle rising ground, commanding an extensive prospect, whilst immediately in front is a broad expanse of meadow, bounded by the high wooded bank of the river Caldew.

In 1300 Edward I. stayed here, but we do not read of it in connection with the see of Carlisle until the reign of Edward II., when it was the residence of Bishop Halton. It must originally have been a Norman keep or Peel castle, and the Strickland tower which stands at the north-east corner of the existing building, and was restored or rebuilt by Bishop Strickland early in the fifteenth century, is probably the remains of the ancient keep. The Norman plan of architecture, as circumstances permitted, was generally adapted to the requirements of a mansion.

In 1322 the buildings were destroyed by Robert Bruce, and in 1336 Bishop Kirby obtained a licence to crenellate his mansion of Ross. The licence gave power to embattle, kernel, and machecollate. Bishop Kirby, besides executing these defensive works, also built himself a more spacious mansion within the walls, and this was doubtless carried on by his successor, Gilbert Welton, who, in 1356, also obtained licence to crenellate. Few of these additions now remain, though we can trace what they were. In the fifteenth century, the hall, which had previously reached its greatest perfection, and was undoubtedly one of the finest specimens of domestic architecture ever produced in England, fell somewhat into decadence, and private sleeping accommodation was increased. Late in the fifteenth century Bishop Bell added a tower on the north front, and in the sixteenth century we find further additions by Bishop Kite, who not only built the tower on the west side, but is said to have built the whole of that side of the quadrangle.

In 1645 Rose Castle was held for the royalists by Mr. Lowther, constable of the castle; was taken by a party of Colonel Heveringham's regiment, and was for some time used as a prison for the royalists. In 1648 it was again garrisoned by a company of the royalists, and after an assault of two hours was taken by storm, and afterwards burnt by order of Colonel Cholmly. "Rose Castle, the Bishop's best seat," says Fuller, writing about this time, "hath lately the rose therein withered, and the prickles in the ruins thereof only remain." So low, in fact, had the fortunes of the castle fallen, that on a survey made by the Puritans in 1649-50 for its sale, it was valued at 1000*l*.; "yet," it is added, "if the same be sold to a gentleman who will purchase the whole estate and make it his habitation, we take it to be worth 1500*l*." It was sold, together with the manors of Dalston and Linstock, for the small sum of 4161*l*. 11s. 10*d*., to Colonel Heveringham, who is said to have fitted up the offices for his own residence. On the restoration, Richard Sterne was nominated to the see, and rebuilt the chapel and other portions, but in such an unskilful manner that his successor, Bishop Rainbow, who was appointed to the see when Sterne was translated to the archiepiscopal see of York, brought an action against him for dilapidations. He recovered 400*l*., and rebuilt the chapel; and spent 1500*l*. in addition. His successor, Thomas Smith, made further additions, with the assistance of William Machel, vicar of Kirkbythore, in Westmorland, in 1688, and the appearance of the castle at that time is illustrated by a view from watercolour drawings taken by Hayman Rooke.

Under Bishop Percy the castle was brought to its present form, and it was somewhat remarkable that whereas Bishop Smith in his alterations employed Machel, who prided himself on being the pioneer of regular or classical architecture in this diocese, Bishop

Percy should have carried out his alterations from the designs of Rickman, one of the great leaders of the Gothic revival. The north and west sides of the quadrangle alone remain, and they are mostly modern.

In the time of Bishop Nicholson the Scots had designs upon the castle, but were prevented from attempting them by the swollen state of the river. During the rebellion of 1745 Rose had a still more narrow escape, which was due to the gallantry of Captain Macdonald, the leader of the Scotch party. At the time of his arrival the infant granddaughter of the bishop, Sir George Fleming, was about to be baptized, and on the captain being appealed to, not only drew off his men without disturbance, but presented the white cockade from his bonnet for the little lady to wear during baptism and as a protection against any stragglers. Rose Mary Dacre, the little lady, as Lady Clerk, survived to a great age.

Visitors to Rose Castle ought to include a peep at Dalston Hall and Highhead Castle. The former stands in a charming situation on the Carlisle side of Dalston village, and comprises a fine specimen of the Peel towers so common in these parts in former times.

Highhead Castle stands 2 miles south-east of Rose Castle, on the bank of a beautifully wooded dell, through which flows the Ivebeck, and near the junction of the streamlets Ive and Roe. It is a comparatively modern mansion built on the site of an ancient castle. It was here that Harcla's brother, Sir Edward Blount, and others, were assembled when Harcla was seized in Carlisle Castle, and when the news arrived they fled hence into Scotland.

The See of Carlisle.

Whatever was the cause, bishoprics and kingdoms were originally conterminous in their limits; and hence, as Cumberland, which extended from the Clyde to the Duddon, and was subject in ecclesiastical matters to the Bishop of Whitherne, was once part of the Welsh kingdom of Strathclyde, we need not be surprised to find the Bishop of Witherne, or Candida Casa, in Galloway, the earliest to exercise ecclesiastical authority in what is now Cumberland. When Egfrid, King of Northumberland, conquered and granted Carlisle and 15 miles round to St. Cuthbert,

Bishop of Lindisfarn, the district so granted became part of the see of Lindisfarn, and then of Durham, which absorbed Lindisfarn.

In 1133 Henry I. formed the see of Carlisle, and its formation was regarded by the Bishops of Whitherne and Durham as a robbery committed upon them. Athelwald, the first prior of St. Mary's, Carlisle, became the first bishop of the new see, which at first had no landed property, but the impropriation of three benefices, Carlton and Dalston in Cumberland, and Meaburn in Westmorland. To the fact that Athelwald was prior and bishop is due the curious circumstance that the Bishop of Carlisle has both a throne and a stall in his cathedral, he enjoying the prior's stall while the dean only has the sub-prior's stall. This duplication of characters also caused confusion as to the property of the see and the priory, and disputes arose which the Papal legate had twice to arbitrate upon—this he did by a partition of the property. When the see did acquire landed property, it acquired it under a very favourable tenure. Carlisle and Rochester are the only episcopal sees that hold their property *in pure alms*, the freest tenure known to the law, and not *in barony*. The see lay vacant for many years while the Scots held Cumberland, and during that time the Bishops of Whitherne and Durham asserted their ancient sway. Indeed the Bishop of Durham about 1255 made good his claim to the profits of the see whenever vacant. The Bishop of Whitherne on this set off to Rome to make a similar claim, but died on the road.

The earliest residence of the bishops of Carlisle appears to have been Linstock, whence they moved to Rose Castle. Both these places were often burnt and robbed by Scottish armies, and the luckless bishops fled to Buley in Westmorland, Horncastle in Lincolnshire, or begged Parliament and the King to give them a house within the walls of Carlisle.

The earlier bishops of Carlisle numbered among them many famous generals, politicians, and diplomatists, such as Halton, Kirkby, Welton, Merks, Kite, and Oglethorpe who crowned Queen Elizabeth. Other famous bishops have been Usher, Archbishop of Armagh; Nicholson, the antiquary; Law, father of Lord Ellenborough; and Vernon, afterwards Archbishop of York. The present bishop is the Right Rev. Harvey Goodwin, D.D. (consecrated A.D. 1869), sometime Fellow of Gonville and Caius College, Cambridge, Incumbent of St. Edward's, Cambridge, and subsequently Dean of Ely.

The Abbey of Holme Cultram.*

Twelve miles to the west of Carlisle, and close to the Abbey station on the Silloth Railway, is the parish church of Holme Cultram, a building which from its outward appearance seems to be little worthy of notice; but some strangers will visit it with interest, as it is the only relic of a once famous abbey.

Sir Walter Scott, in the 'Lay of the Last Minstrel,' speaks of "Holme Cultrame's lofty nave;" and when we enter the church and see the grand proportions of the nave arcade we must admit the justness of the allusion. The walls outside, the stones and monuments, ancient slabs of various sorts and sizes, worn with the storms of centuries, smooth with age, and with inscriptions almost gone, testify to the antiquity of the place. The tourist will wonder how it came to pass that so substantial a building could ever have been so mutilated, for edifices in other parts of the country as old and less substantial still remain. This once noble abbey seems to have suffered every possible misfortune; more than all, it has suffered from that cold neglect which allowed its ruins to be at the mercy of every comer, the nearest and most convenient quarry for building materials. Traces of this cruel destruction may be found in nearly every adjacent farmhouse, and most prominently in the remains of the abbey itself, where large portions have been taken down in order to furnish material for enclosing the poor remnant left.

> "Still do ye stand, fair ruins, like the ghosts
> Of friends departed, mouldering to decay.
> Oh! would that ye might warn us that at best
> Frail are our deeds, and frailer still ourselves—
> That, like the rainbow of a weeping sky,
> We rise, we shine, we change, and pass away."

---

* We have pleasure in stating that Charles J. Ferguson, Esq., allowed us to extract many of the following facts from an article on Holme Cultram, published by him in 1872.

There seems some doubt as to the exact date of the foundation of the abbey. It is variously stated to have been founded in 1100, 1124, 1135 and 1150, the last three of which dates, it is noteworthy, coincide with the accession of David of Scotland in 1124, and of Stephen and Henry I. of England in 1135 and 1150. Though Henry I. of England, and one Alan, have been put down as the founders of the abbey, the real credit seems probably due to Henry, Prince of Cumberland, son of David, King of Scotland, and father of Malcolm, King of Scotland, he himself dying *vitâ parentis*. Stephen of England, on his accession to the English throne, gave up Cumberland and other territory to the Scotch, apparently as the price of their acquiescence in his usurpation, and the heir apparent to the Scotch throne ruled the ceded territory as a nominal vassal to Stephen. The charter of Prince Henry, and his father's confirmation of it, are given in the local histories. It seems probable that, after the example of their brethren at Fountain's Abbey, a small fraternity of monks had settled in the Holme, and that they had been more or less countenanced and benefited by successive rulers and magnates, each of whom the monks successively looked on as their patron and founder for the time being, until eclipsed by a more liberal successor. Thus they might have had founders and benefactors prior to Prince Henry, their undoubted and substantial benefactor; while we find that when Henry II. of England, in the third year of his reign, possessed himself of Cumberland, the monks lost no time in proclaiming him as their founder, and thus acquiring his protection and a confirmation of all previous grants. And, indeed, he would be their founder: coming into Cumberland as a conqueror, claiming under a title hostile to Prince Henry and to Prince Henry's liege lord King Stephen, he would not be bound by the grants of Prince Henry, or the confirmations of the King of Scotland; and thus, in granting to the monks lands already granted to them by Prince Henry, King Henry II. would consider he was giving away his own property, and so entitled to all the honours of a founder. It is probable that the doubt as to who founded the abbey of Holme Cultram arises from the fact that successive lords of Cumberland from 1070 to 1154 claimed, not through one another, but against one another.

Henry, Prince of Cumberland, gave to the monks two-thirds of the Holme, and in the same deed confirms the grant to them of the other third, by Alan, son of Waldeff, who had received it from Henry as a chase. He also gives them Raby. The deed mentions that the bounds had been perambulated, and it and the deed of confirmation by David of Scotland were executed at Carlisle, where were assembled King David, Prince Henry, and his barons. The Bishop and the Prior of Carlisle were among the witnesses to the deeds.

The subsequent grant of Henry II. of England was confirmed by Pope Clement III., who makes no mention of any grant or foundation prior to Henry II. The abbey had many liberal benefactors, and a list of its possessions is to be found in the local histories.

One of its best friends was Christian, Bishop of Candida Casa, or Whitherne, who consecrated Lanercost. He gave the abbey many gifts: by one deed he gave the grange and lands of Kirkwinny in Galway, directed his body to be buried at Holme Cultram, and threatened with terrible evils anyone who molested the house of Holme Cultram or the grange of Kirkwinny. Pope Innocent gave the abbey the church of Kirkwinny, and invoked the indignation of God and St. Peter and Paul on meddlers.

The church at Burgh was given to the abbey by Hugh de Morville, out of the profits thereof to find lights and all necessaries for the ornament of the church at Holme Cultram, and for the service of the altar there.

The church at Wigton was also given to them, and amongst other possessions they acquired houses in Carlisle, one in Richardgate, and two near St. Mary's churchyard towards the castle; lands at Edenhall near Penrith, at Aspatria, Blencoggow, Branslibet, Bromfield, Caldbeck, Distington, Dundrake, Flimby, Gilcrux, Harrais, Hertelpol, Kelton, Kirkbride, Kirby Thore, Newbiggin, Castlerig, Sandstath, Warthebirth, Maidengate, Laysingby, Newby near Carlisle, Newton, Ormesby, Dereham, Sacmirdash, together with possessions in Ireland and Scotland, and numerous fisheries and commons of pasture; also iron mines at Egremont and Coupland, and sundry benefactions in coin, such as the gift of Edward I. of England, of 300 marks yearly out of forfeited estates in Scotland: this last was given by charter dated at Cordoyl in Scotland, and witnessed by the greatest dignitaries of the day.

The monks thus established and endowed, were of the Cistercian order, a reformed branch of the Benedictines, founded by Robert, Abbot of Molesme, at Cistertium or Cisteaux, whence the name, in the year 1098, and afterwards so augmented by the efforts of St. Bernard of Clairvaux, as within a century after its formation to number 3000 affiliated monasteries. In England the first seats of this order were Waverley in Surrey, Furness, Fountains, Kirkstall, Bolton, Tintern, Holy Cross, Roche, Sweetheart, Netley, Buildwas, and many others. This order was considered as especially under the protection of the Virgin Mary; its members were often called White Monks from their habits, which consisted of a white cassock with narrow scapulary, and over that a black gown when abroad, white when in church. They were especially devoted to agricultural pursuits, and to the duty and virtue of obedience. The general characteristics of their churches were extreme simplicity of outline, absence of triforium, a single central tower, a simple west front, and plain undivided windows, while generally a flight of steps led from the transept into the dormitory.

The first object of the monks of St. Mary's, Holme Cultram, on their establishment, seems to have been to make themselves secure; we may presume from the traces we can see, that they set about building their church at once, and that they enclosed the precincts with a great earthwork, protected by a ditch on its outer side; remains of the wall and ditch still exist on the north side, adjoining the Carlisle road. We are further told by Denton that the monks presently erected five granges for husbandry, whose names Hutchinson gives as Old Grange, Grange Determs, Mayberg, Skinburne, Calfhouse, and Raby, six in all; while Burn and Nicholson name them Raby, Mawbergh (Mowbray), Skinburne (Skinburness), Culshaw (probably Calvo), and Newton Arlosh. They are also said to have turned all into arable, meadow, and pasture, or to have extensively reclaimed the wild forest ground, full of red deer, which at first coming covered the isle of Holme Cultram and Raby. They also built themselves a place of safety at Wulstey near the coast, due west from the abbey. This castle is mentioned by Camden as having in his day sufficient remains to prove it had been a place of great strength, with a broad and deep ditch around it. It was finally dismantled, and the materials carried to Carlisle by order of Colonel Thomas Fitch, Cromwellian governor of and M.P. for Carlisle. Tradition says that its gates were re-hung on the Irish gatehouse at Carlisle. "In this castle," says Camden, "tradition reports that the magic works of Michael Scot (or Scotus) were preserved till they were mouldering into dust. He professed a religious life here about the year 1290, and became so deeply versed in mathematics and other abstruse sciences, that he obtained the character of a magician, and was believed in that credulous age to have performed many miracles." Another writer tells us that "Michael Scot was a Durham man, who applied himself to the abstruse Aristotelian philosophy, which he pretended to translate from Avicenna, and dedicated to Frederick II., Emperor of Germany, whose astrologer he was. Some of his philosophical and astrological works have been printed; and Dempster says some remained in his time in Scotland, which his countrymen would not dare to open, for fear of the devilish pranks that might be played by them."

The abbots of St. Mary's Abbey, Holme Cultram, though not mitred, were occasionally summoned to parliament during the reigns of the first and second Edwards, and were entrusted with jurisdiction within their own territory.

In the taxation of Pope Nicholas IV. the revenues of the abbey were valued at 217l. 5s. 10d. In 1266 the abbey was pillaged by Alexander, King of Scotland.

In 1301 we read that Bishop Halton granted to the abbot and convent of Holme Cultram power to erect a chapel at Skinburness. In 1305 we find the abbot petitioning that, whereas he had paid a fine of 100 marks to the king for a fair or market to be held at Skinburness, and whereas that town, together with the way leading to it, is carried away by the sea, the king would grant that he may have such fair and market at his town of Kirkby Johan, instead of the other place aforesaid, and that this charter may be renewed. Skinburness seemed to have been a place of some importance, having been used as a depôt for supplying the armies then employed against the Scots.

In 1303 we find Bishop Halton, by his charter bearing date at Linstock Castle, near Carlisle, the 11th April, grants licence to build a church at Newton Arlosh or Kirkby Johan, with all parochial rights and titles within their territories for the use of the monastery, half a mark to be paid yearly to the bishop in the name of a "cathedraticum," and in token of subjection to him. A second Gregory seems to have been abbot at this time, and it is, recorded of him that he, being more greedy of gain than any abbot before him, petitioned that a parish church should be granted him whereby he might present a priest, and call for tithes. It seems, however, that some of the more stubborn of his parishioners declined to pay, and that therefore their lands were cursed and tithes not exacted, but their rents doubled: be that as it may, these lands still bear the name of "cursed lands," and are tithe free.

In 1322 the abbey was pillaged by Robert Bruce, and threatened by him with destruction by fire, notwithstanding that his father's body was interred here. In 1353 the abbot and convent paid 20*l.* to Lord Douglas to save the monastery from plunder.

Holme Cultram is mentioned in the visitation of Thomas Tonge, Norroy King-at-Arms, in 1530. Later we read of its being cautioned against certain evil practices (such as inviting ladies to dinner and supper), which had crept in, and on the 5th of March, 1537, it was dissolved, Gawin Borrowdale being the then abbot. Abbot Borrowdale was made rector of Holme Cultram, and on his death Queen Mary, in the first year of her reign, granted the rectory and vicarage with the chapel of Newton Arlosh to the Chancellor, Masters and Scholars of the University of Oxford, on condition that they should maintain a graduate clergyman, and that the surplus revenues of tithes and other emoluments should be devoted to the maintenance of the examination schools at Oxford.

Such is an outline of the early history and foundation of St. Mary's Abbey, Holme Cultram, but it must have gone through many varied scenes; exposed as it was to constant inroads from the Scots, and to the no less lawless raids of its border neighbours, it must have been at once a fortress and a monastery. We know that its two churches of Burgh and Newton Arlosh were fortified, so that doubtless the abbey which could build a fortified church for its own aggrandisement would fortify itself, and we can even now trace the remains of the earthworks that once defended it, while curious entries in the parish books show the bitter hatred of the Scots, which long eras of rapine and robbery had engendered. We may notice that Wolstey Castle, the stronghold of the abbey, was extremely well placed in a military point of view. At first sight one would think it exposed to attacks from the sea, but there were few boats in the Solway in those days; deep water was a safeguard; the enemy forded the Solway in the shallows at Burgh, and to get at Wolstey Castle they had to leave in their rear the fortified churches of Newton Arlosh and Burgh, and the earthworks of the abbey itself; unless they first occupied these strongholds, the warlike tenants of the abbey would collect there and cut off the retreat of the marauders. Thus Wolstey Castle was peculiarly a place of refuge.

The whole area about the east end of the present church of Holme Cultram is filled with the ruins of the former tower, choir, and transepts. It is stated in an old document that "Holme Cultram church was 279 feet long and 135 feet broad. The length of the chancel was 96 feet, the breadth 63 feet, from the steeple (which was in the middle) to the lower church door 162 feet; and this church (which was in the form of a large cross) was a good landmark, and a great refuge and defence in time of war and invasion against Scottish and English rebels and outlaws, and the steeple being 114 feet, stood upon the chancel, and fell 9 feet ajaiew for lack of repairs."

The church was cruciform in plan, and consisted of a nave of nine bays, with a spacious aisle and lofty clerestory, of a crossing beyond, with choir and transepts. The conventual buildings were on the south side; few remains of them now exist, the field on which they stood having been thoroughly excavated for the sake of the building material. The abbey is built of a close-grained red sandstone, not from any local quarry, but brought from a distance. Quantities of chippings have been found on the river bank, at the point nearest to the abbey, so that probably the stone was brought from Scotland by sea, and worked where it was landed. All the stones are extremely well wrought, and in some the chisel marks are as fresh as on the day they were executed, and many mason's marks have been found.

One of the earliest and most noticeable features of the existing church is the west door, which is of the transitional period, and is a late example of round-headed Gothic. The nave arcade is of fine proportions, and is transitional in character, slightly more advanced than the west door. The pointed arch first appears, and the earliest types of conventional foliage are to be noticed in the capitals. The columns are clustered, and, on plan, consist of four circular shafts, grouped together with smaller shafts at the angles, all attached, and worked as one column. The fifth shaft from westward differs in plan from the others, and is of a slightly earlier type, being formed of a combination such as one finds in the earliest ornamentation of a jamb—a series of recesses filled in with angle shafts. The respond at the west end is similar to this shaft; possibly the chancel may have extended into the nave to this point, and the rood screen may have been here. This we may learn, if the whitewash and plaster should ever be removed.

The later history of the church seems to have been a series of misfortunes. In 1600, we read that upon the 1st of January the steeple of the church suddenly fell to the ground, and by the fall brought down a great part of the church, both timber, leads, and walls. In 1602-3 the tower was rebuilt, and on the 18th of April, 1604, it was burnt down by the vicar's servant, Christopher Hardon, carrying a live coal into the roof of the church, a sudden gust of wind having blown the light into a daw's nest and set the roof on fire. The vicar and his servant were brought into the Queen's Bench, but acquitted of wilfully burning the church. An old writing states that "the vicar Mandeville hired and agreed with his servant for 40s. to kill the *doues* (i.e. daws or jackdaws) in Holme Cultram church, and that he ripped up the lead to go in and out to shoot at them *during divine service*, and put the people in great fear."

In 1604 the chancel was re-edified by the vicar, and in 1606 the body of the church was repaired by the parishioners. In 1703 Bishop Nicholson's visitation took place, and he thus describes the building: "The inside of the church was full of water, the rain falling in plentifully everywhere. The parishioners, about fifteen or sixteen years before, took off the lead from the south aisle (the arches of which are drooping down), to cover that on the north. The fabric is large, though only the body of the church is standing, of nine arches on each aisle, and very high." The church was brought to its present state about the middle of the last century.

Gretna Green.

Few strangers will visit places of interest around Carlisle without having a desire to see the far-famed village of Gretna Green, which is situated nine miles from the city, on the Glasgow and South-Western Railway.

It was formerly daily resorted to by romantic lovers of all classes of the English people, who, in their pilgrimages here, were often hotly pursued, but immediately they had crossed the bridge over the river Sark, and entered Scotland, and there stated before two witnesses they were man and wife, they were united for ever in the eyes of the law.

At the tollgate close to the bridge, the first house over the river, the poorer couples were often united; but the rich generally went to an hotel in the village, and there were married either by the landlord or by a certain individual who was looked upon by Hymen's votaries as the high priest of Gretna. It has generally been stated that this person was the village blacksmith, but persons residing on the spot say this was a popular delusion, originating, in all probability, from the hot hasty marriage resembling the welding together of heated iron.*

In February, 1875, we visited the place, and found that there were half-a-dozen people who had acted the part of priest; but one, William Long, a hand-loom weaver, seems to have married more than all the rest put together. His father and grandfather had had the same occupation, and he showed us books which reached back for more than a hundred years, and contained thousands of names; the celebrated Lord Erskine, Lord Chancellor of England, Lord Durham, and Lord Coventry being, he stated, among the number. Lord Erskine's name is still on a pane in the window of the village inn, said to have been written by himself.

Sometimes for these marriages a good fee was paid. Lord Erskine, we were told, gave the handsome sum of eighty guineas; and another person, who was married by the landlord of the hotel, gave 60*l.* to the landlord, and 20*l.* to each of his daughters.

The usual custom was for the parties to go to the house of the person who was going to marry them, or they would send for the individual to come to them at the hotel. The ceremony was of the shortest and simplest kind, for marriage in Scotland is merely a civil contract.

* A correspondent informs us that the blacksmith's shop was once the first house in Scotland, and hence the smith was the priest most easily got. Afterwards the tollgate was built nearer England.

Mr. Long told us that not a word was read from any book. He merely asked the parties if they were single and wished to be man and wife. They replying in the affirmative in the presence of two witnesses (male or female, old or young), the two were married. No writings were necessary, but he made it a custom to enter the signatures of all present in a book, and to give the parties married a certificate printed as under:

"Kingdom of Scotland.
County of Dumfries.
Parish of Gretna.

These are to certify, to all whom they may concern, that   , from the parish of   , in the county of   , and   , from the parish of   , in the county of   , being now both here present, and having declared to me that they are single persons, have now been married after the manner of the laws of Scotland.

As witness our hands at Gretna, this   day of   , 187

Witnesses {

It is generally understood that marriages at Gretna are entirely done away with; but such is not the case, for we saw in Mr. Long's book entries as late as January and February, 1875, and one only a few days before our visit. In 1856 a law was passed making Scotch marriages illegal unless either the man or the woman had resided for three weeks previously in Scotland. This had the effect of putting a stop to many hasty runaway weddings, but was chiefly intended to do away with the weddings of the hundreds of servants who visited the place from Carlisle during the time of the hirings. Probably these customs at term time were relics of what was known on the western borders as *hand-fisting* in former times. Hutchinson says: "In the upper part of Eskdale, at the confluence of the White and Black Esk, was held an annual fair, where multitudes of each sex repaired. The unmarried looked out for mates, made their engagements by joining hands, or by *hand-fisting*, went off in pairs, cohabited till the next annual return of the fair, appeared there again, and then were at liberty to declare their approbation or dislike of each other. If each party continued constant, the *hand-fisting* was renewed for life;

but if either party dissented, the engagement was void, and both were at full liberty to make a new choice; but with this proviso, that the inconstant was to take the charge of the offspring of the year of probation. This custom seemed to originate from the want of clergy in this country in the time of popery. This tract was the property of the abbey of Melrose, which, through economy, discontinued the means that were used to discharge the clerical offices; instead, they only made annual visitations, for the purposes of marrying and baptizing; and the person thus sent was called *Book-in-Bosom*; probably from his carrying, by way of readiness, the book in his breast; but even this being omitted, the inhabitants became necessitated at first to take this method, which they continued from habit to practise, long after the Reformation had furnished them with clergy. Persons of rank in times long prior to these, took the benefit of this custom; for Lyndsey, in the reign of King James II., says, 'that James, sixth Earl of Murray, begat upon Isabel James, daughter of the Laird of James, Alexander Dunbar, a man of singular wit and courage. This Isabel was but *hand-fist* with him, and deceased before the marriage; where, through this Alexander, he was worthy of a greater living than he might succeed to by the laws and practices of this realm.'"

How Gretna Green came to have the monopoly of runaway marriages we know not, for any point on the borders between England and Scotland would have answered the purpose. Coldstream Bridge End Toll and Lamberton Toll, near Berwick, were the rivals of Gretna for lovers in the eastern counties. There is a tradition that Gretna received the special privilege by a grant from a king of Scotland, but in all probability it derived its fame from its favoured situation, for it was in old times the first place on the Great Western Mail Road, or Great North Road, from London to Scotland.

Netherby.

Netherby, the seat of Sir Frederick Graham, Bart., is an elegant mansion charmingly situated on the east bank of the river Esk, 11 miles north of Carlisle, and 2¼ miles from Longtown. It was erected in the middle of the last century by Dr. Robert Graham, and commands an extensive prospect in the direction of the heights Burnswark and Criffel, and the estuary of the Solway Firth. The nucleus of the building was a border tower of great thickness, which stood on the site of a Roman station, supposed to be the Castra Exploratorum of the second Iter of Antoninus. Some very fine altars and sculptured stones found in the station are preserved on the spot, but no traces of the camp remain, although both Leland and Camden speak of extensive ruins of walls and buildings.

The Grahams are descended from Malice, Earl of Monteith in Scotland, whose second son, from whom they trace their genealogy, was surnamed *John with the bright sword*. From some disgust, John withdrew himself from the court, and, with many of his retainers, settled in the English borders during the reign of Henry IV. One writer, speaking of the Grahams, says : " They were all stark mosstroopers and arrant thieves, both to Scotland and England outlawed, yet sometimes connived at, because they gave intelligence forth of Scotland, and would rise 400 horse at any time upon a raid of the English into Scotland. A saying is recorded of a mother to her son (which is now become proverbial), *Ride, Rowley, hough's ith' pot*; that is, the last piece of beef was in the pot, and therefore it was high time for him to go and fetch more. Late in Queen Elizabeth's time, one Jock (Grahme) of the Peartree had his brother in Carlisle gaol ready to be hanged; and Mr. Salkeld, sheriff of Cumberland, living at Corby Castle, and his son a little boy at the gate playing, Jock comes by, and gives the child an apple, and says, ' Master, will you ride ;' takes him up before him, carries him into Scotland, and never would part with him till he had his brother home safe from the gallows."

" Richard Grahme, second son of Fergus, when a youth, in the reign of King James I., went to London, and by the recommendation of some friends got entertained in the Duke of Buckingham's service ; with whom he became so much in favour, that the duke made him his master of the horse, and introduced him not only to the knowledge but to the particular favour both of the king and prince. He was one of those few who were entrusted with the secret of the prince's going to Spain, and who waited on him thither. Sir Henry Wotton, in his life of the Duke of Buckingham, giving an account of their travel through France upon this occasion, relates the following circumstance: 'They were now entered into the deep time of Lent, and could get no flesh in their inns. Whereupon fell out a pleasant passage if I may assert it by the way among more serious. There was near Bayonne a herd of goats with their young ones; upon the sight whereof, Sir Richard Graham tells the Marquis of Buckingham that he would snap one of the kids, and make some shift to carry him snug to their lodging. Which the prince overhearing, 'Why, Richard,' says he, 'Do you think you may practice here your old tricks upon the borders?' Upon which words, they in the first place gave the goatherd good contentment; and then while the Marquis and Richard, being both on foot, were chasing the kid about the stack, the prince from horseback killed him in the head with a Scottish pistol.' This Sir Richard purchased the barony of the Earl of Cumberland; after which he was created baronet. In the rebellion which begun in 1641 he armed in defence of his royal master. At the battle of Edgehill he received many wounds, and lay amongst the dead all night. He took his last leave of the king in the Isle of Wight in 1648, and with his permission retired into the country where he lived very private."

If the stranger cross the river Esk by a ferry-boat close to Netherby he may visit Kirk Andrews church and a fine old border fortress. The latter consists of a square tower, with a ground floor, and two apartments above, one over the other. In the first floor it was usual to keep the cattle, in the two last was lodged the family. In those unsettled times everyone was obliged to keep guard against, perhaps, his neighbour, and sometimes to keep themselves shut up for days together, having no other opportunity of taking fresh air but from the battlements of their castles.

A quarter of a mile distant is the Scotch Dyke station, on the North British Railway. It is so named owing to being contiguous to an earth mound which runs four miles across the country, from the river Esk to the river Sark. This mound, locally termed a *dyke*, was raised in 1552 to mark the boundary between England and Scotland. Previously the narrow tract of country between the two rivers had been known as the *debatable land*, and had been the cause of many contentions between the two kingdoms, as it was the abode of outlaws who feared no punishment and obeyed the laws of neither country. In one part of this tract is a flat area of 7 miles in circumference, known as the Solway Moss, where in the time of Henry VIII. a Scotch army was almost completely destroyed during their flight after a disastrous defeat. A skeleton of a trooper and his horse, in complete armour, are said to have been found many years afterwards by some persons who were digging peats. On the 13th November, 1771, in one dark tempestuous night, the vast body of moss gave way and continued spreading for weeks over an area of 500 acres.

The country around Netherby, which was formerly known as the *frontiers, marches* and *debatable ground*, is now well cultivated, owing principally to the improvement effected by the Graham family. One writer, when referring to these changes, says, "The people were changed from being idle to being industrious, from wretched cottagers, grovelling in dirt and poverty, into contented husbandmen and opulent farmers. Still more, they were changed from loose and ignorant barbarians, ever quarrelsome and disorderly, into a peasantry, peaceful and regular, a peasantry, perhaps, more intelligent, and better educated, than most others in the island."

Corby Castle, and Wetheral Priory.

Alighting at Wetheral station, 5 miles east of Carlisle, the traveller finds himself in one of the most lovely spots in England. Stepping on to the handsome viaduct, of five arches, each 80 feet span and 100 feet high, he overlooks that beautiful river appropriately termed the Eden, flowing between thickly wooded banks, past the pretty village of Wetheral, and the renowned grounds of Corby Castle; and glancing along the course of the silvery stream, in a north-west direction, there is spread to view a pleasing and extensive prospect of a plain studded with trees and hedgerows, resembling a great garden, stretching right into Scotland.

From the station Wetheral may be first visited, and then Corby reached by a ferry-boat over the river, charge 1$d.$; or the viaduct may be crossed from the station by a footway, on payment of ½$d.$, and Wetheral reached by ferry-boat after visiting the Castle grounds. There is a large inn close to the station, and smaller ones on each side of the river.

The grounds of the Castle are only open to the public on Wednesdays, and the interior of the house is not generally shown to visitors.

A few yards beyond the village of Corby is the lodge gate, where the park is entered. It is advisable to stroll at once to the top of the hill on the left, crowned with noble trees, as it commands a grand prospect, embracing Carlisle, the Castle and Cathedral—a wide extent of level country, the Langholm monument, the Solway Firth, and Criffel mountain; and by proceeding a few yards farther, Skiddaw and other of the Lake District mountains appear in sight. Passing a farmhouse, pleasant paths are entered, which continue under large old trees on the brow of the cliffs for a mile or two, with here and there glimpses of the stream below. It is well to follow these paths for some distance, and then to return by other paths close to the river.

On the opposite side of the water are observed thickly wooded banks, with here and there fine sandstone rocks, presenting a picturesque appearance; and on reaching a stone statue of a monk-like figure, bareheaded, and with book in hand, some caves will be seen in the face of the opposite cliffs. The figure is that of St. Constantine, a younger son of an early Scotch king, who turned hermit, and is said to have lived in the opposite caves, which are still called St. Constantine's Caves, and sometimes Wetheral Safeguards. These caves must be very ancient, for they are mentioned in the charter of St. Mary's, York, in Henry II.'s time. They may have been the abode of a hermit, but in all probability the monks of the adjacent priory excavated them, and used them as places of refuge or retreat from the Scotch marauders or other enemies. They are 40 feet above the river, and hewn out of the solid rock. There are three cavities, each seven yards in length, three in breadth, and three in height, and each has a window looking upon the water. A ledge served as the foundation for a wall which was built in front of the cells, and formed a sort of gallery or covered passage. There are no traces of steps; the entry must therefore have been effected by a ladder afterwards drawn into the cells which were concealed by hanging wood. They can now be visited after a short, pleasant walk from Wetheral.

Near the cells there is an inscription in the rock, supposed by some to be Roman.

A few yards from St. Constantine's statue is a pretty building, with steps, pillars and sculpture in front. It is used as a summer-house, and commands a lovely view through a long avenue to the Castle. After pacing the green sward of the avenue the tourist reaches some cool pleasant cells with water trickling through them, and then having passed a monster statue of Polyphemus in the attire of a Grecian warrior, by Dunbar, a steep ascent is made to a temple-like building, containing the figures of two females and two mermaids. The traveller is now close to the house, but before going to it it is advisable to descend again to the bank of the river, when he will pass a pool of water, in the centre of which stands a statue of Admiral Nelson. Here is a little picture, exquisitely beautiful, the water descending from the temple above over ledges of rock richly coloured with mosses and lichens of every hue. The path then passes some caverns in the sandstone rocks, and when the Wetheral Priory and Village on the opposite side come in sight, the bank becomes steep, and the path ascends and leaves the river. It is advisable to return a short distance, and then ascend to the Castle, the residence of P. H. Howard, Esq. The Castle stands on the edge of a cliff overlooking the Eden, and is a plain square mansion, built of red freestone, with a Doric portico. A parapet round the house is surmounted with lions, the family crest.

The sight of the lions will remind the tourist of a noted page in English history. The Earl of Surrey, an ancestor of the owners of Corby, had chief command of the English army at the battle of Flodden Field, in 1513, when the Scots were defeated with the loss of their king, the chief nobility, and 10,000 men. Surrey's eldest son, Thomas Howard, Lord Admiral of England, was in charge of the van, and another son, Sir Edmund Howard, knight marshal of the army, was in command of the right wing. In reward for his signal service Surrey was created Duke of Norfolk by Henry VIII., a title which had been conferred by Richard III. on his father, who fell fighting on the side of that tyrant at Bosworth Field. An augmentation was appointed to his arms, expressive of his victory over a king of Scotland, being on the bend thereof the upper half of a red lion, painted like that in the arms of Scotland,

and pierced through the mouth with an arrow, in token that the victory was chiefly owing to the English bowmen. The title of Earl of Surrey was given to his oldest son, the lord Admiral.

Though Corby Castle now presents the appearance of a modern hall, having undergone complete renovation at the early part of the present century, it is said to have been an ancient stronghold. Corby, on the attainder of Andrew de Harcla, Earl of Carlisle, in the reign of Edward II., was forfeited to the Crown, whereupon it was granted to Sir Richard de Salkeld, Knt., whose descendants possessed it for many generations, and finally sold it to Belted Will Howard of Naworth, who made it a provision for a younger son, from whom the present proprietor is descended. There are several monuments of the Salkeld family in the adjoining church of Wetheral.

The interior of the Castle is elegantly furnished, and contains many paintings and works of art of great interest and value.

In the Stuart gallery: Portrait of Charles II., given by himself to Mr. Francis Howard at the Restoration; Lord William Howard, and his grandson Colonel Thomas Howard, slain at Atherton Moor; one, very rare, of the Princess Louisa, sister of Charles Edward, who died in her seventeenth year. In the dining-room: Charles, Duke of Norfolk, by Hoppner. In the library: The Emperor Charles V. and his Consort Isabella of Portugal, by Titian; David and Goliath, by Poussin; Thomas, Duke of Norfolk, victor of Flodden, by Holbein; fine portrait, by Gainsborough, of Ann Witham, wife of Philip Howard; and other more modern family portraits by Hoppner and Northcot. In the drawing-room : St. Catherine and two Angels, typifying divine love and martyrdom, by Leonardo da Vinci, or Luini; Madonna and Child, by Sasso Ferrato, belonged formerly to the late Cardinal Erskine. Besides these, there are the gems of the collection: the Marriage of St. Catherine, by Corregio, and St. Agnes, by Carlo Dolce; and also some beautiful miniatures.

Among the curiosities are many ornaments which belonged to Mary, Queen of Scots, including the rosary and cross worn by her on the scaffold, and sent through Melville, her secretary, to the Earl of Arundel, as the last pledge of affection for a family which had suffered so much for her. The grace cup of St. Thomas à Becket, and another which belonged to Götz von Berlichingen; and a carved oak chair, formerly at Dilston Hall, the seat of the earls of Derwentwater.

In the "Ghost Room," with its tapestried walls and black oak wainscoting, there is a pane of glass on which are the lines written by David Hume:

> "Here chicks in eggs for breakfast sprawl,
> Here godless boys God's glories squall,
> While Scotsmen's heads adorn the wall,
> But Corby's walks atone for all."

Descending to the brink of the river by a pleasant path from the Corby village, the traveller will enjoy a most lovely prospect while being rowed across in the ferry-boat to the Wetheral side of the stream. He will then stroll to St. Constantine's Caves, and afterwards visit the priory and the church.

The priory is only a few yards distant. Hardly any part of it remains; only an embattled tower and an archway, close to which has been erected a farmhouse. It was founded in 1088 for monks of the Benedictine order. On the dissolution of monasteries in the reign of Henry VIII. it was bestowed on the Dean and Chapter of Carlisle. It was afterwards pulled down, and the materials were used for building prebendal residences in that city. It was an appendage to St. Mary's Abbey at York.

Wetheral village is a clean-looking, pretty little place. The principal object of attraction for strangers is a small mausoleum attached to the parish church, built over the vault of the Howard family, and which contains a marble monument by Nollekens, said to be "one of the finest pieces of sculpture in modern times." Upon it is the following inscription: "Maria, the third daughter of Andrew Lord Archer, was married to Henry Howard on the 22nd of November, 1788, and died with her infant daughter on the 9th of November, 1789, in the 23rd year of her age." One writer says: "Mrs. Howard died when she became a mother, and the affecting incident is transferred by the magic chisel to the pure marble. There is the exquisite drapery, and the mother, and the new-born infant on her lap, looking upward from her couch of pain to the benignant figure of religion which is bending over them. 'Tis surely the sweetest group that genius ever created." There is a cast of a monument by Westmacott, representing a lady kneeling, to the memory of Mrs. Petre, Mr. Howard's sister.

A short distance below Wetheral, on the banks of the Eden, is Warwick Church, which was rebuilt five years ago, but the apse, which was retained, is one of the oldest bits of masonry in the district, and is remarkable for its circular shape, with thirteen arcades on the exterior, which is very unusual in England.

The Nunnery.

When at Wetheral some tourists may desire to drive to the beautiful grounds of the Nunnery, distant 10 miles up the river Eden. The road turns to the left half a mile out of the village, and then runs through a richly timbered country, with a prospect across to the Cumberland hills, Skiddaw being very prominent. Two and a half miles from Wetheral the new railway between Carlisle and Settle is crossed, and again 2½ miles farther on; the river Eden is in the hollow a short distance on the left, and on the opposite side of it is the Tindale and Crossfell range of hills. Seven miles from Wetheral the pleasant village of Armathwaite is reached, where, close to the bridge spanning the Eden, is the Red Lion, a comfortable inn, where refreshment may be obtained. The village is so delightfully situated along the wooded bank of the river, that few visitors will leave it without loitering there for a short time, and they cannot do better than enter the gate close to the bridge, and stroll to the mansion known as Armathwaite Castle. It is not a castellated building, and does not present the appearance of a fortified residence, but it stands in beautifully wooded grounds, called the bay, where the river's banks present a charming appearance. A few yards higher up the stream is a high weir, over which, after heavy rains, the water rushes with great fury. Here, at a small corn-mill, the visitor may obtain a man to row him across to the opposite side, where there are some fine rocks and walks among the woods. One of these paths might be followed until the main road is entered leading to the Nunnery.

With a carriage the river must be crossed at the Armathwaite bridge, and the distance thence to the Nunnery is 3 miles.

The visitor who expects to meet with the ruins of an old

monastery will be disappointed. An ancient religious house of Benedictine nuns, founded by William Rufus, is said to have existed here, but the old edifice appears to have been demolished, and on the site of it a mansion of red freestone has been erected, which is now occupied as a farmhouse, the owner, Mr. Aglionby, preferring to live on an estate in Virginia, in the United States of America.

The parties residing in the house kindly allow a visitor to put his horses in the stables, and make no charge for entering the grounds; but all ought to leave a trifle to help to pay the expense of keeping the grounds in order.

Close to the house will be observed a Roman altar, with an inscription; and on a hill, a few yards distant, is an old cross, said to have been the boundary of the ground to which malefactors could flee for sanctuary.

The chief, in fact the only attraction of the place, is the river scenery and the delightful walks in the romantic dell through which flows the Croglin streamlet. Although the grounds are not very extensive, the paths wind about in the woods for miles, and in places are carried close to the water under immense cliffs, and on each side of a finely wooded ravine, down which the streamlet dashes with great impetuosity over high rocks, forming a series of fine cascades, the whole effect being singularly impressive.

Visitors occasionally arrive here from Penrith viâ Kirkoswald, Lazonby, and Eden Hall, a distance of 12 miles.

Brampton.

This is a quiet old market-town, containing 2800 inhabitants. Market day, Wednesday. It stands 1½ miles north-west of the Newcastle and Carlisle Railway, and is reached by alighting at Milton station (now named in the Company's time-tables Brampton station), and then going on a tramway, in a carriage called a dandy, drawn by one horse, the charge being 3d. The place contains a woollen mill, and there are some collieries not far distant. It would be little visited by tourists were it not for the Mote, a steep conical hill, rising between 300 and 400 feet above the town, whence may be obtained a splendid view of the surrounding country, and upon the summit of which was erected, in 1870, a statue of the late Earl of Carlisle, pronounced by competent judges to be well executed and an excellent likeness. Upon the monument is the following inscription: "Erected by the people of Cumberland to commemorate the public services and personal worth of George William Frederick Howard, seventh Earl of Carlisle, K.G. Born April 18th, 1802, died December 5th, 1864. J. H. Foley, R.A., Sculptor, London, 1869. H. Prince & Co., Founders, Southwark."

Standing on the top of the hill the spectator sees the streets of the town close below, and then is spread a vast tract of level country, wooded and well cultivated, like a garden, stretching to Carlisle, the Solway Firth, and Scotland; Criffel and other Scotch hills being to the right, and the Cumberland hills to the left, including Skiddaw, Grisedale Pike, Blencathara, Carrock and Caldbeck fells, Souterfell, and Helvellyn range. To the south-east are Castle Carrock, Talkin and Tindale fells. To the northeast is the vale of the Irthing, backed by high ground, which stretches into Scotland.

Eastward of the Mote is an eminence, named the Ridge, much frequented on summer evenings as a promenade by the inhabitants of Brampton and the adjacent villages. Seats are placed at convenient distances, and a row of trees is on the right. It commands an unobstructed view to the north across a vast tract of level woodland to the Solway Firth, and to Criffel, Burnswork, and other Scotch hills. Castlesteads is also a fine object. At the end of the Ridge a pleasant wood is entered, and the path winds to the right, and descends and enters the Lanercost road three-quarters of a mile out of Brampton.

The old church is 1½ miles from Brampton. After going through the town and proceeding a quarter of a mile on the Longtown road, follow a lane on the left, which takes direct to the church. It is a small unpretending edifice, with a tiny bell-turret and one bell, and would appear very like a barn were it not covered almost entirely with ivy. It is probably of very ancient date, as Robert, Parson (persona) of Brampton, was one of the witnesses of the charter granted by Robert de Vallibus at the foundation of Lanercost Priory in 1169. Some importance must have been attached to this church, for in 1360, when Richard Rydal, the prior of Lanercost, absented himself from duty, Martin, vicar of Brampton, was appointed by the bishop to fill the place in his absence; and in another instance, the vicar of Brampton installed a new prior, on the authority of a commission from the bishop. The adjoining graveyard is thickly studded with headstones, and it is still used as a place of interment for Brampton, though there is no regular service held in the church. In the south wall on the outside of the building is an arch, and beneath it a monumental slab, now grassed over, under which the founder of the church is supposed to be interred. The river Irthing flows close past the grounds, and may be reached by returning on the Brampton road for a hundred yards, and then going through a gate on the right. Tourists who do not wish to return direct to Brampton may extend their walk, and continue by the bank of the stream to the point of junction with the Gelt rivulet, and then along the bank of the Gelt to the Lower Bridge, distant from the church $4\frac{1}{2}$ miles.

Talkin Tarn.

Talkin Tarn is situated half a mile to the south-west of Milton (Brampton) railway station, and two miles from the town of Brampton. At the station enter a road, which runs westward on the south side of the line, and then passes through a gate and winds to left; the tarn being about one mile distant by this route. Half a mile may be saved by following a footpath over ground covered with gorse and heather, on left, a few yards from the station, and then through a plantation. The tarn is a large sheet of water $1\frac{1}{2}$ miles in circumference. Half of its banks are covered with wood, and from the other half rises undulating and cultivated ground, clothed with a few clumps of trees. In the background is the Talkin Fell, hiding the Tindale and Castle Carrock fells.

There are boats on the tarn, which can be hired either from a person generally in attendance, or at a public-house on the Brampton road half a mile distant. There is a rowing club at Brampton, and regattas are held once a year, also sports or picnic parties occasionally. The water is well stored with pike and perch.

The Gelt stream and the 'Written Rocks may be reached from the tarn by following the road which crosses the railway, and then bends to left, and descends to the Lower Gelt Bridge, a distance of two miles; or the stream may be reached after walking direct from the tarn one mile through the fields in the direction of Hellbeck, a rill that drains the lakelet of its surplus water.

On the banks of Hellbeck a battle was fought on the 20th of February, 1570, between 1500 regular cavalry under the command of Lord Hunsden, governor of Berwick, and 3000 men assembled by Leonard Dacre, who had rebelled against Queen Elizabeth. Leonard's army behaved with great courage, and among them "were many stout women who gave the adventure of their lives, and fought right stoutlie for Dacre," but all was of no avail, for his army was defeated with a loss of 400 killed and 300 taken prisoners. Various accounts are given of the cause of the revolt, but the following appears the most probable. During the autumn of the previous year the papists in the northern counties, under the leadership of the Earls of Northumberland and Westmorland, rebelled against Elizabeth, and in support of her prisoner, Mary, Queen of Scots, and they mustered 15,000 strong at Wetherby in Yorkshire. They were defeated, and fled by way of Hexham and Naworth into Scotland, where some were captured, while others found refuge on the Continent. Edward Dacre, Leonard's brother, was an active partisan in this rebellion, and Leonard Dacre himself appears to have countenanced it, and given vague promises of assistance, but taken no part personally. About the same time, his nephew, Lord George Dacre, Baron of Gilsland, a mere child, was accidentally killed by a fall from a wooden vaulting horse. Leonard claimed the estates by right of entail, but Thomas, Duke of Norfolk, who had married the widow of Thomas Lord Dacre, Leonard's brother, sought and obtained the Dacre baronies for his wife's daughters by her first husband, and he afterwards married the girls to his own sons. By this means Leonard and his two younger brothers, Edward and Francis, were deprived of the estates. As he was not able to obtain in the courts of law what he considered his rights, or disdaining probably to prosecute his suit by the slow process of law, and knowing that he was suspected of favouring the late rebellion, he seized Naworth Castle, and called his supporters to arms. After the battle he made his escape to Scotland, whence he and his brother Edward afterwards retired into Flanders. His youngest brother, Francis Dacre, who had taken no part in the rebellion, lived and died in poverty and retirement, and Francis' only son, Randal, appears also to have lived in seclusion, for all that we know of him is that he died in London, and was buried at Greystoke in 1634, his body having been brought down at the charge of Thomas, Earl of Surrey. More than 300 years have passed since Leonard Dacre and his devoted followers fought the battle of the Gelt, and tradition is now almost silent respecting it. All that the stranger can learn from those living near the spot is that Hellbeck is so called because once after a great battle the rivulet ran with blood three days and three nights. Relics of the conflict have at different times been found on the adjacent grounds, and within a hollow tree there was discovered the skeleton of a human body, in all probability that of some wounded soldier, who having crept in for protection had there died. Some corroded vestiges of an iron weapon were lying near the remains.

The River Gelt, and the Written Crag.

The glen through which flows the river Gelt is famed chiefly for having some Roman inscriptions on the face of a rock known as the Written Crag, and although the writings are very curious and interesting to the historian and the antiquary, the glen deserves to be visited independently of these memorials, for it is a most lovely spot and in the highest degree picturesque.

The best plan is to enter the glen at the Lower Gelt Bridge, distant from Milton station 2½ miles, and from the town of Brampton 2 miles. At the railway station enter the road which runs on the south side of the line, and then crosses the rails and bends to the left. Half a mile before arriving at the river the spot is passed where formerly by the road-side stood an old oak, nearly 18 feet in circumference, called the "Capon Tree." This name, according to tradition, was obtained from the judges of assize and their retinue, who, owing to the poverty of the intervening country, could not in their progress from Newcastle to Carlisle procure sufficient refreshment,· and were wont under this oak to regale themselves in the open air on capons and wine. The name, however, in all probability is derived from the Saxon word "kepand," to catch or lay hold of, and at this tree the sheriff and his company met or caught the judges of assize on their way to Carlisle. Macaulay, in his 'History of England,' vol. i., says: "The judges on circuit, with the whole body of barristers, attorneys, clerks and serving men, rode on horseback from Newcastle to Carlisle, armed and escorted by a strong guard under the command of the sheriffs. It was necessary to carry provisions; for the country was a wilderness which afforded no supplies. The spot where the cavalcade halted to dine, under an immense oak, is not yet forgotten."

At the Lower Gelt Bridge is an inn, which was an important place in old coaching days, for it stands on the military road between Carlisle and Newcastle. From the bridge a wide grass-covered path runs through the woods by the east side of the stream, and there are also walks higher up the bank, and on the opposite side. Half a mile above the bridge, a few steps on the left lead to the Written Crag, which overhangs the water. The track to the spot is only a few yards long but very narrow, and in the face of a precipice, thus requiring the stranger to thread his way with care.

Dr. Bruce gives the following translation of the inscriptions:

"A vexillation of the second legion styled the August on account of its bravery, under Agricola the optio (lieutenant)."
"Aper and Maximus being consuls (A.D. 207). The workshop (quarry) of Mercatius. The band of Julius."
"Mercatius (the son of) Fermus Julius Peculiaris, a vexillation of the 20th legion (styled) Valeria and Victrix."

Continuing by the path up the stream for a hundred yards farther, steps are observed on opposite bank leading to a hollow in the cliff known as Abraham's Cave, a place which used to be shown to strangers, but has not recently been opened. A short distance farther an immense vertical sandstone cliff is passed, which has been, in all probability, a large quarry worked by the Romans. The glen all the way is narrow and remarkably beautiful, the channel of the river being in the rock, which in places is curiously hollowed and scooped, forming little cascades and whirlpools, whilst precipitous cliffs arise like rugged walls on either side, covered here and there with wood from base to summit. The pleasant murmur of the water and the majestic grandeur of the surrounding scenes will tempt many visitors to wend their way up the glen by the smooth path close to the stream.

Two miles distant from the Lower Bridge is the middle bridge, where is a public-house and the railway arches spanning the ravine. A narrow track then leads on the west side of the water for half a mile to the hamlet of Greenwell, where are a few farmhouses and green fields, and by following a lane another half mile the Upper Bridge is reached. Here the water flows in a deep, dark, wooded dell, and in places tumbles over ledges of rock and forms beautiful cascades. Crossing to the east side and following an ill-defined track high up the bank, a farmhouse is passed, and a road entered which comes from Brampton by Talkin village, and runs into the recesses of the neighbouring fells of Talkin, Castle Carrock, Gelstone, and Tindale.

The traveller can either return to Milton station *via* Talkin Tarn, or prolong his journey to the summit of Tindale Fell, the hills here being well grouped and very tempting for a mountain ramble.

GILSLAND SECTION.

GILSLAND.

GILSLAND * is situated on the Newcastle and Carlisle Railway, 20 miles from Carlisle, and 40 miles from Newcastle; exactly on the boundary line between Northumberland and Cumberland; and on the watershedding to east and west; the river Irthing flowing past the village to the west, into the Eden, and thence to the Solway Firth; and the Tipalt, to the east, into the South Tyne, and thence by Newcastle to the German Ocean.

To the north is a vast tract of common, or undulating mossy pasture land, called the *Waste*, rendered classical

* Until within the last few years the railway station was called Rose Hill, and only the ground near the sulphur well was known as Gilsland. At present the village is sometimes spoken of as Rose Hill, but formerly that appears to have been merely the name of a small mound, which was removed to afford a site for the station, and the houses close by were called Runnerfoot, Buff Head, The Crooks, and Mumps Hall.

Camden, in his 'Britannia,' offers two or three suggestions as to the origin of the name of Gilsland, which in the middle ages embraced a wide tract of the neighbouring country. He says: "Gillesland Barony is a tract so cut and mangled with the brooks (which they call *Gilles*) that I should have thought it had taken the name from them; if I had not read in the book of Lanercost church that one *Gill* the son of Bueth (called also *Gilbert* in a charter of Henry II.) was possessed of it, so that probably it had its name from him." To this, in Gibson's edition of Camden, there is added the following note: " A gill signifies in the Northern dialect a *low ground* near a water side encompassed with hills, but nowhere the *brook* or *rill* itself. *Hubert de Vallibus* probably might give the name to the country, for de Vallibus (Vaux) and *Gills* signified the same thing, unless one should say that it comes from the river *Gelt* which runs through the middle of it."

in romance by Sir Walter Scott's vivid description of it in 'Guy Mannering.' It extends for many miles right into Scotland, the division of the two countries being about 14 miles distant. Three or four miles to the south of the village rises the Tindale Fell, the beginning of the Pennine mountain range extending past Crossfell to the south-west of England. To the east is the South Tyne, and a long cliff-like ridge with its face to the north, presenting for miles a fine escarpment of rock; whilst westward is a fertile and well-wooded district, containing Naworth and Corby castles, and the ruins of Lanercost and Wetheral priories. The Roman wall passed close to the site of the railway station, and a small part of it is to be seen in the vicarage garden 300 yards distant. There is a fine Roman camp at Birdoswald, 1½ miles to the west; and 2 or 3 miles eastwards are the ditch, and portions of the wall in a good state of preservation. One mile to the south of the village, and parallel with the railway, is the turnpike road between Carlisle and Newcastle, provincially known as the Military Road. It was begun in 1751 and constructed by Government, chiefly for the transit of soldiers and war material during the unsettled period when the Stuart family troubled the new Hanoverian dynasty of England. Previous to this time the roads were so bad that in 1745, when the Pretender, Charles Edward, invaded England from Scotland, the governor of Carlisle, on applying to the commander of the troops at Newcastle for assistance, received a reply that the country being impassable for artillery, the enemy would have to be met in Lancashire.

Gilsland is a favourite resort of the Newcastle, Shields, and Sunderland people; and many visit it from Scotland and different parts of Cumberland; and also tourists often stay here a few days when travelling to and from Scotland. It is considered to be one of the healthiest places in England, the air being remarkably pure and bracing, but it is chiefly resorted to on account of its mineral waters, there being an excellent sulphur spring, and also a chalybeate or iron well.

In the village, close to the station, there are three small inns, the Station Hotel, the Samson Inn, and Bridge House, and about a dozen lodging houses; and a mile and a quarter distant, and visible from the railway, is a large handsome hotel, delightfully situated on an eminence 610 feet above the level of the sea, upon the wooded banks of the river Irthing, and close to the wells. It is generally called "Shaw's Hotel," Shaw being the Teutonic word schawe, a thicket. Burns in " My Nannie's Awa'," says:

"While birds warble welcome in ilka green shaw."

The edifice, erected at a cost of nearly 10,000*l.* by the late George Gill Mounsey, Esq., of Castletown, Carlisle, is built on the site of an old hotel which was burnt to the ground on the 27th of August, 1859. It is capable of accommodating 200 visitors, and connected with it, and managed by the same proprietor, Mr. James Gelderd, are three other large houses which were formerly private residences. The principal of these, the Orchard House, stands half a mile from the station, and three-quarters of a mile from the hotel. It is charmingly embowered by trees, and is a favourite retreat for private families and young ladies. There is a public coffee-room, and the usual custom is for parties to provide for themselves and have the cooking done by the servants of the house. The other two houses are the Villa, and Wardrew House. The former stands on its own grounds close to the hotel, and commands an excellent prospect. The latter is situated on a wooded eminence on the opposite banks of the river, three minutes' walk from the hotel. It is a pleasant residence, half mansion, half farm, built in 1752 on the site of one much older; and a more healthy secluded spot could not be desired. The poet Burns appears to have stayed here one night during his Border tour in 1787, for he writes: "June, Wednesday.—Left Newcastle early and rode over a fine country to Hexham to breakfast, from Hexham to Wardrew the celebrated spa where we slept." A pane of glass in one of the windows, with Sir Walter Scott's name upon it, said to have been written by himself, was taken out about eight years since, when the house was rented by Mr. Hodgson Hinde, M.P. for Tynemouth, owing to the annoyance caused by the hundreds of strangers who visited the place to see the writing. Parties residing here can either be entirely alone and undisturbed, or they can mix with the visitors at the hotel, and take part in the balls, excursions, and other festivities of the place. Those staying at the Orchard House, and at the Villa, are allowed the freedom of the hotel grounds, bowling green, &c.; and in the evenings they can visit the hotel and join in the dancing. Private lodgings, not connected with the hotel, can also be had at the Shaw's Cottages, behind the Villa, and at the Green Grove Cottages near the sulphur well.

Visitors staying at the hotel are divided into three classes. The charge (including attendance) for board and lodging, for first class, is 8s. per day; for second class, 6s.; and for third class, 3s. 6d. Separate sitting and dining rooms are provided for each class, and private rooms can be had by paying a small extra charge. At so healthy a place, where almost everyone quickly finds that he can eat twice or thrice as much as at home, it is important to know the hours appointed for the meals, and to the stranger it is amusing to hear the constant recurrence of the bell calling the visitors to the prime occupation of the place. The first class have breakfast at 9 A.M., luncheon at 1 P.M., dinner at 5 P.M., and tea at 8 P.M.; the second class have breakfast at 8.30 A.M., dinner at 1.30 P.M., tea at 5.30 P.M., and supper at 8.30 P.M.; the third class have breakfast at 8 A.M., dinner at 12.30 P.M., tea at 5 P.M., and supper at 8 P.M.

In the hotel are billiard and bagatelle tables, library and news-room, and a ball-room. There is dancing every week-day evening during the season from 9 P.M. to 11 P.M.; and for those who do not care to trip about on the "light fantastic toe," chess, draughts, and cards are provided. During wet days the visitors often while away a few hours very pleasantly by arranging impromptu concerts. The grounds around the house are tastefully laid out, and well wooded, and the terrace commands an extensive and pleasant prospect across the vale, in which lies the village, and through which runs the railway and road between Carlisle and Newcastle. Anciently it was the course of the Roman wall, and now traces may be observed of both the north and the south ditches which accompanied the wall. Beyond the village is the gentle rising ground of Denton Fell, backed by the heath-clad height of Tindale Fell; and, looming in the distance to south-west, are the bulky masses of Skiddaw and Blencathara, reminding the on-looker of the lovely lakeland of Cumberland and Westmorland. Close to the terrace is a large bowling green and croquet ground, where visitors of both sexes may loiter happily enough for hours on a hot summer's day under the shade of the trees.

As the hotel is a mile and a quarter from the railway station, most visitors will avail themselves of the omnibus which meets every train, the charge being 6d. Those who walk may have a pleasant change in the route by leaving the road in the village at the Hydropathic Bath Establishment, and then proceeding by a footpath through the fields. Close to the baths a small stream, called the Poltross Burn, flows into the river Irthing. It, and the Irthing, are the boundary line here between Northumberland and Cumberland, so that part of the village is in Northumberland and part in Cumberland, along with the hotel and Orchard House. The footpath runs by the side of the river, and allows of a charming view of the hotel and Wardrew House perched at the top of the wooded eminence. The public path proceeds on the south bank of the river to the Irthing farmhouse, but to reach the hotel and the wells, the river has to be crossed at a footbridge, where there is a notice board stating that it is a private road. By paying 1d., however, to the boy who is sometimes in attendance, the stranger can cross the bridge, proceed through the fields by the side of a small dell, and gain the main road a few yards below the church.

Gilsland Church.

This building was erected in 1854 by the late George Gill Mounsey, Esq., who also provided the greatest portion of the endowment. The church was built principally for the accommodation of visitors. About one-half of the ancient parish of Lanercost, comprising 18,240 acres, is united to this church, and formed into a separate ecclesiastical district, by Order in Council. The parish of Over Denton, with its quaint little church, more ancient than the priory of Lanercost, is united to Gilsland, to be held as one benefice. Here a church and an endowed vicarage existed in early times, but the endowment is gone, like "the poor man's ewe lamb." The spoliation of the church property was complete, even the ancient parish churchyard being taken and treated as private property. The old baptismal font is used as a trough for cattle, and may be seen just inside the gate, at the dilapidated cottage on the west side of the road near the church gate. The curious old building in the north-east corner of the churchyard, a border peel with its massive walls, is yet, and always will be known as the ancient vicarage. Standing in close proximity to the church, and on land yet known as *glebe land*, it is evident that the tradition is true. The present vicar informed us that for two centuries the rectors and patrons neglected to appoint a vicar. It is easily seen that during that long vacancy of the living, the church, churchyard, vicarage, and glebe land, would be without a claimant. On the 28th November, 1566, Christopher Dacre leased the "advowson, rectory, and parsonage of Over Denton, together with all those his glebe lands, tithes, &c., to Nicholas Twydall of Over Denton for twenty-one years, at forty shillings a year;" and from the Tweddles the ancestors of the Earl of Carlisle purchased the property. This case affords an illustration of the unsettled state of the borders three centuries ago.

At the time of Robert de Vallibus, the founder of Lanercost, there was an ancient church existing in the parish of Over Denton. It was then that Robert, the son of Asketil, with the concurrence of De Vallibus, conveyed the rectory and right of presentation to the prior and canons of Lanercost, who, on each vacancy, were to present to the bishop a perpetual vicar of the parish. The vicar was to have his livelihood ("*victum suum*") out of the endowment, and to pay half a mark a year to the rectors. There is historical evidence to prove that this arrangement was faithfully carried out for about four centuries, and that it was only from the time of the dissolution of the priory that the parish was left without a minister, and that episcopal knowledge of its existence appeared to be lost. It was in the diocese of Durham; but Bishop Nicolson, of Carlisle, was the first to rediscover and restore the lost and spoliated parish. One pound a year salary for four quarterly sermons, and two shillings for communion wine, appear to have been the utmost that Bishop Nicolson could accomplish.

An eminent authority kindly supplies the following note on this subject: "The vicar was replaced by a poor incumbent, who received the magnificent stipend of twenty shillings per annum. The neighbouring living of Lanercost was worth about twenty pounds per annum, obtained by the painful collection of threepence each cow and calf, fourpence each foal, and such like miserable dues, to be collected over a parish of 40,000 acres. Farlam was also equally poor, and the three were enjoyed for sixty years prior to 1845 by the Rev. George Gillbanks, who held alternate services at Farlam and Lanercost. His income was helped out by some addition from Queen Anne's Bounty. These livings had all been appropriated to the priory of Lanercost, which took the revenues, and gave a monk some small stipend to do the services. On the dissolution of the monasteries those who obtained the revenues enjoyed by the priory obtained them subject only to these small stipends, sufficient for a monk who lived free at the priory, but not for an incumbent who had to live on the stipends."

The times of service are—at Gilsland church, every Sunday, 10.45 A.M. and at 6.30 P.M.; and at Over Denton, 3 P.M. The Rev. Adam Wright is the present vicar.

Near the Gilsland railway station there is a Wesleyan Methodist chapel, where service is held every Sunday at 10.30 A.M., and also at 6 P.M. during the summer.

The Sulphur Well.

As soon as the visitor has fixed his quarters at the hotel, or some lodging-house, as the case may be, he will take a stroll to the sulphur well, which is situated on the west bank of the river Irthing, at the base of high perpendicular cliffs, and in a beautifully wooded and secluded dell, about 350 yards from the hotel. The descent is steep, but the grounds all around are very pleasant. Close to the well are a few modest buildings, one containing a bazaar, another a refreshment house, and a third baths and an engine for pumping the sulphur water to the hotel. Hot or cold sulphur baths can be had here, the charge being 1s. 6d. each. They are also provided in the hotel at 2s. each.

Throughout the day the well is constantly frequented by visitors from the hotel and village, with their drinking glasses and jugs; and the stream gives forth a never-failing supply of pure and cold water. The river flows close by over a rugged bed strewn with blocks of freestone; and the overhanging cliffs, composed of layers of sandstone and shale, are quite perpendicular, and not less than 100 feet high, and charmingly diversified with plants and trees. The geologist will look with interest on these rocks, and picture in his mind the far-bygone time when each alternate layer was formed by a never-ceasing but long-continued process.

The strata through which the water percolates are deposited in the following manner: Surface soil, 1 foot; irregularly stratified sandstone, 33 feet 5 inches; bituminous shale, 22 feet 9 inches, which includes a stratum of aluminous schist 4 feet 2 inches deep; porphyry slate, containing minute crystals of felspar and iron pyrites, 22 feet 10 inches. From under this stratum the sulphuretted water issues, through a leaden pipe, at the rate of two gallons and a half per minute. Below the spa are the following strata: Bituminous shale, 4 feet, through which run four thin strata of clay ironstone; coarse greenstone, 2 feet; bituminous shale, containing eight thin strata of clay ironstone, 6 feet; and cubical coal, 9 inches.

Dr. Reid Clanny, of Sunderland, who gave great attention to the mineral waters of Gilsland, and published a treatise on them in 1816, says: "In general a half-pint tumbler of this water is a sufficient dose for an adult, but the quantity ought to be augmented as the stomach becomes accustomed to it, and may be increased, if needful, to the extent of two or three quarts in the forenoon. It acts powerfully upon the kidneys, and as a diuretic stands unrivalled amongst mineral waters. Its diaphoretic effects are of no ordinary nature in severe and obstinate diseases of the skin. It has been found to be very efficacious in the cure of dyspepsia or indigestion. The water is also highly esteemed as a remedy for the cure of those who are affected with scrofulous habits, for the cure of ill-conditioned and irritable ulcers; it is often used with great benefit as an external application, and a course of it, and a few tepid baths, have effected several cures of chronic rheumatism. The water is also a valuable remedy in atonic gout, which, being a distressing and obstinate disease, requires the greatest attention and reflection. In those diseases which are attended with a copious secretion of bile, it cannot be too much extolled; and in some instances in which the waters of Cheltenham have failed, this water effected a cure. In worn-out constitutions it has done wonders, as its tonic powers are called into action in strengthening the system.

THE SULPHUR WELL.

One gallon of this water contains—

	cubic inches.
Sulphuretted hydrogen gas	17·0
Carbonic acid gas	6·2
	23·2

The following are the gaseous and solid contents of a wine gallon of this water:

	grains.
Common salt	20·05864
Carbonate of soda	4·50296
Carbonate of lime	1·462
Silica	1·1696
	27·19320

In 1858 the late Dr. George Wilson, of Edinburgh, gave the following analysis:

COMPOSITION OF AN IMPERIAL GALLON.

Proto-carbonate of iron	0·66
Carbonate of lime	2·39
Carbonate of magnesia	0·73
Sulphate of lime	0·41
Sulphate of potash	0·11
Sulphate of soda	2·62
Chloride of sodium (salt)	5·07
Carbonate of soda	21·49
Sulphide of sodium	1·78
Organic matter	1·92
Silica	0·81
	37·99

Specific gravity	1·0003

	cubic inches.
Combined carbonic acid gas	22·56
Free carbonic acid	·44
Total in one gallon	23·00

	cubic inches.
Oxygen gas in one gallon	2·2
Nitrogen gas	5·8
Sulphuretted hydrogen	21·0

The Popping Stone.

Had it not been that there are always some shy bachelors, we would not have given our usual practical directions for finding this stone, for the orthodox plan is to obtain the companionship of one of the fair sex, who, somehow, generally are aware what direction to take, and not unwilling to render assistance to the puzzled stranger.

A wooden footbridge spans the river, a few yards from the sulphur well, but, when the water is low, the opposite bank may be gained by walking over stepping stones. The lover of the picturesque will delight in wandering up and down the stream, along the stones over which the water is constantly flowing with a musical sound at the base of high towering and well-wooded cliffs, and he may readily find haunts secluded enough for the play of the imagination, and the abode of water nymphs.

When over the stream and through the plantation the river, if not too high, is again crossed at some stepping stones in front of the Green Grove Cottages,* and then the traveller wends his way for a few hundred yards over green sward on the bank of the river and through as charming a dell as it is possible to imagine.

"Poetic fields encompass me around,
And still I seem to tread on classic ground."

Presently, at a bend in the glen, the *Popping Stone* is reached, where Sir Walter Scott is said to have popped the question, and close to it is a thorn tree known as the *Kissing Bush*, where the compact is supposed to have been sealed. The stone, though large, is now much rounded, and only half its original size, owing to people constantly chipping off bits to take away with them, as these pieces are said to have great efficacy when placed under the pillows of the unmarried of the fair sex, causing them to dream of their future partners. Gilsland being a small

* Formerly these cottages were called "The Hulks," and it is supposed the name originated with the people of the hotel in their desire to get a word that would sufficiently describe the inferiority of the place.

homely place, few visitors remain any length of time without considerably enlarging their circle of acquaintance, and amongst the young people a visit to the Popping Stone sometimes assists in cementing a friendship which lasts for life.

A more lovely or secluded nook Scott could not have chosen for making known his love to Miss Carpenter, who soon afterwards became his wife. It is easy to understand how supremely happy a young man, full of enthusiasm and poetry, and alive to all that was lovely in nature, would feel in such a spot, in the presence of one so charming as was then the object of his affections.

In July, 1797, Scott set out on a tour to the English lakes, accompanied by his brother John, and a friend. They visited Carlisle, Penrith, Brougham Castle, Mayborough, Arthur's Round Table, Ullswater and Windermere; and at length fixed their headquarters at the then peaceful and sequestered little watering-place of Gilsland, making excursions thence to various scenes of romantic interest. Scott was, on his arrival, not a little fascinated with the beauty of one of the young ladies who lodged under the same roof with him, but this was only a passing glimpse of flirtation. A week or so later commenced a more serious affair.

Riding one day with his friend, they met, some miles from Gilsland, a young lady taking the air on horseback, whom neither of them had previously remarked, and whose appearance instantly struck both so much that they kept her in view until they had satisfied themselves that she also was one of the party at Gilsland. The same evening there was a ball, at which there was no little rivalry among the young travellers as to who should first get presented to the unknown beauty of the morning's adventure. Though the other two gentlemen had the advantage of being dancing partners, Walter succeeded in handing the fair stranger to supper, and such was his first introduction to Charlotte Margaret Carpenter. Without the features of a regular beauty, she was rich in personal attractions; "a form that was fashioned as light as a fay's"; a complexion of the clearest and lightest olive; eyes large, deep-set, and dazzling, of the finest Italian brown; and a profusion of silken tresses, black as the raven's wing; her address hovering between the reserve of a pretty young Englishwoman who has not mingled largely in general society, and a certain natural archness and gaiety that suited well the accompaniment of a French accent. A lovelier vision could hardly have been imagined, and from that hour the fate of the young poet was fixed. She was the daughter of Jean Carpenter, a French royalist, who held an office under Government. On her father's death, her mother escaped with her and her only brother, first to Paris and then to England, where they found a warm friend in Arthur, the second Marquis of Downshire, who had, in the course of his travels in France, formed an intimate acquaintance with the family, and, indeed, spent some time under their roof. Her father had, on his first alarm as to the coming Revolution, invested 4000*l.* in English securities—part on a mortgage upon Lord Downshire's estates. On the mother's death, which occurred soon after her arrival in London, this nobleman took on himself the character of sole guardian to her children; and the son received, through his interest, an appointment in the service of the East India Company, in which he had by this time risen to a lucrative situation. Miss Carpenter had been educated in the Protestant faith—the religion of her mother. Her brother had settled upon her an annuity of 500*l.* After a courtship of six months, Scott was married to the lady on the 24th of December, 1797, in the parish church of St. Mary, Carlisle.

The Chalybeate Well.

A very pleasant walk may be had through the plantation on the brow of the cliffs overhanging the western side of the river, by taking the higher path in front of the hotel door. Seats are placed at convenient distances, from some of which charming views are had down to the stream, and the people may be observed below walking to the sulphur well and to the Popping Stone. The path leads to the chalybeate or iron well, which hardly deserves the name of a well, as the water comes merely in small drops, and to obtain a tumblerful the tourist has to wait some minutes. Independently of the well, however, the spot is deserving a

THE CHALYBEATE WELL. 71

visit, and the stranger may continue for a few yards farther to the Green Grove Cottages, and thence to the Popping Stone; or he may, by making a slight ascent from the well, or from the cottages, gain the Common, or Waste, and then wander at his will almost any distance. Those who visit the Popping Stone from the sulphur well may return this way, or *vice versâ*; and when the river is high, and the stepping stones cannot be crossed, this is the only way that can be taken. The chalybeate well has been known only about half a century, though the sulphur well was frequented in remote times.

The following are the strata through which the chalybeate water flows: Surface soil from 2 to 4 feet; coarse sandstone, cemented by an argillaceous basis, from which the spring flows, 3 feet. Beneath this there is a coarse sandstone, 4 or 5 feet thick, with gravelly bottom. In Dr. Clanny's treatise we read: "The iron suspended in this water is in the state of a sulphate, which is uncommon. The dose should be half a wine glass at first, twice a day, which may be increased to a small tumbler. Perhaps the best mode to be used would be to commence the use of it by putting a tablespoonful of chalybeate into a common-sized tumbler, and taking it to the sulphuretted water, with which it may be filled, and immediately afterwards drunk. The sulphuretted hydrogen and carbonic acid gases of the sulphuretted water will cause the chalybeate to sit more lightly upon the stomach, and by this process the dose may also be more readily augmented. The sulphate of iron, which is the most valuable ingredient in this water, gives so strong an impression upon the tongue, that the twentieth part of a grain of it, in a pint tumbler of warm water, may be readily distinguished. This mineral water may be kept for any length of time, provided the bottles be well corked, is very valuable for the cure of dyspepsia, and as an external application in foul ulcers, for which, from its stimulant and astringent properties, it is likely to be very serviceable. As a tonic it is also of great value. Under its use the stomach will be strengthened, the vascular system excited, the secretions promoted, and, consequently, the muscular power increased. Its virtues, therefore, are unquestionable in diseases of debility, in excessive discharges, local pain, and irritation, or affections of lungs and head.

Dr. Wilson analyzed this water, with the following result:

COMPOSITION OF ONE GALLON.

Proto-carbonate of iron	1·16
Carbonate of lime	5·89
Sulphate of potash	1·41
Carbonate of magnesia	1·82
Sulphate of soda	·94
Carbonate of soda	1·24
Chloride of sodium (salt)	·69
Silica	1·28
Organic matter	2·92
	17·35

Specific gravity .. 1·154

	cubic inches.
Combined carbonic acid gas	9·57
Free carbonic acid	2·63
Total in one gallon	12·20

	cubic inches.
Oxygen gas in one gallon	1·6
Nitrogen gas	5·7

Both the springs at Gilsland flow most copiously during the wet season, when they are comparatively weak in quality. In summer and autumn, when visitors most resort to them, they are at their best.

The Cramel Linn Waterfall.

This fall is situated up the river, 2 miles from the hotel. When the water is low some persons will delight in wandering leisurely along the rugged bed of the stream, stepping from stone to stone, and thus obtaining almost every minute lovely vistas, as the river winds through charming miniature dells, overhung with picturesque rocks, clothed with plants and trees; the only obtruder in these delightfully secluded nooks being the curlew, which flies wildly overhead, and with its shriek appears to resent the intrusion. Many times have we thus strolled for a few hours between meals, and always with increased interest, for it is a place where, if anywhere, one feels the truth of the well-known line of Keats:

"A thing of beauty is a joy for ever."

Here, we fancy, when on his visits to Gilsland in the heyday of his youth, would the "Northern Magician" delight to saunter, and with his strong imaginative genius people these secluded nooks with beings to us unseen, and

"Find tongues in trees, books in the running brooks,
Sermons in stones, and good in everything."

There being trout in the stream the angler may enjoy his favourite sport, and the geologist and botanist will find innumerable objects of interest.

Those who object to travel along the rugged bed of the river will reach the fall by entering the common from the chalybeate well, or from the Green Grove Cottages. Having gained the open ground, an extensive prospect is had of the surrounding country, with Skiddaw in the distance. Many persons fond of being alone and safe from intrusion will delight in gaining this ground, where they may walk for hours unmolested, and have the benefit of a pure, healthy breeze, or sit reading under the shade of the trees which fringe the brows of the cliffs overhanging the river. By keeping behind the plantation one or two stone fences are passed at stepping stiles, or through gateways, on the north of which is a wide extent of open grass-grown land, known as Spadeadam Waste, which contains only here and there, at wide intervals, single farmhouses, and these are mostly hidden in the hollows. Keeping in the direction of the stream, pleasant glimpses are obtained of it in its course, and no difficulty will be found in discovering the fall. On the sloping and overhanging banks of the river there are some sheep tracks which may be mistaken for paths. These are not always safe. The water flows over a wide ledge of rock about 25 feet high; the ravine both on the north and south sides of the cascade being solitary and picturesque. To realize the beauty of the fall it is necessary to descend to the river bed. This can be done without much difficulty even by ladies. Though there is nothing about the place very wild or grand, it possesses many charms, and cannot fail to please and beguile the true lover of nature. Tourists fond of a long ramble will follow the course of the river for 2 miles farther to a place called Wylie Syke, where are two or three farmhouses and a few green fields. For some distance above the fall the rocks on each side present features interesting to the geologist, there being some thin seams of coal, and in one place a small working, but afterwards the rocks subside and the banks are covered with grass to the water's edge. When the river is low the return journey from the waterfall may be agreeably varied, and good views obtained, by crossing to the east side and walking over grass-covered ground; the direction of Wardrew House being taken, or a descent made to the river after proceeding some distance.

Temple Heap.

After crossing the river by the footbridge near the sulphur well, a pleasant stroll may be enjoyed by following the path on the right which ascends the hill and passes through the plantation to Wardrew House, and thence by a road in front of the house to a small height crowned with a dozen trees, and known by the name of "Temple Heap." From this point an extensive prospect is obtained of the surrounding country. The village of Gilsland is fully displayed close below, and the river Irthing is seen winding along the wooded vale, and past the foot of the Roman station of Birdoswald. The practised eye will trace the route taken by the Roman wall from Birdoswald to the Carvoran Camp. The towers of Thirlwall Castle are visible 2 miles distant, at the beginning of the long cliff-like ridge known as the "Nine Nicks of Thirlwall," or more correctly the Walltown Crags, and the ivy-covered towers of Blenkinsop Castle may also be observed a little to the right of Thirlwall. Tindale Fell is the dark heath-covered mountain to the south; farther west are the Skiddaw and Criffel mountains, and between them on a clear day may be seen the Solway Firth. To the north, behind the hotel and Wardrew House, lies the Waste, which stretches to the Beacon and to the sources of the Irthing.

A descent may be made by the road which leads past

Irthing House to the village and railway station; or, at the house, the footpath may be entered, which conducts either to the village or over the river by the footbridge, and thence to the hotel.

Mumps Hall and Upper Denton Church.

Mumps Hall, which stands in the village, opposite the Methodist chapel, was formerly a public-house, and is celebrated as being the scene of the first rencontre of Brown, Dinmont, and Meg Merrilies, in the novel of 'Guy Mannering.' Unfortunately even the magic wand of Sir Walter Scott has been unable to preserve the old building, and now it is a private residence, presenting a new and modern appearance.

In a note appended to the above novel, and headed "Mumps Ha'," Scott says:

"There is, or rather I should say there *was*, a little inn, called Mumps Hall—that is, being interpreted, Beggar's Hotel—near to Gilsland, which had not then attained its present fame as a spa. It was a hedge alehouse, where the Border farmers of either country often stopped to refresh themselves and their nags in their way to and from the fairs and trysts in Cumberland, and especially those who came from or went to Scotland, through a barren and lonely district, without either road or pathway, emphatically called the Waste of Bewcastle. At the period when the adventures described in the novel are supposed to have taken place, there were many instances of attacks by freebooters on those who travelled this wild district, and Mumps Ha' had a bad reputation for harbouring the banditti who committed such depredations.

"An old and sturdy yeoman, belonging to the Scottish side, by surname an Armstrong or Elliot, but well known by his soubriquet of 'Fighting Charlie of Liddesdale,' and still remembered for the courage he displayed in the frequent frays which took place on the Border fifty or sixty years since, had the following adventure in the Waste, which suggested the idea of the scene in the text:

"Charlie had been at Stagshaw-bank fair, had sold his sheep or cattle, or whatever he had brought to market, and was on his return to Liddesdale. There were then no country banks where cash could be deposited, and bills received instead, which greatly encouraged robbery in that wild country, as the objects of plunder were usually fraught with gold. The robbers had spies at the fair, by means of whom they generally knew whose purse was best stocked, and who took a lonely and desolate road homewards—those, in short, who were best worth robbing, and likely to be most easily robbed.

"All this Charlie knew full well, but he had a pair of excellent pistols and a dauntless heart. He stopped at Mumps Ha', notwithstanding the evil character of the place. His horse was accommodated where it might have the necessary rest and feed of corn, and Charlie himself, a dashing fellow, grew gracious with the landlady, a buxom quean, who used all the influence in her power to induce him to stop all night. The landlord was from home, she said, and it was ill passing the waste, as twilight must needs descend on him before he gained the Scottish side, which was reckoned the safest. But Fighting Charlie, though he suffered himself to be detained later than was prudent, did not account Mumps Ha' a safe place to quarter in during the night. He tore himself away, therefore, from Meg's good fare and kind words, and mounted his nag, having first examined his pistols, and tried by the ramrod whether the charge remained in them.

"He proceeded a mile or two at a round trot, when, as the Waste stretched black before him, apprehensions began to awaken in his mind, partly arising out of Meg's unusual kindness, which he could not help thinking had rather a suspicious appearance. He therefore resolved to reload his pistols, lest the powder had become damp; but what was his surprise, when he drew the charge, to find neither powder nor ball, while each barrel had been carefully filled with *tow*, up to the space which the loading had occupied! and, the priming of the weapons being left untouched, nothing but actually drawing and examining the charge could have discovered the inefficiency of his arms till the fatal minute arrived when their services were required. Charlie bestowed a hearty Liddesdale curse on his landlady, and reloaded his pistols with care and accuracy, having now no doubt that he was to be waylaid and assaulted. He was not far engaged in the Waste, which was then, and is now, traversed only by such routes as are described in the text, when two or three fellows, disguised and variously armed, started from a moss-hag, while, by a glance behind him (for, marching, as the Spaniard says, with his beard on his shoulder, he reconnoitred in every direction), Charlie instantly saw retreat was impossible, as other two stout men appeared behind him at some distance. The Borderer lost not a moment in taking his resolution, and boldly trotted against his enemies in front, who called loudly on him to stand and deliver. Charlie spurred on, and presented his pistol. 'D——n your pistol!' said the foremost robber, whom Charlie to his dying day protested he believed to have been the landlord of Mumps Ha'. 'D——n your pistol! I care not a curse for it.' 'Ay, lad,' said the deep voice of Fighting Charlie, 'but the *tow's out now!*' He had no occasion to utter another word, as the rogues, surprised at finding a man of undoubted courage well armed instead of being defenceless, took to the moss in every direction, and he passed on his way without further molestation.

"The author has heard this story told by persons who received it from Fighting Charlie himself; he has also heard that Mumps Ha' was afterwards the scene of some other atrocious villany, for which the people of the house suffered. But these are all tales of at least half a century old, and the *Waste* has been for many years as safe as any place in the kingdom."

Margaret Carrick, the treacherous landlady above referred to, and whose soubriquet was "Meg of Mumps Hall," having passed her days amid these wild and often sanguinary deeds, and in the company of those reckless characters with which the borders were once filled, died in peace on the 4th of December, 1717, "the last of the iron race of the olden time," at the advanced age of one hundred, and sleeps in the churchyard of Upper Denton, where her daughter, Margaret Teasdale, who died 1777, aged ninety-eight, is also interred.

The church, distant from Mumps Hall one mile, will be visited with interest, as it is said to be one of the oldest and smallest parish churches in England. The road must be entered which passes on the south-west side of the Methodist chapel. A few yards farther is the Vicarage, a new house on the left, in the garden of which may be seen a small portion of the old Roman wall, 7 feet 8 inches broad, and 2 or 3 feet high. The road slightly ascends and crosses the railway at the school-house gates, and runs parallel with the line for half a mile to the hamlet of Upper Denton. Near the Hare and Hounds inn the railway is again crossed to the church, distant about 100 yards. It is a plain unpretending edifice, evidently built of stones from the Roman wall. It is 17 yards long and 6 yards broad, and contains a small bell-turret and tiny bell. In the burial-ground is a row of four noted gravestones, one being that of Margaret Carrick and Margaret Teasdale of Mumps Hall, mentioned above. Another is George Teasdale, Margaret's husband, who died 1753, aged thirty-five; the third is their daughter Bridget, who died 1779, aged fifty-nine; and the fourth their son John Teasdale, who died 1788, aged seventy-five. The inside of the church may be seen by obtaining the key at the neighbouring farmhouse. In the centre of the small chancel there is a vault, but no stone or other record to tell us whose remains are contained in it. On the north-east corner of the churchyard there is an ancient building now used as a byre and barn. This is the ancient vicarage, built in the form of a border peel. Hutchinson, in his 'History of Cumberland,' under the head of Vicarage, says: "The walls standing in the churchyard; the lower floor a keep for cattle; the upper floor for the inhabitant; the walls 5 feet thick, such as are seen on the borders of Northumberland." The ancient glebe land extends from the church to the river-side below Birdoswald. This belongs to the vicar, who, according to the deed conveying the patronage to the prior and canons of Lanercost, was to have his maintenance out of it, subject to the payment of half a mark annually to the patrons and rectors. The deed is in the chartulary of Lanercost, and Hutchinson gives a copy of it. Upper Denton was then in the county of Northumberland and diocese of Durham; it is now in Cumberland and in the diocese of Carlisle.

After visiting the church the tourist will have pleasure in strolling to the adjoining bank of the river Irthing, to see what is called the "petrifying well." A few yards beyond the hamlet, cross the line and enter a field at a wooden step-stile. Descending to the bed of the river at the north-west corner of the field the south bank is found to be composed of cliffs covered with beautiful moss and plants, and crowned with trees; and the moss is petrified in many places by water which is incessantly dropping from the rocks above. It is a cool, pleasant place, but one only to be visited by those who do not fear a rough stony path, and an occasional wetting from the drops above or the stream below.

The Roman Wall between the Poltross and the Irthing.

The Poltross is the streamlet which flows past Gilsland railway station, and enters the river Irthing close to Mumps Hall. It forms there the boundary line between Northumberland and Cumberland. The visitor will be repaid if he cross the railway behind the school-house and walk up the bed of the stream for a short distance. The water flows through a tiny wooded dell, and over stones and ledges of rock forming one or two small cascades, presenting here and there a pleasant little picture.

On the west side of the stream, just behind the line, and about 50 yards from the railway station, will be observed the ruins of part of a Roman mile castle. It is overgrown, but would, in all probability, if excavated, be found to form a good specimen; and is very conveniently situated for inspection by strangers. Believing as we do that the vallum, or south mound and ditch, was merely a Roman military road, we were agreeably surprised on being shown by the Rev. Adam Wright, the vicar of the parish, some stones on the west bank of the stream, which presented the appearance of having been Roman masonry, and the foundation of a bridge across the stream at the very spot it ought to have crossed to be in a line with the vallum. Mr. Wright also states that when clearing the school ground a belt of stones about 14 feet broad was discovered, which appeared to be the foundation of a road.

On again crossing the railway to the school-house a fine specimen of the wall will be observed in the Vicarage garden. The Vicarage house is built on the north fosse, and the school is near the line of the vallum. By entering the field opposite, and following the course of the wall for a short distance, there will be found, close to an ash tree, three courses of facing stones bared, and in as perfect a condition as when placed; and if the accumulated rubbish were removed from the bottom of the fence it is probable much of the lower part of the wall for two or three hundred yards would be found in a good state of preservation. On the opposite side of the fence the lower courses of facing stones are still perfect and visible for a score of yards, the wall here being about 8 feet thick. At the north-west end of the field the river makes a bend, and here the wall overhangs the precipitous banks for a few yards, without leaving room for the north fosse, but immediately on passing this place the fosse reappears in a very perfect condition, with its northern side high and sloping direct down to the river, and some of the wall in a good state. It is curious to observe that the wall here is about eight yards distant from the fosse, although it generally stands directly above it. Passing in the rear of a farmhouse, called Willow Ford, the ditch has been filled up, but the wall, though in a dilapidated condition, descends through another field, and may be traced by the great quantity of large, square, and rounded stones in the fence, overgrown, and almost entirely covered with trees and underwood. It continues in this way until within fifty yards of the river, and in a straight line with it, on the top of the opposite high cliff, may be seen the beginning of the wall running to Birdoswald. Of the bridge which must, in all probability, at one time have crossed the stream a few yards lower down, we could find no trace, but if the accumulated sand were removed it is likely the foundation stones would be seen.

Birdoswald and Coome Crags.

One of the favourite short excursions from Gilsland is to the Roman station of Birdoswald, and to Coome Crags; the former is 2¼ miles, and the latter 4 miles from the hotel, but half a mile may be saved by following the footpath through the fields.

A few yards below Orchard House enter the road which branches to the right. It leads over a little dell through which trills Red Beck, and then gradually ascends and commands a view of the river winding through a miniature vale at the foot of the Birdoswald cliffs.

On the right is passed a height called Rock Mount, upon which is a cluster of trees (two rows of beech and one of holly) surrounding a gravestone inscribed with the following: "Here lies Rock, a faithful and sagacious dog, in attachment and fidelity to his master he was an emblem of his name; died July, 1830." Rock's grave may be visited from Hill House, the mansion on the right. On the top of the mount is seen an extensive prospect embracing Skiddaw, Birdoswald, river Irthing, Tindale Fell, Gilsland, and the heights of Carvoran, or "Magna," above Thirlwall Castle.

A short distance beyond Hill House the road divides, the right hand leading to Triermain, Askerton Castle, and Bewcastle. The left-hand way has to be followed, and presently a glimpse is caught of a tower-like object, the only remaining portion of the ruin of Triermain Castle, and then the farmhouse of Birdoswald is reached, where the road again turns to the west.

As the ground is rather hilly, it is advisable for all who can do so, to leave the conveyance and walk through the fields by a footpath, which is entered at the first gate on the left after passing Hill House, and which conducts direct to the road close to Birdoswald. After crossing the first field, and a small dell down which runs the Kiln Hill beck, there will be observed, behind a mound, some heaps of grass-grown rubbish, apparently traces of ancient buildings, perhaps for camp followers during the time of the Romans, or even more ancient still. Here, on the slope towards the glen, and near to a thorn bush, there was formerly a mosstrooper's cottage.

Another way of reaching Birdoswald, but one suitable only for those who are not afraid of a little rough work, and only practicable when the water is low, is that of strolling for a mile along the banks of the river; commencing at Mumps Hall bridge. A few hundred yards below the bridge, the stream pours over large ledges of rock, and divides into two, flowing thus for some distance, and forming a small island. It then winds along over a rough bed, the banks being low and covered with foliage, until directly under the high cliff of Birdoswald, upon the brink and summit of which may be observed some of the old Roman wall. The height is composed of loose sandy soil, and must have weathered and worn greatly since the time of the Romans, so that it is now impossible to say whether the wall descended to the stream or not. The stranger may, by proceeding a few yards farther, wind his way without difficulty to the summit of the cliff.

There is a farmhouse at Birdoswald on part of the site

G

of the ancient station, and the residents supply excellent milk, or provide tea, &c., for picnic parties. It is a pleasant spot, being elevated, and commanding an extensive prospect. Just outside the station the cliffs descend steeply to the river Irthing, and are well clothed with wood. From them is had a beautiful view of the river winding through a tiny vale, whilst in the distance are the Thirlwall heights, Tindale Fell, Skiddaw, and Blencathara. This view is referred to by the late Earl of Carlisle, in his 'Diary in Turkish and Greek Waters.' He says: "Strikingly, and to anyone who has coasted the uniform shore of the Hellespont, and crossed the tame low plain of the Troad, unexpectedly lovely is this site of Troy, if Troy it was. I would give any Cumberland borderer the best notion of it, by telling him that it wonderfully resembles the view from the point just outside the Roman camp at Birdoswald; both have that series of steep conical hills, with rock enough for wildness and verdure enough for softness; both have that bright trail of a river creeping in and out with the most continuous indentations; the Simois has, in summer at least, more silvery shades of sand."

On the ground is a board containing the following notice:' "Persons wishing to examine the camp must obtain permission to do so at the farmhouse. Visitors are urgently requested to refrain from pulling down or displacing stone, mortar, &c., or otherwise injuring the walls or gateways."

The remains of this station are the most perfect on the line of the Roman wall, with the exception of that at Borcovicus or Housesteads, near the Northumberland Lakes. It is supposed to be the Roman Amboglanna, and to have been garrisoned by a strong force of Dacians from the districts now known as Wallachia and Moldavia. It is the largest station now found on the line, having an area of 5¼ acres, which is almost a quarter of an acre more than Chesters, and half an acre more than Housesteads. The eastern gateway is still in a fine state of preservation, with large blocks on each side of the double portal, placed in their original position, and still containing the pivot holes. The arch which would anciently stand above the gateway is destroyed, but some of the stones which formed it lie strewn about. In 1787 a similar gateway with an arch entire was discovered at Ellenborough, near Maryport, but unfortunately destroyed by the workmen. Close to the gate are the ruins of a building, apparently a guardhouse, and a portion of the boundary wall, 6 feet in breadth. The western and southern gateways and walls are also well preserved, the walls having five or six courses of facing stones, and being 7 or 8 feet thick. Dr. Bruce says: "Although the wall adapts itself to the north rampart of the fort, the station is entirely independent of the wall, and must have been built before it. Probably the first step taken in the construction of the barrier, in every case, was the erection of the stationary camps." Close to the garden in front of the house are remains of buildings which look as though they had been sleeping apartments or small barracks. Within the boundary wall are heaps of grass-grown rubbish, where formerly existed the temples, streets, &c.; and outside, to the east, are similar mounds, apparently the former abodes of camp followers and native inhabitants. Slight traces may also be observed of the moat or fosse which surrounded the walls of the station. In the rear of the house, close to the road, the northern gateway and wall are destroyed, but to the west of the station the wall runs for about 500 yards close to the road in as good a state of preservation as on any other part, being in some places 7 feet broad and 7 feet high. The best portion is observed inside the field. Not a single turret remains of the hundreds which were originally on the line of the wall. This is to be regretted; especially as one existed here until within the last few years. Hodgson says: "In 1833 I saw a turret opened about 300 yards west of Birdoswald, the walls of which were standing to the height of six courses of stones, and 34 inches thick—the doorway on the south and the internal area 13 feet square; all of it, in 1837, was taken away."

Sir Walter Scott in the prime of youth often visited this spot, and it was probably here that he penned the following:

"TO A LADY, WITH FLOWERS FROM THE ROMAN WALL.

"Take these flowers, which, purple waving,
  On the ruin'd rampart grew,
Where, the sons of freedom braving,
  Rome's imperial standards flew.
Warriors from the breach of danger
  Pluck no longer laurels there,
But they yield the passing stranger
  Wild-flower wreaths for Beauty's hair."

In the grounds at the west end of the house are some broken Roman altars and millstones, and inside the house is a beautifully-sculptured stone (being part of a figure in drapery), the head having been removed to the museum at Newcastle, and two or three small altars. The latter are such as were used by the soldiers in their private devotions.

Coome Crags.

After leaving Birdoswald the Roman wall disappears, and the road occupies its site, which is rendered evident by the perfect state of the north ditch, running along, close to, and parallel with the road, just behind the right-hand hedge.

When three-quarters of a mile beyond Birdoswald the antiquary will do well to leave the conveyance for two or three minutes, and stroll through a field along a cart-road leading to the first farmhouse on the left, called High House, in order that he may inspect what is perhaps the best specimen of the vallum or ditch and earth mounds, which ran at a little distance from the Roman wall, on the south side, and about the origin of which there has been much dispute. These mounds are so high that the traveller will easily distinguish them at some distance.

On gaining a slightly elevated portion of the road, with a single tree on the top, called "Wallbour's Tree," the view opens to the west over an undulating well-timbered district, with the Tindale and Castle Carrock fells on the left, and in the distance Skiddaw, Blencathara, and other Cumberland mountains. On the opposite side of the ravine, through which flows the river Irthing, is the Nether Denton Church, a new edifice.

A few yards farther is the Coome Crags cottage in a small plantation close to the road. The grounds have been planted within the last few years by the Earl of Carlisle, and the cottage built specially for the accommodation of visitors. In the house may be obtained a guide to the crags, and hot water is provided for picnic parties; also a room is set apart for retreat in case of rain. The stranger is, however, allowed free access to the spot, and he may wander alone, and at his will.

After walking a few hundred yards along a grass-grown path, a wooded bench is gained on an eminence overlooking the river. Here there is a lovely view embracing a wide extent of undulating woodland, whilst immediately at the spectator's feet is a charming dell with high rocks and cliffs beautifully timbered, and the river winding musically at their base over a rugged stony bed. This spot is most lovely on an autumn afternoon, when the trees are clothed in their varied and rich autumnal tints, with the sun shining from the south-west along the course of the river. The effect is truly charming, far surpassing the boldest efforts of the painter's skill, and recalling the poet's lines:

"Who can paint
Like Nature? Can Imagination boast,
Amid its gay creation, hues like hers?
Or can it mix them with that matchless skill,
And lose them in each other, as appears
In every bud that blows? If fancy then
Unequal fails beneath the pleasing task,
Ah! what shall language do?"—THOMSON.

Following the path which winds in and out amongst the woods, vantage points are obtained allowing of lovely vistas. Paths descend in different directions to the brink of the river, and then wind and ascend by other routes, over soft green-sward, and under bowers which ever and anon hide the stream; but where are heard the soft sweet murmurs of the water, whilst it appears to sing in the words of Tennyson:

"I chatter over stony ways,
  In little sharps and trebles,
  I bubble into eddying bays,
  I babble on the pebbles.
With many a curve my bank I fret
  By many a field and fallow,
And many a fairy foreland set
  With willow-weed and mallow.
I chatter, chatter, as I flow
  To join the brimming river—
For men may come, and men may go,
  But I go on for ever."

The combination of wood, rock, and water is such as to make the spot a little earthly paradise, where the lover of nature may loiter for hours in a listless contemplative mood.

The Romans appear to have used the place as a quarry; for, on the east side of the narrow ridge over which a path leads down to the river, may be observed on the face of the rock some ancient Roman inscriptions, which some individual, fancying that a coat of paint was necessary to preserve from decay what had defied the storms of seventeen centuries, has bedaubed with white, with one exception, thereby destroying their antique character.* These rude memorials even the learned in antiquarian matters have been unable satisfactorily to interpret. It has been suggested that one inscription may be read "Severus Augustus;" and another, "In the consulship of Faustinus and Rufus," who were consuls A.D. 210, the year before Septimus Severus died, at which time extensive repairs were no doubt effected in the Roman wall.

Some visitors will be tempted to walk along the path which continues up the bank of the stream for a good distance, passing directly under a bold cliff where has evidently been an ancient quarry. They might follow the course of the river to Birdoswald, or if the water be not too high the stream might be crossed to the petrifying well, and thence to Denton Church. See page 78.

Those who cross the river a little below the Coome Crags may have a romantic scramble up the opposite bank, and wind amongst the rocks by a path known as the "Fairy Walk."

Gilsland to Lanercost Priory and Naworth Castle, viâ Birdoswald and Coome Crags; and back by Upper Denton Church.

Birdoswald, 2¼ miles; Coome Crags, 4 miles; Lanercost Priory, 6¼ miles; Naworth Castle, 7½ miles; Upper Denton Church, 12¾ miles; Gilsland (Shaw's) Hotel, 15 miles.

For a wagonette or other conveyance, to carry six persons and the driver, 18s.
For a wagonette or other conveyance, to carry eight persons and the driver, 24s.
For a four-wheeled break, 3s. each person.

Most visitors to Gilsland look upon this as their favourite excursion; and it is deserving the honour, for it passes through a beautiful part of the country, and affords a treat to the antiquary, the lover of works of art, and of natural scenery.

* Dr. Bruce, in his 'Lapidarium,' says the microscope shows this to be not paint, but a rare lichen.

For a description of Birdoswald and Coome Crags refer to pages 80 and 84.

Leaving Coome Crags, the road runs in a perfectly straight line, and makes a gradual ascent to the hamlet called Banks, the road still being on the site of the ancient Roman wall, with the north ditch well defined close to on the right: here and there are traces of the vallum in the fields on the left. To the south is seen the Low Row railway station, and in the rear in the distance are the heights of Thirlwall. From the high ground, on a clear day, most of the Cumberland mountains are visible, and those acquainted with them will distinguish Skiddaw, Blencathara, the Helvellyn range, Grisedale Pass, Fairfield, Red Screes, Robinson, and High Stile. When the summit of the hill called the Pike is gained, there is also spread to view a wide extent of level and well-timbered country stretching past Carlisle to the Solway Firth, with Criffel, Burnswark, and other Scotch hills, and it is said that on a clear day the Isle of Man is visible. The river Irthing is observed in the hollow on the left. At the hamlet of Banks is a small public-house, called the Traveller's Rest, with the following distich on the sign:

"This house stands high and troubles none;
Drink and pay, and travel on."

Leaving the inn the road bends to the left, and descends steeply to Lanercost Priory, situated in the midst of a level tract of pasture land watered by the river Irthing, and environed by rising ground thickly covered with timber. In the midst of the wood, on the other side of the stream, is Naworth Castle, though out of sight from this point.

On reaching the abbey the stranger will be delighted with its picturesque and antique appearance. The tower, transepts, and chancel are roofless, but otherwise in a tolerable state of preservation, and beautified by a covering of ivy, and a few shrubs sticking here and there aloft in the niches of the walls. The nave has recently been restored by Messrs. Cory and Ferguson, of Carlisle, at the expense of the Howard family. It has long been used as the parish church, where service is held every Sunday.

Beneath the wings of the structure are the vicarage, a farmhouse, and the parish graveyard, whilst all around are large venerable trees. The antiquary will observe that the surrounding walls are built of stones from the Roman wall, which barrier crossed the vale only a few hundred yards distant, and the principal part of the old building is of the same material, although additions and renovations appear to have been effected with new red sandstone from quarries in the neighbourhood. Some persons have been led to think that the priory stands upon, or near, the site of a Roman station, all vestiges of which have disappeared, owing, perhaps, to the whole of the stone being used in the building of the monastery. Such a supposition appears quite natural, when we take into account that along the whole length of the wall the Romans erected stations about four miles apart, and Birdoswald is eight miles distant from Castlesteads. It is, however, very unlikely that the low ground would be selected for a camp, when there existed close by such a suitable height as that where now stands the hamlet of Banks, corresponding in character with the sites of Birdoswald, Carvoran, and other stations, and commanding a view along the course of the wall for many miles, both to the east and to the west. The people at the hamlet have often dug up coins, and in 1808 they found two altars, which are now at Lanercost, and also in 1832 a broken slab bearing the name of Antoninus Pius.

Lanercost Priory was built, according to tradition, by Robert de Vallibus or Vaux, the second lord of Gilsland after the Norman conquest, in expiation for the crime of having slain the dispossessed Anglo-Saxon proprietor, Gilles Bueth, who, after making many attempts to regain his inheritance, had been invited to a friendly meeting for settlement of differences, and then treacherously murdered.

Although Denton, the father of Cumberland history, gives this story as authentic in his MSS., it has been treated as fabulous by Mr. R. S. Ferguson, in a recent little book written by himself and his brother Mr. Charles J. Ferguson, entitled 'Lanercost Priory,' a work from which we have gleaned most of the following facts. We can hardly think that Robert de Vallibus was capable of so dark a deed, for we are told by Denton that "he was a valorous gentleman and well learned in the law of the land," and that "he became of so much account with King Henry II. that the king did little in Cumberland without Robert's advice and counsel." Whether or not there be truth in the above story, all agree that Robert founded the priory, and that the building was consecrated in the year 1169, in the name of Mary Magdalene, and granted to Black Canons of the order of St. Austin.

A tablet placed in the church by the vicar in 1761, gives 1116 as the date of the foundation, but this cannot be correct, for although after the grant some years would in all probability be occupied in preparing parts of the building before the place was consecrated, yet the original grant or charter of Robert de Vallibus, which has no date, is witnessed by Walter, prior of Carlisle, and the said Walter was not prior of Carlisle until 1133. The language of the grant also shows that Hubert de Vallibus, the father of Robert, was dead when the grant was made, and the date of his death was 1164.

The members of the order of St. Austin held a somewhat intermediate position between the regular and secular clergy, being not so much monks as a community of parish priests living under rule. Their garb consisted of a long black cassock, with rochet above it, and a black cloak and hood over all. Though the order had a previous existence, yet its rules were first imposed by Pope Innocent II. in 1139. Carlisle and Hexham were also priories of this order, and Lanercost received priors from both these places.

A manuscript known as the Chronicle of Lanercost, which is a monkish history of the times, and now deposited among the Cottonian MSS. in the British Museum, has generally been considered a production of the canons of this priory; but it has been proved by Mr. William Stevenson, who edited it for the Bannatyne Club, that it derived its name merely from having somehow got into the library of the priory of Lanercost, and that it is really the work of a friar minor of Carlisle, and not of Lanercost, which place it merely mentions. The principal source of the historical facts connected with this priory is obtained from a MS. entitled the Chartulary or Register of Lanercost, the original of which cannot now be found, although it was at Naworth Castle in 1777, and had been annotated by Lord William Howard, "Belted Will." A copy of it was fortunately made by Mr. Nicholson, one of the editors of the History of Cumberland, and deposited in the library of the dean and chapter of Carlisle. Mr. Ferguson thinks it probable that the original may be found in the muniment room of Greystoke Castle. The existing copy has been edited by Mr. Mackenzie Walcott, and will be found in the Transactions of the Royal Society of Literature (vol. viii., new series); it has also been printed in a separate form. As its name implies it is a list or register of the muniment deeds of the priory, and close examination brings to light many curious pieces of information.

Among the deeds we find confirmations of charters by popes Alexander III., Honorius III., Lucius III., Innocent III., and Gregory XI. The earliest of these confirmations is one by Alexander III., dated 1181. By it the pope takes the priory under his protection, and confirms all the gifts that have been made to it. He grants to the priory the right of sanctuary for clerics or laics flying from the law, and prohibits any of the canons "after profession" from leaving without the prior's licence. He directs that the priory shall choose and present to the bishop the priests of all the churches held by it, who are in spiritual things to be subject to the bishop, but in temporal matters to the priory. In times of a general interdict the priory might celebrate in its own church, in a low voice, with closed doors and without ringing of bells; the priory might also give burial within their church to all who desired it, except persons excommunicate or under an interdict, so however as not to interfere with the rights (burial fees) of the parish churches, from which the bodies were brought. After providing for the quiet election of new priors, the pope concludes his confirmation with a curse on all who molest the priory. In the Chartulary are found instances of the Roman Catholic parish clergy being married, for their sons and daughters are mentioned. There are instances of all sorts of quaint rights and tenures; nominal rents of $1d.$ or $2d.$, or of a pound of pepper, of cumin, or of wax, payable on a fair day, frequently occur as reserved for property. Amongst the many gifts of land, houses, cattle, oak-bark, skins of deer and foxes, fishing in lakes and rivers, &c., there are mentioned grants of serfs, their wives, and all their issue and goods.

Little is known of the history of the priory, and probably owing to its exposed situation in the wild border country it was often subject to depredations from the

Scots, and thus prevented amassing those riches which fell to the lot of religious houses in more peaceable southern quarters. The height of its prosperity appears to have been in the reign of Edward I. This king being constantly at war with the Scots in the latter years of his reign, spent much of his time in the northern part of his dominions, and in 1280 he visited Lanercost, along with Eleanor, his queen, and they were met at the gate by the prior and canons. On this occasion the king presented a silk cloth to the priory, and the chronicler tells us it was said he took in his hunting two hundred stags and hinds in Inglewood Forest. In 1296 a Scottish army of 40,000 men stayed one night at Lanercost, and next morning hastened homewards on hearing that the English king was close at hand with a large force. They behaved with great barbarity, and burnt the conventual buildings, but not the church. The following year the priory was again plundered by William Wallace and his men. On Michaelmas Day, 1306, King Edward I. arrived here, and the prior had the honour of entertaining his majesty until the following Easter. This was the king's last visit to the north. He was too ill to head his army in person against Bruce, and had travelled to Newcastle, and thence by Hexham and Haltwhistle, in a litter carried by horses. The small tower at Lanercost, which stands close to the vicarage, is said to be the place the king occupied during his illness, and it is still called the Edwardian tower. On leaving Lanercost he proceeded to Carlisle, and thence to his army, which was encamped on Brough Marsh, where he died on the 7th of July.

Many important documents and writs are dated from Lanercost during the time of the king's visit, among others a grant of certain churches to the priory of Hexham. The judges were sent hence to Berwick, where "they tried hundreds and thousands of breakers of the peace and conspirators, many of whom were hanged, and the Countess of Bowen was enclosed in a cage, whose breadth, length, height, and depth was 8 feet, and was hanged over the walls of Berwicke." From Lanercost, too, was issued the writ which banished for ever Piers Gaveston from the kingdom as a corrupter of the Prince of Wales. During this visit one Dungall Machduel, a noble of Galway, captured alive two brothers of Robert Bruce, namely, Thomas Bruce and Alexander Bruce, Dean of Glasgow, and also Reginald de Crawford; these he sent prisoners to the king at Lanercost, and with them the heads of a small Irish king, a gentleman of Cantyre, and two unnamed nobles, all adherents of Bruce. Thomas Bruce was sent forthwith to Carlisle, dragged by horses round that city, then hanged and beheaded, and his head put on a spike on the Castle of Carlisle. The others were merely hanged and beheaded, and their heads and those of the small Irish king and company divided among the three gates of Carlisle, being two heads for each gate. On leaving Lanercost at the end of his visit, the king presented the churches of Mitford, in Durham, and Carlattan, to the priory. The grant is dated Carlisle, 17th March, 1307. A copy of the grant is in Prynne and Rymer, and also copies of letters addressed by the king to the pope, and to the cardinal vice-chancellor of the Romish Church, praying to have the gift confirmed by the pope. From this we learn that the king's reasons for his liberality were his special devotion to Mary Magdalene, and the restoration of the status of the priory of Lanercost, which was much impoverished, both through the burning of its houses and the plundering of its goods by the Scotch, and also by reason of his own long stay while he was detained by bad health, an honour which doubtless fell heavy on the impoverished treasury of the priory.

In the month of August, 1311, the prior, much against his wish, had the honour of entertaining another illustrious visitor in the person of Robert Bruce, King of Scotland, who came with a great army and stayed three days. He imprisoned most of the canons and did infinite evils, but at length the canons were liberated by him. In 1346 David, King of Scotland, paid the priory a visit. His army entered with haughtiness into the holy places, they threw out the sacred vessels, stole the treasures, smashed the doors, played practical jokes, and reduced "in nihilum," into nothingness, everything they attacked. After this invasion Lanercost dropped its head and relapsed into obscurity; henceforth the register of the bishops of Carlisle, which had up to this time made some scant mention of the names of the priors, is silent as to either prior or priory. From other sources we learn that in 1409 the priory was in mournful condition, for the Archbishop, Bowet, of York, in a letter to his suffragan bishops, says that he has turned his attention to the poor canons, prior, and convent of Lanercost, whose monastery and most of its buildings, as the prior with a lamentable voice tells us, are threatened with ruin; their buildings and possessions, in consequence of frequent attacks from the Scots, are in ruins and burnt; their lands for the same reason lie uncultivated; in short, that the prior and convent are reduced to such poverty that they cannot nowadays live without the help of other Christians, nor serve God according to the rules of their order or duty. The archbishop, who was a Black Canon himself, requests his bishops, when deputations from the priory arrive to collect money, to receive them well, to explain their errand thoroughly by means of the parish priest in each church, and to let him have the money collected without any deduction, and further grants subscribers to the restoration fund an indulgence of forty days. How far this appeal was successful we know not; we may presume it to some extent enabled the priory to restore its ruined buildings and fallen fortunes. Nothing is known at present of the history of the priory between 1409 and 1536, the date of its dissolution. It probably lingered on in poverty, its canons but little superior to the rude peasants by whom they were surrounded. How different this from the days of King Edward I., and of the time of Thomas de Hextoldesham, a canon of Hexham, who became prior of Lanercost, and was admonished by the Bishop of Carlisle on his installation "not to frequent public huntings, or keep so large a pack of hounds."

In 1536 the Act for the dissolution of smaller religious houses having become law, Lanercost was disestablished and disendowed, and the prior, John Robyson, became rector of Aikton, and probably the canons got small pensions and went adrift.

After the dissolution the property of the priory was granted to Sir Thomas Dacre, the lineal descendant of Robert de Vallibus, the founder. He was commonly called Dacre the Bastard, being an illegitimate son of one of the Lords Dacre of the north. The reason assigned for the grant was good, true, and faithful service. On failure of male issue the site of the priory and demesne lands reverted from the Dacres to the Crown, and were until lately under a lease to the earls of Carlisle, who have recently purchased them. Other portions of the estate, which had not been limited in the grant to heirs male, descended in the female line to the Applebys of Kirklinton, who took the name of Dacre. A curious fireplace from Lanercost is now in the drawing-room of Kirklinton Hall. When in possession of the Crown the buildings were allowed to fall into extreme squalor; the very vaults were open to heaven, and, according to some writers, the corpses were exposed to view—one in particular, that of a venerable man with a long white beard, is mentioned as being visible. The following advertisement, taken from the Newcastle papers, speaks to the neglect with which the place was treated:

"Whereas some evil-disposed person did some time this spring enter into the ruinous part of Lanercost Church or Priory, and did felonously take away from out of a vault in the said church a lead coffin, which contained the remains of Lord William Dacre, Knight of the Garter. A reward of ten guineas on the conviction of the offenders.
"Naworth Castle, 9th May, 1775."

At a later period the local volunteers were wont to practice with ball at the ruins. The Commissioners of Woods and Forests recently aided in the restoration of the parsonage and the parish church.

On application at the vicarage strangers are allowed free admittance to all parts of the priory ruins between the hours of 10 A.M. and 5 P.M. Whilst waiting for the cicerone, the old cross which stands in the green will be examined. It probably marks the site where buying and selling took place, and where public preachings were occasionally delivered.

Judging from the gradual progress in style of architecture, from the very Early Transitional to the perfected Early English, which is observed in different parts of the building, it would appear to have been begun about the middle of the twelfth century, the whole being completed in about seventy or eighty years; during which period the canons gradually grew in wealth, and availed themselves of any new development of style as it arose. The west front appears to be the most modern, and has a noble and beautiful appearance. It has a finely-recessed doorway, surmounted by an arcaded gallery, and a window of seven lancets. The niches in the arcading probably contained figures of Christ and the twelve Apostles. The nave, now renovated and used as the parish church, has an aisle to the north but not to the south. The transepts, tower, chancel, and chapels are roofless, and in ruins, but the remains have a picturesque effect. The massiveness of the pillars gives great dignity and stability, and the small groining shafts and multiplicity of parts lend delicacy and finish.

In the north transept is the tomb of Sir Roland Vaux of Triermain; and in the chapel at the east of the north transept that of Humphrey or Hugh Lord Dacre, Lord Warden of the Marches in the reign of Richard II., and his wife Mabel Parr. The chapel on the south side of the chancel was restored and re-roofed by the Dacres, judging from the fact that their badge appears on the corbels carrying the roof-timbers; and the window might have been inserted by the puissant Thomas Lord Baron Dacre of Gilsland, the representative of the great families of Multon and Vaux, and in right of his wife Elizabeth of Greystoke, Baron of Greystoke, Greymethorpe, and Wemme. He commanded the reserve force at Flodden Field, and died in 1526, the seventeenth year of King Henry VIII.; his is the magnificent altar tomb which stands in the archway between the south chapel and the choir, exquisite in design and cunning in workmanship, carved over with the arms of the various baronies, and still a study for lovers of heraldry. In the choir and also in the north chapel are the remnants of a piscina, where the sacred vessels were washed. Visitors in general ascend some steps and stroll round the tower and transepts along a winding arcaded gallery, and the cicerone tells how a cow once made its way up here and startled the canons by ringing the bell. He also points out a stone effigy laid in the graveyard below, which is supposed to cover the grave of a workman who was thrown from the building by his brother masons after having given them some offence.

To the south of the church was situated the cloister garth, now converted into a garden, and around it were the prior's lodge, the refectory, dormitories, cellars, &c. In 1539, after the dissolution of the monastery, the prior's lodge and other buildings were converted by the Dacres into a dwelling-house. The alterations were commenced by Sir Thomas Dacre, and carried on by his successor

Sir Christopher Dacre, as we learn by the inserted fireplace in the hall bearing the initials C. D. and the date 1586. The alteration seems to have been effected in this wise: the various rooms comprising the west front of the cloister were thrown into a large hall, and new windows inserted; the fireplaces seem originally to have been on the west side of the hall, and to have been done away with, and a grand open fireplace inserted in the centre of the east wall. The use of the large hall as the common room of the house for every purpose had at this time become obsolete; this apartment would be used as a reception hall and a banqueting hall on great occasions; from it were entered all the other rooms of the house. The north end seems to have been the dais end, and at the south end we find remains of what probably was the minstrels' gallery. In the time of Christopher Dacre it must have been a fine hall, being about 100 feet in length; although only 18 feet wide in its narrowest part, at the north end it widened out considerably. A portion of the decorations remain, and can be distinguished under the whitewash.

In the cellar or vault are several interesting Roman altars and millstones, &c. One altar is dedicated by the hunters of Banna to the holy god Silvanus. It is not known where Banna was, but it must have been in the neighbourhood, and some have suggested Bewcastle as the place. Another altar was found at the hamlet of Banks; it reads: "To the god Cocidius, the soldiers of the twentieth legion, styled the Valerian and the Victorious, dedicated this altar, in discharge of a vow to an object most worthy of it in the consulship of Aper and Rufus." The boar at the foot is the emblem of the twentieth legion. On another stone is a representation of Jupiter and Hercules. A metal thunderbolt (probably gilt) was no doubt inserted in the hole in the right hand of Jupiter. All these altars are engraved in that most magnificent work, 'The Lapidarium Septentrionale,' edited by Dr. Bruce for the Society of Antiquarians of Newcastle-on-Tyne.

At the door of the farmhouse is a centurial stone, which may probably be read, "The century of Claudius Priscus." In the west wall of the cloister garth is another, which may be translated, "The century of Cassius Priscus." In the south-east angle of the choir is an altar which may be translated, " To Jupiter, the best and greatest, the first cohort of the Dacians, styled the Œlian, commanded by Julius Saturninus, the tribune (dedicated this)."

The Edwardian tower is separated by a few yards from the priory. It was probably used as a defence and refuge, and as a lodging for guests of distinction. To the west of it stood the stables, barn, and buildings connected with the farming operations. The porter's lodge stood close to the ancient round-headed gateway, which still forms such a picturesque feature in the landscape and figures so prominently in views of the place.

The gateway conducts from the grounds to the road, which presently crosses the Irthing at an antique bridge, close to which is a small public-house, called Abbey Bridge Inn, and the entrance gate to Naworth Park.

It is a pleasant walk or drive through the park to the castle, but some tourists will prefer following a footpath near the river which leads through the woods and up a delightful dell. This path may also be gained direct from the priory by crossing the river at some stepping-stones. Those who go through the park ought to stroll into the dell after seeing the castle, descending by one path and returning by another on the opposite side. Two gushing streamlets, forming some pretty cascades, descend between high banks richly clothed with trees, ferns, and mosses, and the spot is one where, if the stranger have time, he may spend one or two pleasant hours.

" The water it sings merrilie
   Alang the castle dean;
The water it rins merrilie,
   The grassy banks a-tween:

An' merrilie the birdie sings,
   A-top o' the greenwood tree;
An' there's a heart that has a part
   In the sweet harmonie."
      PETER BURN'S *Border Ballads.*

The park consists of a large tract of undulating land, with here and there patches of timber, and all around are cattle and sheep, but no deer, although both fallow and red deer are said to have existed here in large numbers in ancient times. On each side of the carriage-way are aged trees; one, an immense oak, which throws its branches across, was, according to tradition, the gallows where Lord William Howard ("Belted Will"), the famous ancestor of the Earl of Carlisle, is reported to have hanged those depredators who came into his clutches when appointed Warden of the Marches by King James I., and from the window of his private room in a tower of the castle he is said to have been able to see his victims dangling in the air. We are told that once when employed in his library a servant came to tell him a mosstrooper had just been captured, and desired to know what should be done with him. Vexed at being disturbed, he answered peevishly, Hang him! A few hours afterwards, when he had finished his work, he called and ordered the man to be brought before him for examination, but was told that his order had been complied with, and the man was dead. He kept here constantly 140 men in arms, as his guard. The approach to his apartments was secured by plated doors, several in succession, fastened by immense locks and bolts of iron, defending a narrow winding staircase, where only one person could pass at a time. His prisoners were kept in dungeons difficult of approach, and were there chained to rings fastened in the walls. The borders were a wild country in those times, and inhabited by a still wilder race of men, the result of centuries of contention between the English and Scotch, and when plunderers were taken in the act, swift and stern justice had to be administered. The cause of contention ceased when James I. ascended the throne of England; but to bring order out of chaos, it required Wardens of firm resolve and dauntless courage. Belted Will appears to have been equal to the work, and to have spread terror among all evildoers. Though in his official capacity he was a man of iron, tradition has much belied him, and little reliance is to be placed on these stories of summary execution. In all probability convictions were almost always previously obtained at the annual assizes at Carlisle, Newcastle, &c., or before the local courts of the Warden, who administered *march law* or the law of the marches, or borders. The Wardens were, however, invested with despotic power, and could imprison and hang at pleasure. Belted Will was a studious and well-read man, and spent much of his time in a carefully-selected library, many of the large folios of which still remain in their old bookcase in his favourite room, mute evidences of the real character of the man. In the old histories of the district he is constantly mentioned as corresponding with the learned of that era, and taking an especial interest in antiquarian and kindred pursuits. Camden, who visited Naworth in 1607, speaks of him as "a singular lover of venerable antiquities, and learned withal." Sir Walter Scott thus refers to him in the "Lay of the Last Minstrel:"

"Costly his garb—his Flemish ruff
  Fell o'er his doublet, shaped of buff,
  With satin slashed and lined;
Tawny his boot, and gold his spur,
His cloak was all of Poland fur,
  His hose with silver twined;
His Bilboa blade by marchmen felt,
Hung in a broad and studded belt;
Hence, in rude phrase, the Borderers still
Call noble Howard, 'Belted Will.'"

He was born on the 19th December, 1563, being the third son of the Duke of Norfolk and Lady Margaret Audley. His mother died a few weeks after his birth, and nine years afterwards his father was beheaded for an unfortunate attachment to Mary, Queen of Scots. Being thus deprived by the act of attainder of title and estates, his only hope of retrieving his fortunes was by marriage with Lady Elizabeth Dacre ("Bessie with the braid apron"), to whom he had been betrothed at a very early age, while his two brothers were betrothed to, and afterwards married, his bride's two sisters, thus bringing to the Howards the three great Cumberland baronies of Greystoke, Burgh, and Gilsland; two of which the Howards still hold, while Burgh has been sold to the Lowthers. The three sisters, heiresses of the Dacres, had been committed by Queen Elizabeth to the guardianship of the Duke of Norfolk, who, without the queen's leave, arranged these marriages, and so incurred her wrath. Belted Will is said to have been married in October, 1577, when he was only fourteen years old, and his bride some months younger. When about twenty-one, he and his elder brother, Philip, Earl of Arundel, having espoused the Roman Catholic faith, and being suspected of disaffection to the Government, it was thought advisable to place them in the Tower of London, where they remained some years. After their release Lord William got possession of the barony of Gilsland, his wife's portion of the Cumberland estates of the Dacres; and after the accession of James I., being in favour at Court, he was appointed, in 1605, Warden of the West Marches. He lost his wife in 1639, and in the following year he died on the 9th October, at the age of seventy-seven.

Before entering the castle the stranger will like to know something of its history, and that of its former occupants, the ancestors of the present Earl of Carlisle.

The statement that William the Conqueror granted Cumberland to Ranulph de Meschines, and that Ranulph gave the barony of Gilsland to a relative, Hubert de Vallibus, has been proved to be a blunder, traceable to a marginal note interpolated in a MS. of Matthew de Paris. The grant of Gilsland to Hubert de Vallibus was made by Henry II. in these words: "Totam terram quam Gilbertus filius Boet tenuit die quo fuit vivus et mortuus," and no reference is made to any previous grant by the Conqueror, or by De Meschines; indeed, until the time of Henry II. the Normans had no possessions in Cumberland, except a garrison at Carlisle. In the reign of Henry III., Hubert, the fifth baron of Gilsland, dying without male issue, his only daughter Matilda succeeded to the estates and married Thomas Multon, Lord of Burgh, whose mother was the heiress of the Morvilles, of Kirkoswald Castle. Male issue again failing in the reign of Edward III., the barony devolved to Margaret, the sister of Thomas Multon, the eighth baron. Margaret at the age of sweet seventeen eloped by moonlight from Warwick Castle with Ranulph, Lord Dacre, whom she married, and the estates passed in a direct male line to eleven of their descendants. On the accidental death of the infant Lord George Dacre, baron of Gilsland, Greystoke, and Wemm, during the reign of Elizabeth, the sisters of the deceased laid claim to the estates, but were opposed by their uncles. After a delay of many years it was decided in the courts of law that the girls were the rightful heirs; but the queen had seized the baronies, and would hardly give them up. To the eldest, Anne, was apportioned Dacre and Greystoke, and she married the Earl of Arundel, eldest son of the Duke of Norfolk. The second daughter, Mary, got Burgh, and married Thomas, Earl of Suffolk, the second son of the Duke of Norfolk, and dying childless, her barony of Burgh was sold and purchased by the Lowthers. The youngest, Elizabeth, got Gilsland and Wemm, and married Lord William Howard (Belted Will), the youngest son of the Duke of Norfolk, and their greatgrandson Charles was created Earl of Carlisle by Charles II. for his services in bringing about the Restoration.

The present proprietor of the castle, the Earl of Carlisle, thus springs from an illustrious ancestry, being descended from the great family of Norfolk, and a lineal descendant, on the female side, of the ancient barons of Dacre and Gilsland.

It is uncertain when the castle was built, and it can hardly have been before the time of Edward I., for that king twice took up his abode at Lanercost Priory, which he would probably not have done had Naworth then been in existence. Some are of opinion that the Barons of Gilsland had a fortress at Castlesteads, the site of a Roman station, and where now stands the beautiful mansion of G. J. Johnson, Esq., but no vestiges remain of any such building. Tradition says that the baronial residence at Castlesteads was pulled down and its site sown with salt, as a place accursed, the scene of the murder of Gilles Bueth, or of some dark deed. It is on record that Ralph Dacre, who had married the heiress of Gilsland, obtained a licence in the ninth year of King Edward III. to make a castle of his house at Naworth, and it is again mentioned in the time of Richard II. It stands on rising ground overhanging two deep but narrow dells, and is surrounded by venerable trees. It consists of two large square towers, united by other buildings, and enclosing a quadrangular court. The castle of Kirkoswald, situated a few miles to the north-east of Penrith, which had formerly come into the possession of the barons of Gilsland by marriage, and had been apportioned, on the division of the Dacre estates, to Lord Dacre of the South, was dismantled in 1604, when Lord William Howard ("Belted Will") purchased many of its ornaments and brought them to embellish his castle at Naworth. Among these was an oak ceiling and wainscoting, which he had placed in his hall and chapel. The ceiling was divided into panels, and on every panel was painted a portrait of the kings of England, from Brute down to Henry VI. Brute is given by Malmesbury as an ancient king of England. The whole of this antique oak work, except a little in Belted Will's chapel, perished by a fire which burnt down most of the castle in 1844. Since that date the building has been entirely renovated, but every endeavour made to retain its character of an old border fortress.

Visitors to the castle enter the courtyard by a gateway, above which are the Dacre arms, and then the services are obtained of Mrs. Reeves, the housekeeper, who is an excellent guide. The most convenient times are from 10 A.M. to 1 P.M, and from 2 P.M. to 5 P.M. Everyone is treated with the utmost courtesy, and the family of the Earl of Carlisle are exceedingly kind in allowing the interior of the castle to be inspected. The portraits, tapestry, ancient armour, and other relics of the past are well worthy of a visit. The hall itself suggests ideas of lordly gatherings and magnificent hospitality, or oftentimes the daylight assembling of retainers preparing for a moonlight raid over the border to secure and punish the lawless freebooter. On entering the hall the visitor will see on the left the armour of Lord William Howard (Belted Will); and at the east end the portraits of Lord William and of the Lady Elizabeth Dacre, his wife. The tapestry, and the various armorial bearings on the corbels, being the arms of the families allied to the Earl of Carlisle, will be examined with interest. The partial destruction of the castle by fire, and subsequent restoration, are referred to in the quotations over the fireplace in the hall. In the drawing-room there is a picture of a mosstrooper by Glass, an American artist. The present library is the ancient chapel. After seeing this the stranger ought to visit the bedroom, oratory, and library of Belted Will; and the entrance to the secret staircase from his bedroom to the dungeon.

Leaving the castle the straight road is taken, which gradually ascends and commands a glorious retrospective view of the castle and neighbourhood, and across a cultivated and wooded tract to the Scotch hills in the far distance. On emerging from the park, at the lodge gate, the turnpike road from Carlisle to Newcastle, locally known as "the military road" is entered, close to a milepost stating 12 miles to Carlisle and 44 miles to Newcastle. Here a turn must be made to the left; the direct road leads to the railway station, which is situated about 300 yards distant. Presently the Newcastle and Carlisle railway is passed over by a bridge, and the station is observed pleasantly situated amongst the woods on the right. When passing the Low Row Tollgate the road commands a view of a wide tract of level country, also Tindale Fell, Crossfell, the Scotch and Cumberland hills, and a strip of the Solway Firth. Here, quitting the military way, a turn is made to left, and when over the railway the right-hand road has to be followed. It passes the Nether Denton rectory and church, both new elegant buildings erected through the exertions of the Rev. Canon Shipman, who had previously built a rectory and restored the church at Scaleby. The old church here was unsightly and without antiquarian claims to recommend it. The site of the rectory and church was, however, full of interest, having been a Roman camp, as was proved, when the alterations were being made, by the large quantity of coins, pieces of pottery, lamps, and other interesting relics which were found, and are now in the possession of Mr. Clayton of Chesters, near Chollerford.

Denton Hall in Nether Denton is situated near to Low Row station. It was many centuries ago the seat of the ancient family of the Dentons del Hall de Carlisle. Denton Hall formerly consisted of a tower with massive walls; it is now a farmhouse with no external feature to indicate its antiquity and importance, but some of the old thick walls exist in the present building. The Rev. C. J. Denton, M.A., Vicar of Askham Richard, Yorkshire; and Wm. Denton, Esq., J.P., Keswick, are the present representatives of the ancient family of the Dentons of Denton. The pedigree of the family is considered to be the oldest and best authenticated of any in Cumberland, and one of the members, who lived in the sixteenth century, left a manuscript history of the county that has been the fountain from which all historians of Cumberland have since drawn the bulk of their information. A copy, or possibly the original, of this MS., is in the possession of Mr. Denton, of Keswick, who kindly lent it to us, and from it we have gleaned facts which appear here and there in this work. There are said to have been two Denton MS. histories of Cumberland: one by John Denton, of Cardew, above referred to, and another by Thomas Denton, of Warnell, which is lost.

About half a mile west of Denton Hall is a farmhouse, which also was a border "peel" with massive walls. It is now converted into a comfortable farmhouse. Between Denton Hall and Bowsteads is a barn-like building, which also deserves the attention of the antiquary.

As the traveller proceeds on the journey he will be interested in observing to the left, on the opposite bank of the river, the position of the Coome Crags, and Birdoswald, which were passed during the early part of the drive, and he will not fail to discern the hotel as soon as it appears in its commanding position in the distance. When driving through Upper Denton, those who have not previously visited the interesting old church will be tempted to leave their conveyance for a few minutes and stroll into the churchyard and look at the tombstones, which are described at page 78.

Persons who do not desire to drive to Naworth can of course go by train, as the railway station is only half a mile from the castle, and it would be a pleasant walk back to Gilsland *via* Lanercost, Coome Crags, and Birdoswald. A very pleasant day's excursion may also be had by taking the train to Naworth, thence walking to the Castle, Lanercost Priory, Brampton by the Ridge and Mote, the river Gelt and Written Crag; then to Talkin Tarn and the Milton railway station, thus making the walking distance about 9 miles.

Gilsland to Triermain Castle, Askerton Castle, and Bewcastle.

Triermain, 2½ miles; Askerton, 6 miles; Bewcastle, 10 miles.

For a wagonette or other conveyance, to carry six persons and the driver, 25s.
For a wagonette or other conveyance, to carry eight persons and the driver, 30s.
For a four-wheeled break, 5s. each person.

Starting from the hotel, enter the road which branches to the right, a few yards below the Orchard House. It is the same way as that leading to Birdoswald, but after proceeding another mile the Birdoswald road is passed on the left. Keeping straight forward high ground is attained, and on passing a house by the roadside the ruin of Triermain Castle appears a short distance in front. There appears to have been a mansion or castle here during the time of the Norman conquest, and it was afterwards the property of the lords of Gilsland, and the residence of a branch of that family. A single strip of the outside wall, standing on a mound strewn with lumps of cemented rubble stone, is all that remains of this famed border fortress, rendered famous principally by Sir Walter Scott, who fixed here the scene of, and hence obtained the name for, his poem "The Bridal of Triermain." Many thoughts will rush into the mind as the stranger stands on its site and sees less than a mile distant the Roman station of Birdoswald. The ancient Romans, the former conquerors of the world, the uncivilized Britons and Caledonians, the fierce Barons of the middle ages and their followers, and the modern Magician of the North, all appear to pass in review, and thus render the visit one of unusual interest. The ruin is the property of the Earl of Carlisle. The adjoining farmhouse is occupied by Mr. Thomas Milburne, two generations of his ancestors having lived here before him. The visitor may obtain some excellent milk at the house.

Leaving Triermain the road proceeds for a mile without any object of particular interest, and then a rivulet, called King's Water, is crossed close to a small inn and blacksmith's shop. One mile beyond the inn the road bends to left, and care must be taken not to enter the road on the right, which merely leads to some farmhouses and to the common. A pleasant cultivated district is passed through, with occasional views of distant hills, including Tindale and Castle Carrock fells; the Lake District mountains, Skiddaw, Blencathara, and Helvellyn range; and also the Scotch hills, Criffel, Burnswark, and others. Directly opposite the Lees Hill brick and tile works, enter the right-hand road. It makes a gradual ascent, commanding fine retrospective views across the vale to the Tindale and other fells, and leads direct to Askerton Castle.

The edifice belongs to the Earl of Carlisle, and is a good specimen of the old border fortified residences. Two of the towers remain almost perfect, and are connected by old buildings still used as a farmhouse, whilst around are outbuildings of modern construction. The whole when seen from the front entrance presents an ancient and pleasing appearance. On a stone outside of one of the towers is carved T. D., supposed to be the initials of Thomas Lord Dacre, who occasionally resided here when Lord Warden, in the reign of Henry VIII. In ancient times this castle was the usual residence of an officer called the Land Sergeant, whose duty it was to take the command of the inhabitants in repelling the mosstroopers. The tenant, Mr. Thomas Tweddle, kindly allows people to enter the house and ascend to the summit of the towers, standing upon the leaden roofs of which a wide extent of country is spread to view, with the Tindale and Castle Carrock fells, Skiddaw, and a host of the Lake District mountains; also Solway Firth, Criffel, Burnswork, and Christenbury Crags. Though there are now only two towers standing, in all probability there were originally four, and there yet remain a few steps which appear to have led up to one at the north-west corner.

From the castle the road runs through an open country, covered with coarse grass, and tenanted with sheep and cattle, whilst here and there is a thorn bush or a clump of trees. As the traveller wends his way he has a good prospect of the hills of Cumberland and Scotland, and now and again the silvery streak of the Solway Firth is visible. When Bewcastle comes in sight it is found to consist of two or three houses, a church, and the ruins of a castle, situated in the middle of a tolerably wide vale, from which rise low heath-clad hills. The whole district appears open and undulating, with a verdant tract extending to the south-west, but in the opposite direction we appear to be on the confines of cultivation, for to the north and north-east stretch a wide tract of low hills and heathy moorland. The country around was in former times of bad repute, being the abode of the worst specimens of robbers and freebooters; and the evil fame of the district had spread so wide that there was a by-law of the corporation of Newcastle prohibiting any freemen of that city to take for apprentice a native of certain of these dales. An amusing story is told of one thief here. He had stolen a fat hog, and the bailiff and his assistants being in pursuit with a search warrant found him rocking a cradle, when he received them with the utmost composure and courtesy. On being informed of their errand, he coolly observed, "Aye, you are much in the right to search; pray search well, and examine every corner; let me request you only not to make a noise, as the *child* with which my wife has left me in charge is cross and peevish; I beg you not to awaken it." The pig was in the cradle, and of course could not be found. At one time the place was much inhabited by dealers in horses and cattle, called "Border Coupers." They were generally men full of a rude and ready kind of wit, continual talkers, hard drinkers, and often quarrelsome companions. One of these " coupers" attempted to recommend himself to a travelling Scotchman by claiming kindred, affirming that he was a border Scot. "Gude faith, I dinna doubt it," quoth the canny

Scotchman, "*the coarsest part of the cloth is aye at the border.*"

On descending into the vale the Limekiln Inn will be entered. It is a small house of modern entertainment, and contains one of the old large open chimneys which will be glanced at with interest by some visitors. Crossing the Kirkbeck streamlet by a wooden footbridge, a slight ascent is made to the church and castle, which are said to be built on the site of a Roman station, and to be on the line of the Maiden Way, which leaving the great Roman road from York to the north at Kirkby Thore, in Westmorland, ran by Alston, Birdoswald, and Bewcastle into Scotland.

The late Mr. Maughan, formerly rector of Bewcastle, who wrote a pamphlet on the subject, thought he could trace the Maiden Way* running past the station, but we think the tourist will find the task rather difficult, and may prefer to listen to the schoolmaster here whilst he relates that the Maiden Way was not a Roman road at all, but was made in order that one of Edward I.'s daughters, who was going to Scotland to be married to a Scotch prince, might accomplish a vow she had made that she would walk the whole way to Edinburgh without dipping her foot in water.

Mr. Maughan tells us that the place was not destitute of memorials and evidences of ancient occupation, there having been found at different periods several Roman coins, rings, urns, pieces of red Samian and black pottery, both plain and figured, vases, querns, flanged tiles, bricks, oxidated iron, beads, glass, votive tablets, inscribed altars, and other relics. Pieces of coal are also often found, showing that the Romans were probably acquainted with the coal mines of the district. The outer wall of the station appears to have been of considerable thickness, but it is now in ruins and covered with turf. In some places it is nearly level with the ground, but it still shows distinctly the site of the wall.

There is nothing striking in the church, but in the graveyard is a most interesting Runic monument, which has given rise to much antiquarian discussion. It is an

---

* The word Maden or Madien is an old Celtic or British appellation, and signifies "raised or elevated." Hence the term Maiden Way, simply means "a raised road" or "highway."

obelisk 15 feet high, 2 feet square at the base, and 16 inches at the upper part, where has been broken off a cross that would formerly surmount it, but is now lost.

On the west side is a long inscription in Runic characters, which is rendered by Mr. Maughan as follows: "Hwætred, Wæthgar, and Alwfwold set up this slender pillar in memory of Alcfrid, a king, and son of Oswy. Pray thou for them, their sins, their souls." This Alcfrid is supposed to have died about the year 664, and to have been an Anglo-Saxon king of Northumbria, a district which in all probability then embraced all the counties in England north of the Humber, and the southern counties of Scotland nearly as far as Edinburgh. Below the inscription is a human figure, with a bird like a hawk or eagle perched on his arm. Above the inscription is a cloaked figure, with a nimbus or glory encircling the head, and surmounted by two lines of Runes, which, when rendered into English, are said to be simply " Jesus Christ." Above this are two figures, thought by some to be the Virgin and Child, and by others to be St. John the Baptist and the Holy Lamb. On the top are two or three fragments of letters.

The sculpture on the south side is divided into five compartments. In the bottom, central, and top divisions are magical knots. In the second are two vines intersecting each other, and in the fourth is another vine, in one of the curves of which a vertical sun-dial has been placed, somewhat resembling the dial placed over the Saxon porch on the south side of Bishopstone Church in Sussex, and also resembling the Saxon dial placed over the south porch of Kirkdale Church, in the North Riding of Yorkshire; a short description of each of which may be found at p. 60 of the eleventh volume of the 'Archæological Journal.' In the Bewcastle dial the principal divisions are marked by crosses, as on the forementioned dials, which are considered examples of a very early date, the Kirkdale dial having been made, as it is supposed, between the years 1056 and 1065. At the top of this side of the monument is a defaced inscription. Between the other compartments are four inscriptions, which are said to read, " In the first year (of the reign) of Egfrid, King of this Kingdom of Northumbria." Egfrid ascended the throne A.D. 670, and therefore this would appear to be the date of the erection of the monument.

On the north side are also five compartments occupied

by sculpture. In the highest and lowest divisions we find vines with foliage and fruit, which some have considered to be the Danish symbols of fertility, as Amalthea's horn was among the Greeks. In the second and fourth divisions are two curiously devised and intricately twisted knots, often called " magical knots." The third division is filled with a quantity of chequerwork, "which is pronounced by Mr. Smith to be 'a Scythian method of embellishing funeral ornaments'; and is regarded by Bishop Nicholson 'as a notable emblem of the tumuli or burying places of the ancients.' Camden says, 'Seeing the cross is chequered like the arms of Vaux, we may suppose that it has been erected by some of them.' Hutchinson thinks that 'the cross must of necessity be allowed to bear a more ancient date than any of the remains of that name; which cannot be run up higher than the Conquest.' He also thinks that 'armorial bearings were not in use at the same time as the Runic characters.' It is probable, however, that this chequerwork had no reference to the family of Vaux or De Vallibus, as they were not really and legally possessed of the lordship of Bewcastle until the reign of Henry II., or about the middle of the twelfth century, which is too late a period for the decoration of this monument. The late ingenious Mr. Howard, of Corby, suggested that 'very possibly the family of De Vallibus took their arms from this column, being one of the most remarkable things in the barony.' The cheque appears to have been a device used by the Gauls and Britons long before the erection of this cross. The Gaulic manufactory of woollen cloth spoken of by Diodorus and in Pliny's 'Natural History' was woven chequerwise, of which our Scottish plaids are perfect remains. Bishop Anselm's book concerning 'Virginity,' written about the year 680—the era of the cross nearly—when the art of weaving in this country was probably in a comparatively rude state, contains a distinct indication that chequered robes were then in fashion; and many of the figures in Rosselini's Egyptian work are dressed in chequered cloths. The cheques are still retained in common use to this day among the inhabitants of Wales, the descendants of the Ancient Britons; and so great is their veneration for their ancient emblem that whenever a Welshman leaves his native mountains to reside in an English town, he is sure to carry this symbol along with him. Shops with the sign of the chequers were common even among the Romans, as is evident from the views of Pompeii presented by Sir W. Hamilton to the Antiquarian Society. A human figure in a chequered robe is sculptured on the side of an altar which was found in digging a cellar for the Grapes Inn, on the site of the Roman station at Carlisle, thus establishing the probability that the cheque was used among the Romans in Britain. We read also of nets of chequerwork in the days of King Solomon." Immediately above the lowest compartment is one line of Runic characters, said to be "Cyneburga," the daughter of Penda, King of Mercia, and the wife of Alcfrid. Between the second and third compartments (from the bottom) is another line read "Kyneswitha," the sister of Cyneburga. Between the third and fourth compartments is another line of Runes which, though indistinct, appears to read "King of the Mercians," and it appears to have been connected with another line between the fourth and fifth divisions, which may be read "Wulfhere," who was a son of Penda, brother of Cyneburga, and King of the Mercians. He succeeded his brother Peada in the year 657, according to the Anglo-Saxon chronicle.

On the eastern face a vine branch laden with bunches of grapes and figures of birds and animals runs from the bottom to the top. The sculpture on this side of the cross has suffered very little damage from the corroding effects of the weather. It contains no inscription, but it is probable there have been some letters near the top of the shaft on a part which has been broken off. In all probability all the hieroglyphics had a meaning, although some have thought they were merely the fancy of the sculptor.

Before leaving this burial-ground it is curious to note the following on one of the headstones:

"Jonathan Telford, of Craggy Ford, who died April 25th, 1866, aged 72. Deceased was one of the moor game-shooters in the north of England; in the time of his shooting he bagged fifty-nine grouse at seven double shots."

Two or three years ago, the clergyman being ill, there were a few interments here without the burial service being read. The vicar of Gilsland offered to go over to officiate if he could be driven the distance one way, but he was never solicited on these terms, and the interments took place without the presence of a clergyman.

Close to the church are the ruins of the castle, consisting almost solely of a large patch of the southern wall, of great thickness, and 42 feet in height; and evidently built of stones of the shape and size used by the Romans. A part of the western turret remains, but the northern and eastern sides are overthrown and lie in confused heaps to the very edge of the broad fosse which formerly surrounded the building. The form of the castle was a square of 87 feet. The bleak and lonely appearance of its still stately ruins awakens in the mind of the moralizing visitor the idea of fallen greatness proudly and sternly smiling even in desolation and neglect.

The first historical record we have of Bewcastle is, that previous to the Conquest it was possessed by the family of Bueth, who built the castle, whence it took the name of Bueth Castre, or Both Castle, and by corruption Bewcastle. Bueth, who was also Lord of Gilsland, taking part with the Scots against Stephen, was obliged to fly with his son into Scotland. His possessions were afterwards given by Henry II. to Hubert de Vallibus; and in the time of Henry III. another Hubert de Vallibus was the last of that name, whose daughter and heiress Matilda married Thomas de Multon. After the Multons, it was in the possession of the Swinburnes for several generations, and in the seventh year of Edward I. John Swinburne obtained a grant for a fair and market to be held here. In the reign of Edward III. it came into the possession of Sir John Striveling, by marriage with the heiress of the Swinburnes. It appears to have been in the possession of the Crown in the reign of Edward IV., and was by him given to Richard, Duke of Gloucester, though some authors suppose that grant was of a place bearing the same name on the borders of Wales. In the reign of Henry VIII. it was in possession of the Musgraves. James I. demised it to Francis, Earl of Cumberland, for forty years' term, and Charles I. granted it to Richard Graham, knight and barrister, to hold of the Crown *in capite*. In 1641 the castle was reduced to a ruinous state by the Parliament forces under Cromwell, and the inhabitants still point out the place where he planted his cannon, a few hundred yards distant. In the days of Charles II. one Jack Musgrave, "a most pestilent fellow," was captain of Bewcastle. In the life of Lilly, the famous astrologer, will be found a most amusing account of how he made Jack very drunk, and got from him a document Jack held, highly compromising to Sir William Pennington, ancestor of the present Lord Muncaster.

Tradition relates that the castle was burnt by the retainers of the family of Johnstone of Loch Wood, in Annandale. A deadly feud had long existed between Nixon, the governor of Bewcastle, and the Johnstones of Loch Wood; and during the minority of a young heir of Loch Wood, Nixon determined to plunder that estate, and for that purpose sent his band of armed ruffians across the border. It happened that the young heir, inheriting all the inflexible malice of his ancestors, had at the same time formed a resolution to imbrue his yet untried sword for the first time in the blood of the hereditary foes of his family; and arrived at Bewcastle during the darkness of that night on which the retainers of Nixon were foraging the estate of Loch Wood. Here, it is said, through a window he beheld the aged and hoary form of Nixon asleep in his elbow-chair by the fire, near to which also sat his lady, and in another part of the room the menials were busily employed in arranging supper. Whilst the young savage was satiating his eyes on the object of his hatred, now seemingly within his power, Nixon awoke, and told his lady "that he had dreamed the youthful foe of his family was come to Bewcastle, and was then looking in at the window." She soothed him by observing that his dream would be reversed, for by that time the retainers of Bewcastle would have plundered Loch Wood, and were then, doubtlessly, returning with the booty. Young Johnstone no sooner heard this than he ordered every entrance to the castle to be secured, and having set fire to it, hastened homewards. Meeting the plunderers of Loch Wood, near the banks of the river Liddal, after a desperate conflict the Johnstones recovered their property. Old Nixon essaying to make his escape through a window, stuck fast, and in that position fell a prey to the flames. The recollection of his fate has furnished a simile still current among the peasantry of Bewcastle. When anyone has suffered severely, they figuratively term it, "He has 'bidden' (or suffered) Nixon's glow." The traveller on surveying the massive thickness of the walls, and the height of the small window from the ground, through which Johnstone is said to have reconnoitered his victim, and through which Nixon endeavoured to escape, will discover the improbability of this traditional legend.

The castle, demesne lands, and manorial rights of Bewcastle, are now the property of Sir F. U. Graham, Bart., of Netherby.

Whilst at Bewcastle the tourist ought to spare time, if possible, for a visit to *Christenbury Crag*,* distant seven miles. When we first arrived at Bewcastle we inquired the distance to the top of the crag, and were told three miles by one person, another said five, a third six, and a fourth ten. We frequently learned to our cost that the natives hereabouts have very vague notions as to distances of places, and, like the hero of Guy Mannering, we were often told the distance was "*a gey bit;*" then the "*gey bit*" was more accurately described as "*Ablins three mile;*" then the "*three mile*" diminished into "*like a mile and a bittock;*" then extended themselves into "*four mile or thereawa';*" and lastly, a female voice, having hushed a wailing infant which the spokeswoman carried in her arms, assured us, " It was a weary lang gate yet, and unco' heavy road for foot-passengers."

Halfway between Bewcastle and Christenbury Crag is a hamlet named the Flatt, at which place is a handsome hunting seat, belonging to Sir F. Graham, and it is usual to drive to this point and then ascend to the summit of the crag on foot.

Between Bewcastle and the Flatt formerly lived one Thomas Armstrong, well known in oral tradition by the nickname of Socky Tom. He was a daring freebooter, and the hero of many determined deeds, cunning stratagems, and hairbreadth escapes. His house was on the summit of a steep declivity, rising almost perpendicularly from the margin of the brook. For some more than ordinary crime, the civil officers of justice, after repeated and unsuccessful attempts to capture him, had called in the aid of a party of military from Carlisle, and at break of day surrounded the barn in which the redoubted Socky had for some time lain concealed. His favourite grey mare, which had borne him off safely from many a hot pursuit, stood ready saddled beside him, and Tom was awakened out of his sleep by her neighing. The officers stood near the door, and for once deemed the marauder in their power. Aware of his desperate situation, he in-

---

* Derived, according to one writer, from "crista," a crest; and "bury," the Saxon term for a particularly formed hill, and signifying the crested hill—a distinction very appropriately bestowed.

stantly mounted, and calmly awaiting till the officers burst open the door, he dashed at one bound, through the midst of his foes, headlong down the declivity. The officers fired, but only slightly wounding the mare, she safely bore off her master to the not far distant fells, where all search, if made, was ineffectual. The place still bears the name of "Socky's Leap," and the place where the first footprints of the mare indented the ground is still pointed out to the curious traveller.

About forty years ago a writer thus described the ascent of Christenbury Crag:—"After passing the White Leven or Line river, which here is only a mountain brook, the eye of the traveller is arrested by two large conical heaps of stones, or cairns, blanched by exposure to the storms of a thousand winters to an almost perfect whiteness, and which are said by antiquaries to mark the place of sepulture of some renowned Celtic warrior. These are about 100 yards apart, and one of them has been partially removed by some person, no doubt under the vulgar delusion, still prevalent, that treasure was deposited underneath such piles. After surmounting the steep bank on which the cairns are placed, the rocks of Christenbury appear at only a short distance, and so exactly resemble in appearance an immense ruined fortress that it requires some little exertion of mind to dispel the illusion. The traveller is yet 2 miles from the rocks. Owing, however, to the smooth surface of the intervening bog, upon which the eye can find no particular object to dwell, nor estimate by any comparison of magnitude how far the crags are removed, the distance does not appear more than a few hundred yards. On a nearer approach, however, they increase in apparent magnitude, and the anxiety of the visitor is proportionally excited, until, on attaining the summit of the mountain, the whole bursts on the view. The face of the crag, which is a soft sandstone, is not on an average more than 30 feet in height, but the amazing disorder in which the immense blocks, which by some dreadful convulsion have been severed from the parent rock, are piled and tumbled around in every direction, fills the mind with emotions of astonishment. These masses, many of them from 20 to 30 feet in length, and from 15 to 20 feet in depth and thickness, appear heaped upon one another, as if human art had been employed in their compilation, and form dark passages and unshapely dismal caverns, amongst and around which the mountain breezes howl and whistle in melancholy and dreary concert. Amid these solitary masses is one isolated rock, named the 'Long Crag,' which is 48 feet high, and appears at a distance like a quadrangular tower, and may, though not without some difficulty, be ascended. On its summit are a few scanty tufts of heath, and amid its clefts the mountain crow builds her nest and brings forth her young in safety."

In returning from Bewcastle to Gilsland the adventurous pedestrian may shorten the distance from 10 to 7 miles by taking a direct course across Spadeadam Waste. Half a mile out of Bewcastle, at a bend in the road, go through a gate on the left, and ascend by ground covered with brushwood to the rear of a stone fence. During the ascent there is a wide extent of country visible, with the Solway Firth and the distant hills Criffel and Burnswark; and gradually as the tourist advances he will see spread before him a vast panorama stretching across a level cultivated plain to the Tindale and Castle Carrock fells, and the Cumberland Lake District mountains. The highest point passed after leaving Bewcastle is Side Fell : this is 1012 feet above the level of the sea. The stranger will have some difficulty in pushing his way, and must choose his steps with care and deliberation, for he will have to proceed along what Sir Walter Scott terms a *blind road*, a track so slightly marked by the passengers' footsteps, that it can only be detected by a slight shade of verdure from the darker heath around it, and being only visible to the eye when at some distance, ceases to be distinguished while the foot is actually treading it. Sometimes it sinks between two broken black banks of moss earth, sometimes crosses narrow ravines filled with stuff of a consistence between mud and water, and sometimes along heaps of gravel and stones which have been swept together by some torrent that has overflowed the marshy ground. The Maiden Way, which ran between Birdoswald and Bewcastle, is said to have crossed this tract of country, and to be still visible in one or two places. On the top of a hill, called the Beacon, which the traveller has close on his right, is the ruin of a Roman watch tower. From this point a south-east direction must be taken almost in a line with the Thirlwall heights. Leaving a farmhouse and small plantation on the right, and soon afterwards three or four other farmsteads, the hollow is crossed through which flows the King Water streamlet, and then the trees around the hotel gradually come in sight. In passing over the Waste in a mist, or when darkness overtakes the traveller, it is sometimes necessary to notice the direction of the wind in order to keep in a direct line. By this means two travellers walked safely across through mist, rain, and darkness. They left Bewcastle Rectory at a quarter to five o'clock in the evening, and arrived at Gilsland Railway Station at ten minutes past seven.

Ascent of Tindale Fell.

A pleasant change from the general character of the excursions usually taken from Gilsland may be had by ascending Tindale Fell. Those who are fond of a ramble amongst the heather, the freedom of the hills, a fine bracing atmosphere, and lovely views of a wide extent of country, will in all likelihood make more than one visit to this northern outlier of the Pennine mountain chain.

It may be ascended in many ways. On the east side, Lambley railway station is a good starting point. From thence the traveller may proceed in the direction of Glen Dhu, and then have a long gradual climb to the summit of the mountain; or he may walk up Hartley Burn, and follow the course of the Black Burn streamlet into a wild but beautiful mountain recess, where are some small cascades and most interesting geological sections of the rock strata.

From Gilsland village a direct course may be taken by crossing over Denton Fell, and through the head of the Hartley Burn vale.

Those who take the train to Low Row will follow the road which runs southwards from the station, and when it enters the Military Road turn to left for a few hundred yards, then proceed by a footpath through some fields and by a small dell to the Cleugh Head farmhouse, the residence of Mr. Tweddle. Hence to some spelter or zinc works, and by Black Burn to the summit.

Perhaps the easiest and simplest course is to take the train to Milton or Brampton station, and then proceed by road, or by the colliery railway, to the village of Hall Bank Gate, 2½ miles from Milton station. Another 1½

ASCENT OF TINDALE FELL. 117

miles along a good road brings to Tindale Tarn, a large sheet of water with a farmhouse on its bank, situated close at the foot of the mountain. After a good steady climb over short smooth grass, the tourist cannot fail to gain the top, where is a large cairn or heap of stones, sometimes denominated a stone man, at a height of 2038 feet above the sea level.

Another plan is to track the river Gelt to its source, or walk past Talkin Tarn and Talkin village. In many respects the ascent of Tindale Fell by this western side will be preferred, for it enables the traveller to see the fine recesses in the Geltside and Castle Carrock mountains, and from some points of view those hills look very beautiful.

On gaining the summit of Tindale Fell an extensive panorama is spread to view. To the north is a wide tract of woodland and desolate moors reaching to the Scotch hills. To the east, the South Tyne is seen winding its way in the direction of Hexham, and the course of the Roman Wall is tracked for miles over the Walltown and Sewingshields Crags. To the west are Burnswark, Criffel, Skiddaw, Carlisle, the vales of the Irthing and the Eden, the Solway Firth, and the Irish Sea.

If the day be fine, the hardy mountaineer might descend to Alston, on the south-east, or into the vale of the Eden, on the south-west; and some may even think of continuing on the tops in the direction of Cross Fell. A very pleasant ramble might also be had to the tops of Geltside and Castle Carrock.

A Walk to Thirlwall Castle.

Thirlwall Castle is situated 2 miles to the east of Gilsland, and half a mile from the Greenhead railway station. It is included in the excursions given at pages 119 and 136; but some persons may prefer strolling to it direct from the hotel.

After crossing the river and passing Wardrew House, a foot-track must be entered, which branches to the right, and leads in a south-east direction. Leaving Temple Heap, with its dozen trees, on the right, and on the left the house called the Lodge, and an outbuilding, the ridge known as the "Nine Nicks of Thirlwall" presently appears, and a fine view is had of the wooded ground to the west.

At a corner in the stone fence a stile is crossed, and here come into view the ruins of Thirlwall, about a mile distant, and in the opposite direction the village of Gilsland, with Tindale Fell to the south. From this point a descent must be made to the farmhouse in a direct line with the Castle. The house is reached by passing through a gate and then following a cart-track; when through the farmyard the road leads over a small rill. Here follow the foot-track which first winds to left and then to right, and ascends the hill. The track leads to a small house standing behind a large ash tree. At this house pass through a gate and follow a cart-road taking direct to the Castle. The ruins are not yet visible, being hid in a hollow in front; but a view is had of the village of Greenhead and the ivy-covered towers of Blenkinsop Castle beyond. Presently Thirlwall Castle is reached, and the traveller may return to Gilsland by the same route, or by rail. If the trains are not convenient, a pleasant walk of 2¾ miles, along a good road, will bring the tourist back to the hotel.

Gilsland to Carvoran.

Those who desire to make a special visit to the Roman station of Carvoran, or *Magna*, can travel by rail 2 miles to Greenhead, and then walk along the military road past Glen Whelt. After making a rather steep ascent for half a mile the first road on the left is entered, and by proceeding along it a few hundred yards the farmhouse is reached: it stands in the midst of a cluster of trees. Lying about in the yard, and built into the walls, are many altars and other relics, such as millstones, figures, and parts of columns, which have been dug up and carted from the camp. In the house are two beautiful Roman altars, of the medium size. The site of the camp has been, in recent times, levelled and cultivated; but before this, we are told, there were many vestiges of buildings. Some portions of the north rampart and fosse still remain, and are seen to the west of the house. This camp was situated about a hundred yards to the south of the wall, and between the two ran the vallum or south ditch. Heaps of grass-covered rubbish are all that remain here of the wall; but the north fosse is in a perfect condition, and descends to the banks of the Tipalt, close to Thirlwall Castle, which, half hidden by trees, presents from this point a picturesque appearance.

From the castle the traveller may proceed to Greenhead station, situated a few hundred yards distant, or walk to the hotel by the route described at page 117.

Gilsland to Haltwhistle, and thence to Bellister, Featherstone, Blenkinsop, and Thirlwall Castles.

This excursion may be taken with carriage, a distance of 15 miles, but most persons will go by train to Haltwhistle, and then visit the four castles on foot, a walk of 7 miles, and return by train from Greenhead station; or, if it be inconvenient to catch the train, the hotel may be reached by adding to the walk the 2½ miles, *viâ* Thirlwall Castle, as given at page 117.

Those who are anxious to visit the castles, but object both to the carriage drive and the pedestrian excursion, may visit the places by railway, as Thirlwall and Blenkinsop Castles are near the Greenhead station; Bellister Castle is near to Haltwhistle station; and Featherstone Castle is near to Featherstone station.

Haltwhistle contains 1500 inhabitants. The principal hotels are the Crown, Sun, Manor House, and Temperance Hotel. It is pleasantly situated on the north bank of the South Tyne river, and is a respectable town of considerable antiquity; but it appears to find it a hard struggle to emerge from its antique tranquillity to the active commercial life of the present day. Within the last twenty years it has greatly improved, owing that improvement, no doubt, to its being the centre of an extensive and prosperous agricultural district, and also to the development of mineral wealth immediately around it. A weekly market was granted to the town by Edward I., when he rested there a night on the 11th September, 1306, on his last journey into Scotland. Thursday is the market day, but there is now no regular market, as the district has been in a great measure converted from arable into pastoral, and the railway enables the inhabitants to visit Carlisle, Hexham, and Newcastle. The dairy produce is, however, still brought into the town, and few places can boast of being better supplied with butcher meat, butter, eggs, milk, and poultry. There are some good shops, and also a banking establishment—a branch of the Cumberland Union Bank. Tourists staying in Gilsland often find it convenient to run down here to make a few purchases.

In olden times Haltwhistle had its share of the feudal and predatory wars which devastated the borders, and its principal guardians appear to have been the Musgraves, Blenkinsops, Featherstonehaughs, and Ridleys. The tower of Hautwysill, mentioned in a list of the castles and towers in Northumberland in 1416, was no doubt the venerable manorial Peel which stands in the rear of the Castle Hill, at the east end of the town. It has a loopholed turret, built on corbels; the floors consist of stone flags laid on joists composed of oak trees roughly squared. Although it now presents an insignificant appearance by the side of modern structures, in ancient times it would, no doubt, be the official residence of the bailiffs of the town. It is a pity that such a genuine relic of antiquity should be neglected and dilapidated.

The Castle Hill, which commands a good view, is a diluvial bank, artificially formed at a remote period into its present shape, and fortified with earthworks. To the south the Tyne has swept its base; Haltwhistle Burn gurgling down its deep glen cuts it off from the adjacent hill; a wide ditch has defended it on the north, while to the west the ground has been cut away to render it as inaccessible as possible. The earthen rampart is about 4 feet high, and encloses an area of about 200 feet from east to west, by 100 from north to south. A recent writer says, the meaning of Hautwysill is the Holy Hill on the high water; thus showing that the hill was used not only as a defence for the inhabitants and their cattle against any sudden inroad of the enemy, but also as a place for public worship, and probably for the administration of justice.

The castellated house, now used as a temperance hotel, near the market place, is a more modern structure than the old Peel, and was probably used at a later period as a residence for the bailiffs. One of the towers presents an antique appearance at the back of the house, but in front it has been cemented and coloured.

It is said that in the time of Queen Elizabeth, when Sir Robert Carey was Warden of the West Marches, the Liddesdale mosstroopers having plundered the town of Haltwhistle, the English Wardens, in retaliation, entered Liddesdale in a hostile manner and laid waste the lands of the freebooters. Upon this occasion an Armstrong was killed by one of the Ridleys of Haltwhistle, which procured the town another visit from the Armstrongs, who reduced a great part of it to ashes, but not without losing one of their leaders. Sir Robert followed the freebooters; but upon his approach they abandoned their dwellings and retreated to a place of defence. Whilst Sir Robert invested their stronghold, the freebooters sent him a piece of one of his own cattle, telling him that fearing he might fall short of provisions during his visit to Scotland, they had taken the precaution to send him some English beef.

Haltwhistle is said to be one of the healthiest places in England, and the ages which are recorded on the headstones in the churchyard bear out this statement in a remarkable degree. Very few indeed of the gravestones are without the record of some one who lived to be above sixty years of age. We took a note of all above that age (341 in number) with the following result:

Age.	No.	Age.	No.	Age.	No.
61	7	74	12	87	7
62	9	75	15	88	4
63	9	76	15	89	4
64	9	77	20	90	3
65	16	78	13	91	3
66	10	79	4	92	2
67	11	80	16	93	1
68	17	81	14	95	1
69	18	82	6	96	1
70	14	83	—	97	1
71	9	84	11	99	1
72	18	85	8	101	1
73	17	86	13	108	1

One gravestone, recording the ages of seven of one family is so remarkable that we copy it entire. The eighth member of the same family, a son, died a few months ago, above ninety years of age:

"In memory of John Carrick, of Carvoran, who died November 4, 1814, aged 82.

"Also of James, his wife, who died June 29, 1816, aged 73.

"Also of Elizabeth, their daughter, who died December 18, 1839, aged 69.

"Also Robert, their son, who died February 5, 1848, aged 75.

"Also John, their son, who died September 11, 1855, aged 86.

"Also Ann, their daughter, who died May 28, 1868, aged 85.

"Also Margaret, their daughter, who died September 2, 1869, aged 91."

The vicar of the parish informed us that in the register there is an entry of a man who died at the age of 117.

An old lady, M. Beattie, lately died at Pott's Loan, near Bewcastle, aged 107, and was buried at Lanercost.

The church is a very ancient building, and has recently been restored. It contains a remarkable old tombstone, which is figured (under the 14th century) in 'Boutell's Christian Monuments.'

Bellister Castle is half a mile from Haltwhistle. To visit it the traveller must go under the railway, and over the South Tyne river, close to the station; then turn to the right, and after proceeding 700 or 800 yards, a branch road on the left will be observed, leading direct to the building. The ruins are not very extensive, there being merely part of the outside walls remaining of what, in its best days, must have been but a small border tower. It stands on a boss of whinstone, and is shaded by an immense sycamore tree. A modern farmhouse, built in the castellated style, is attached to the ruin. In the rear is a belt of trees, and in front an extensive view of Haltwhistle and the surrounding country. The manor is very ancient, and belonged to Robert de Roos in 1296, but the castle does not make its appearance in border history till 1470, when it was the property of Thomas Blenkinsop, a younger branch of the family of that name. In 1715, the castle was purchased by John Bacon, whose son John married the widow of John Blenkinsop; and their grandson, the Rev. Henry Wastel, in 1818, sold it to John Kirsop, of Hexham, who left it to Mr. Robert Williams, of London, the present owner.

Tradition tells us that when Bellister Castle was occupied by the Blenkinsops, a wandering minstrel sought the protection of its roof. The evening was far advanced, and the old man was gladdened on being invited to the family hearth. This favour had not been long granted before suspicion entered the bosom of the Lord of Bellister. At that time animosity existed between him and a neighbouring baron, and the thought that the minstrel might be a spy in the employ of his enemy at once took possession of his mind. The stranger was not slow in noticing the change distrust had written upon the features of the baron, and this knowledge had the effect of checking his cheerfulness in return. This circumstance soon communicated itself to the entire circle, and it was, therefore, with more than usual alacrity that the order for withdrawal was obeyed. No sooner, however, was the lord left to himself than suspense rose to passion, and the attendants were summoned to bring the harper into his presence. Great was his surprise on being told he could not be found—the minstrel had escaped from the castle—arguing, no doubt, distrust at the hands of his entertainer. The baron was now confirmed in his suspicion, and his embittered spirit thirsted for revenge. The bloodhounds were let loose, and by them the unfortunate stranger was torn to pieces before the baron and his dependents could reach the spot. It is added, the spirit of the murdered man haunts the place, and visitors to the neighbourhood hear from the story-loving people strange accounts of the doings of "The Grey Man o' Bellister."

Featherstone Castle, distant 2½ miles, is reached by following the main road in front of Bellister. A gradual ascent is made, and then the river is on the right, and Alston railway on the left, and an extensive view is had of Haltwhistle and the high ground to the north and south. The large handsome building on the opposite side of the river is Blenkinsop Hall. Presently the rearward view is lost to sight; but this is amply compensated by the woodland scene displayed in front; with the dark heath-clad hills of Tindale, Blacklaw, Thornhope, and Coanwood in the distance. After passing a branch road, on the left, leading to Park village, a sharp descent is made to the large and beautifully wooded park of Featherstone, with the South Tyne flowing round its north and north-west sides. Few strangers will visit the spot without being surprised and delighted to find such a charming sylvan scene in, what will appear to many, an out-of-the-way place, and where nothing but heath and moorland might have been expected. The road runs through the park on the south bank of the river, the opposite side of the stream being a high slope beautifully clothed with wood.

After passing a farmhouse the castle comes in sight, its ivy-mantled battlements presenting a picturesque appearance. The Featherstonehaughs, who formerly lived here, were a noted family in these parts in ancient times. The origin of their name is thus given by an old writer:—
"Their house was formerly upon a hill, where there are two stones, called Featherstones, and was moated about for

defence against the Scots; but upon the ruin of this, the house was afterwards built in the holme or valley under the hill, which they there call Haugh, and thence it was called Featherstonehaugh. Courts of manor were anciently, and many of them to this day are, held in the open air; the place is distinguished by a large stone, which the steward uses as a table, at which the homage take the oath. It seems probable that the stones here mentioned were used for such purpose in former ages, and were called the *Feuderstones*, where the feudal tenants of the manor were assembled." Helios de Featherstonhalf was in possession of the castle in 1212. Thomas Featherstonehaugh was conservator of a truce between England and Scotland in 1327, and in 1335 Edward II. gave him a mandate to array all the men at arms in South Tindale. In 1374 Alexander Featherstonehaugh, being about to proceed to the king's foreign wars, made a settlement of his estate before the high sheriff. About 1460, Alexander de Featherstonehaugh engaged to marry Maud, daughter of Sir Richard Salkeld, in case his brother should die before he married the same lady. Sir Albany Featherstonehaugh was High Sheriff of Northumberland in 1530. He was murdered at Greensilhaugh, near the farm-house of Wydon Eals (situated on the opposite side of the river, about a mile from his castle), by Ridley, of Unthank, on the 24th October, 1530. The event is quaintly told in Surtee's famous ballad:

> "Hoot awa', lads, hoot awa',
> Ha' ye heard how the Ridleys and Thirlwalls and a'
> Ha' set upon Albany Featherstonehaugh,
> And taken his life at the Deadman's haugh?
>   There was Williamoteswick,
>   And Hardriding Dick,
> And Hughie o' Harden, and Will o' the Wa',
> I canna' tell a', I canna' tell a',
> And many a mair that auld Nick may knaw."

Richard Featherstonehaugh, D.D., was chaplain and manager for Queen Catherine of Arragon in the affair of her divorce, which he conducted with great zeal; but refusing to subscribe to the king's supremacy, he suffered death, July 30, 1540. Henry Featherstonehaugh was appointed receiver-general by James I. of all the king's revenues in Cumberland and Westmorland. Timothy, his son, who during the civil wars in the reign of Charles I. raised a troop of horse at his own expense, was knighted under the king's banner for his gallant conduct, but he was taken prisoner at the battle of Worcester, and beheaded at Bolton, in Lancashire, in 1651. The castle and estate continued in the male line of the family for twelve generations, but their interest in it disappeared in Abigail, only surviving daughter of the last of their line. Tradition assigns her a most romantic death (see page 128); but history marries her unromantically to Mr. Peter Dodson, of Kirby Overblows, Yorkshire, and brings her quietly and timely to a natural end. The castle and estate afterwards came into the possession of Matthew Featherstonehaugh, of Newcastle; his son, Sir Matthew Featherstonehaugh, sold them to James Wallace, Esq., barrister-at-law and Attorney-General of England, in 1780 and 1783. He died in 1783, and was succeeded by his son, Thomas Wallace, of Ash Holme, Knarsdale, Carlton Hall, and Featherstone, who was sworn of the Privy Council, 21st May, 1801, and for his distinguished services under four sovereigns he was created Baron Wallace, of Knarsdale, in 1828. In 1814 he married Lady Jane Hope, daughter of John, second Earl of Hopetoun, and widow of Viscount Melville. Lord Wallace died in February, 1844, when the title became extinct, and was succeeded by the Hon. James Hope, second son of John, the great Earl of Hopetoun, who took the command at Corunna after the death of Sir John Moore. Mr. Hope Wallace died January, 1854, and was succeeded by his son, John Hope Wallace, Esq., the present proprietor. On Mr. Hope Wallace coming of age, in 1860, he so improved the whole of the castle and grounds, that as they now stand they may fairly be called the work of the present possessor. The flower and kitchen gardens have been brought to surround the castle, and are all enclosed by an embattled wall. The highest part in the centre of the castle is the ancient tower of Featherstone, but with that exception, the whole of the castellated edifice has been altered and rebuilt. Mr. Hope Wallace was High Sheriff of Northumberland in 1871.

The Featherstone railway station being only half a mile distant, some tourists may stroll there and return to Gilsland by rail. It is reached by ascending the high ground in the rear of the castle. It is close to the boundary of the park, and a few yards distant is the comfortable snuggery of the Wallace Arms. A short distance beyond is the hamlet called Featherstone Rowfoot.

Those who do not return by rail can have a pleasant walk to Greenhead station, visiting Blenkinsop and Thirlwall Castles. Near the Bridge End farmhouse, in the middle of the park, the river is crossed by a picturesque bridge which spans the stream with one arch. The antiquary will be interested in examining two old oak coffins which are kept at the house, and were found along with some other similar ones in a field on the Wydon Eals farm, situated half a mile distant on the north side of the river. The place, which appears to have been a very ancient burial ground, is reached by going through a gate on the right after crossing the bridge. Some workmen accidentally found the coffins when making drains. Each coffin consists of the hollow trunk of part of an oak tree rudely split from end to end, the two halves being fastened together by means of oaken pegs driven into holes. The interior contained human bones, and consisted of a cavity of about 6 feet by 20 inches, rudely shaped, apparently with some very primitive kind of instrument. In 1859, Mr. Clark, land agent, Featherstone Castle, wrote a report on the subject at the request of the Archæological Institute of Great Britain, and it was printed along with the 'Transactions' for that year. Similar oak coffins have been found, though rarely, both in England and Scotland; but there seems to be no close agreement amongst antiquaries as to the age in which they were made. In a deed, dated 1223, the place is called the Temple Land, and paid 19s. per annum to the Dean and Chapter of Carlisle.

On his way back to the road the tourist may turn up the Pynkincleugh burn, and follow a track which ascends through the wood. He will thus pass through a small dark glen, where, by the side of two venerable thorns, stands the *Witch's Cot*, a crumbling ruin, consisting merely of a wall and gable covered with moss and fern. About 150 years ago this lonely and rude hut was inhabited by an eccentric old woman, named Janet Pearson, familiarly known in the neighbourhood by the characteristic cognomen of Beardie Grey, from her singularly long beard. She enjoyed the unhappy privileges of a reputed witch and prophetess, and consequently lived upon her neighbours, "getting more for her ill than her good." Many of her oracular utterances are handed down from father to son. One of these resembles some that are widely current in the traditionary lore of Scotland, and reminds us of Scott's 'Border Minstrelsy,' where it is said, "At Pynkinscleugh there shall be spilt much gentil blood that day." The tradition is that at the west corner of Beardie's hut there stood a huge grey stone, on which she used to rock to and fro whilst venting her maudlin ravings to the midnight blast, and she prophesied that when that stone was covered with moss a great battle would take place here that would make the burn run three days red with blood. This stone, which was being rapidly overgrown with moss, was destroyed some years ago, and no doubt that untoward accident saved the credit of the prophetess or averted the dreadful consequences of the strife. The last time the dreaded old witch was seen she was making her way to her lonely hut on a stormy night, when the burn and river were considerably swollen with rain. The next day her neighbours missed her on her accustomed round, and on the most courageous among them breaking open the door of her hut, it was found empty, and the current belief was that the de'il had wafted her away amid the howling of the tempest on that dismal stormy night.

"When a land rejects her legends;
Sees but falsehoods in the past;
And its people view their sires
In the light of fools or liars,
'Tis a sign of its decline,
And its splendours cannot last!"

After dwelling a few minutes on the mysterious fate of wrinkled old Beardie, the traveller gains the road close to a bridge, which, according to tradition, is the site of the death of lovely Abigail, the last of the line of the Featherstonehaughs. It is said, the last Baron of Featherstone had an only daughter of great beauty, named Abigail, and the baroness being dead, his whole affections were centered on this charming girl, who at "sweet seventeen" was wooed, in all the devoted fervency of the times, by two gay and gallant lovers. The baron's favourite was Timothy Featherstonehaugh, a distant relative; the other was Ridley of Hardriding, who was secretly loved by the daughter, and the favourite with the vassals; but owing to an ancient feud between the families his suit was rejected by the baron, and he was forbidden the castle, and an immediate marriage decided upon with Featherstonehaugh. Neither tears nor entreaties could prevail, and ere she had time to thwart the baron's designs, the Prior of Lambley was summoned to perform the ceremony, which took place in a small chapel adjoining the castle. After the sacred vow and plighted troth, a hunting party took place in honour of the occasion. The numerous vassals who were enjoying the hospitality of their chief were soon in readiness; and, characteristic of the times, the charming bride was to be one of the party. Mounted on a beautiful palfrey she took her place in blushing loveliness by the side of her gallant lord, and the gay calvacade burst from the ivied archway, and rushed into the thickets of the forest glade, accompanied by the fervent blessings of the baron, who was unable, from age and infirmities, to pursue and enjoy the sport. Amid the woody glens of Hartley Burn the harpers' notes made every spirit light. The blast of the horn came echoing through the dales to call all up when twilight grey told it was banquet hour. The chase terminating on Notterish Hill, the party were returning by the gloomy glen of Pynkinscleugh, when at the bridge they were met by the rejected lover, at the head of a well-appointed band of vassals, who attempted to carry away the bride, willingly, tradition saith, but whether by appointment we know not. The bridegroom not willing to lose his prize, offered resistance, and both parties closed in deadly combat, but the vassals of Featherstonehaugh having come lightly armed for the chase, were soon overpowered and cut down. The fair prize was now within Ridley's grasp, but the chivalric spirit of the times forbade the victorious vassals taking so foul an advantage of the chances of the conflict. In single combat it must now be decided, and the steady parrying and desperate thrusts of the two combatants told that valour held death equal in the scales, when the heroic bride—the guiltless cause of all the strife—flung herself between the combatants. As if anticipating her purpose, they made a superhuman effort to close the deadly scene, and ere they could stay the overstrung nerves of their uplifted arms, their reeking blades had pierced her breast; the purple stream told the blow was mortal. Casting a look of forgiveness on both she sank among the slain. Both paused for a moment, and but for a moment, for then the furious clashing of steel announced the regardlessness of life, now that the prize worth living for was gone. They both fell, and expired by her side. Such was the melancholy fate of the last of the direct line of the Featherstonehaughs. The fragment of a stone long marked the spot to the passing stranger.

The road ascends steeply in a straight line, and is bordered on each side by plantations. When the top of the high ground is gained, which is called Notterish Hill, a splendid view of the surrounding country is obtained, and presently the ivy-covered battlements of Blenkinsop Castle present a picturesque appearance directly in front, with Greenhead village beyond. Within the ruins is a chimney or ventilating shaft connected with the working of an old coal mine, and portions of the building are now tenanted by persons connected with the adjoining colliery. It was the seat of the ancient family of Blenkinsop, and is supposed to have been built in 1339, when "Thomas de Blenkinsopp" had a licence to fortify his mansion on the borders of Scotland. It occurs as the residence of John de Blenkinsope in the list of Border castles about the year 1416; and in 1488, its proprietor of the same name, and his son Gerard, committed the custody of it to Henry Percy, Earl of Northumberland, who at that time was Warden of the West and Middle Marches, and no doubt thought this a desirable situation for a garrison on the borders. Under the protection of their castles, the people in this valley so strongly resisted the Act of Parliament made in Henry VII.'s time, to incorporate them with the county of Northumberland, that in 1550 it was reported to Government that the sheriffs of the county had, often to ride to attack offenders at Thirlwall, Blenkinsop, and other places on the South Tyne; "for both they and the people of North Tindale always claimed and used their old liberties, and were therefore more obedient to the keeper of Tindale, or the Lord Warden than to the sheriffs of Northumberland." In 1542 this castle is described as a tower of the inheritance of John Blenkinsope, damaged in the roof, and not in good reparations. When it was finally deserted as a residence by its owners we have no account. In 1727 it came into possession of 'the Coulsons, of Jesmond, near Newcastle, by the marriage of William Coulson with Jane Blenkinsop, the heiress of the estate. In 1785, the names of the two families were blended, and John [Blenkinsop Coulson left the estates to his nephew, Colonel John Blenkinsop Coulson, who built for his resi-

K

dence the fine castellated mansion of Blenkinsop Hall, and whose portrait hangs in the town hall of Haltwhistle. He was called the heather chieftain, from having ridden to Morpeth at the head of the voters of South Tynedale during the fiercely-contested election of 1826, with a sprig of heather in his hat. He died in 1863, and was succeeded by his son, Captain John Blenkinsop Coulson, who married the eldest daughter of the seventh Lord Byron, representative of the celebrated poet. He died in 1868, and was succeeded by his eldest son John Byron Blenkinsop Coulson, the present proprietor.

There is a legend connected with the castle of Blenkinsop, called "The White Lady o' Blenkinsop," which is somewhat as follows: Bryan de Blenkinsop, a brave and handsome youth, was lord of the castle. He possessed many good qualities, which won him favour amongst his neighbours, but he had one failing, which ultimately wrecked his fortune; namely, an inordinate love of wealth. Being present at the marriage of a brother warrior with a lady of high rank and fortune, amongst other toasts was given " Bryan de Blenkinsop and his ladye love." The youthful lord passionately replied, "Never shall that be until I meet with a lady possessed with a chest of gold heavier than ten of my men can carry into my castle." The effect this announcement made upon the assembly was noticed by the speaker, who, ashamed of having disclosed his secret thought, suddenly left the castle, and ultimately quitted the country. After an absence of some years he returned, bringing with him a wife, and a box of gold which took twelve men to carry into his castle. But his married life was not all sunshine: his lady, jealous and revengeful, had her chest removed to a secret vault, when the baron, aggravated by her conduct, left the castle and was never heard of again. The lady, after repeated efforts to find her lost lord, also disappeared, and the lives of the two became enveloped in mystery. It is said the lady, filled with remorse, cannot rest in her grave, but must needs wander back and mourn over the chest of gold, the cursed cause of all their woe.

Half a mile from Blenkinsop Castle is the Greenhead railway station, and half a mile from the station are the ruins of Thirlwall Castle, upon an eminence on the west bank of the Tipalt streamlet. Dr. Bruce, in his book entitled 'The Roman Wall,' says: "Thirlwall Castle is, as Hutchinson calls it, 'a dark, melancholy fortress' of the middle ages. It was for many centuries previous to its purchase by the ancestors of the Earl of Carlisle, the residence of an ancient Northumbrian family of the name of Thirlwall. Amongst the witnesses examined on the occasion of the famous suit between the families of Scrope and Grosvenor, for the right to bear the shield 'azure, a bend or,' which was opened at Newcastle-upon-Tyne in 1385, before King Richard II. in person, was John Thirlwall, an esquire of Northumberland. The witness related what he had heard on the subject of the dispute from his father, who 'died at the age of 145, and was when he died the oldest esquire in all the north, and had been in arms in his time sixty-nine years.' Such is the language of the record of these proceedings, preserved in the Tower of London."

We extract the following story from Mr. Peter Burn's 'English Border Ballads': "A tradition is linked to Thirlwall Castle, called 'The Gold Table o' Thirlwa.' We are told that one of the barons of Thirlwall returned from the wars laden with treasures, amongst which was a table of solid gold. Not only did he become an object of envy amongst his neighbours, but he excited the covetous dispositions of the numerous bands of freebooters with which the borders abounded; yet the baron held the possessions against all comers; brave himself, he boasted of true and daring followers. Furthermore, the gold table was said to be guarded day and night by a hideous dwarf, represented by many to be the foul fiend himself. But a change came to the house of Thirlwall; a Scot more bold than his neighbours, came with his men; they stormed the castle by night, and the baron and his retainers, after a desperate resistance, were slain. Search was made for the treasure, but dwarf and gold table had disappeared; a further search was made, but without success, when, after having set fire to the castle, they departed. It is said that the dwarf had, during the heat of the engagement, removed the treasure; and after having thrown it into a deep draw-well, jumped in, and by his infernal power closed the top of it. So much for the tradition, which, wild as it is, finds a place in the faith of the people. Many speak of the treasure which lies at the bottom of the 'dwarf's well.'"

Glen Dhu.

This is a small, but an exceedingly pretty ravine, situated one mile from the Lambley railway station, on the Alston line; and it contains one of the best waterfalls in the district.

Formerly there was a small nunnery at Lambley, which was destroyed by the Scots in 1296. In the reign of Queen Elizabeth the South Tyne ran among the ruins of the building, and now it has swept away every vestige of it.

The Lambley viaduct is a fine object in the landscape, and before leaving the bridge a small Roman camp, called the Castle, at the east end of the bridge should be visited. Here, too, the geologist will get the best section to be seen of what is known by geologists as the 90-fathom dyke. It brings in the Newcastle coal-field, which is being worked at different places in the neighbourhood. For 6 or 7 miles along the dyke the geology is most interesting, and the traveller can stand as it were with one foot on the Newcastle coal measures and the other on the millstone grit and the mountain limestone.

Glen Dhu may be reached by a rather circuitous road from the station, but a better plan is to proceed close to the line for one mile to the place where are five arches. Here cross the right-hand fence, and proceed up the glen with the stream on the left. It is a very beautiful, narrow, rugged dell; the water tumbling over large blocks of freestone, and the overhanging cliffs being luxuriantly clothed with trees, shrubs, ferns, and mosses. Three-quarters of a mile up the dell there is a delightful cascade, the water having a fall of about 30 feet over a ledge of rock, and tumbling into a deep pool below. The spot is most secluded and romantic. The cliffs are high and charmingly covered from base to summit with a profusion of vegetation, trees and shrubs growing on every rock, through the leaves and branches of which glance rays of the sun on the mosses and ferns that fill every crevice. After a steep climb the top of the ravine is gained and the road entered that runs from Brampton to Alston. From this point the mountain ground might be entered and a gradual ascent made to the summit of Tindale Fell. Those who keep the road will walk in a north-western direction up the vale called Hartley Burn; here are some collieries, and a private single line of rails running from Lambley station to Milton station, and used almost solely for the transit of coal; sometimes a traveller may, however, succeed in getting a ride on the engine. When half-way up Hartley Burn, Gilsland can be reached by following a road which crosses the vale and ascends the opposite high ground, called Denton Fell. Any of the natives will tell the stranger where to leave the road and strike across the fell in order to descend close to the Gilsland station.

Gilsland to the Northumberland Lakes, and to Housesteads.

Greenhead, 3¼ miles; Common House, 7 miles; Twice Brewed, 10 miles; Northumberland Lakes, 12 miles; thence to Housesteads, on foot, 14½ miles; by carriage, 17 miles; to Housesteads direct from Gilsland, 13 miles.

These distances are from Shaw's Hotel, Gilsland.

For a wagonette or other conveyance, to carry six persons and the driver, 30s.
For a wagonette or other conveyance, to carry eight persons and the driver, 35s.
For a four-wheeled break, 5s. each person.

Leaving Gilsland by the road which passes under the railway, close to the station and the hamlet of Crooks, a good view is had of the Hotel and Orchard House, and surrounding woodland; and in front appear the Nine Nicks of Thirlwall, and the cluster of trees close to the site of the Roman station of Carvoran. Presently the ruins of Thirlwall Castle appear, and near to them the north and south ditches are observed ascending the hill. The road crosses the line of the Roman wall, passes within a few hundred yards of the castle, and joins the military way at the village of Greenhead. After going over the railway and the Tipalt streamlet, a house called Glen Whelt is passed, which, in old coaching days, was an inn, and the place for changing horses; in the house are a pair of red deer's horns, taken out of the Roman well at Carvoran. From this point a very steep ascent is made, and the view embraces a wide extent of country. Close below on the right is seen Blenkinsop Castle, and across a field on the left is the Carvoran farmhouse on the site of the Roman station of *Magna*. From Carvoran the Roman wall crosses over the tops of the long ridge of hills on the left, stretching to the east for many miles. The road now runs for a long distance in a straight course over high ground, which hides Haltwhistle on the right and the vale through which runs the railway and flows the South Tyne, whilst beyond are heath-clad hills stretching to Crossfell. Where a descent begins to be made, the Roman station of Great Chesters can be discerned close to a farmhouse half a mile on the left. A small stream is crossed, which flows from Green Lee Lough, one of the Northumberland lakes, situated a short distance north of Housesteads and the Roman wall; and then a small inn, called the Common House, is reached, at the point where the road branches to right for Haltwhistle, 1½ miles distant. At the house the traveller will observe Cawfields mile station, a few hundred yards on the left. It is the most perfect castle of the kind on the whole length of the wall.

After passing the public-house the road runs in a straight course on high ground. The Roman wall is visible half a mile on the left, following in an up and down course the hills and hollows of the cliff-like ridge facing to the north. Half a mile beyond the inn there are two upright stones on a mound on the left; they are known locally as the Mare and Foal, and are in all probability the remains of a Druidical circle, or denote the burial place of some ancient Norse or Danish warrior. In a map published in 1769 they are called "The Three Stones." The country around is bare of trees, and thinly studded with houses, but the traveller will feel braced with the pure breeze, and will occasionally catch pleasant glimpses of distant hills as he proceeds along the road, which runs up and down in an almost perfectly straight course. Moreover he cannot fail to take an especial interest in the journey when he observes the Roman wall running on the ridge for miles, a few yards on his left, and pictures in his mind those far-off times when the Roman warrior, day and night, paced and jealously guarded every inch of that mural barrier.

On reaching the public-house known as Twice Brewed, a large round stone will be seen in front of the building. It is evidently part of a Roman milestone, such as that mentioned at page 139. The original and far-famed

"Twice Brewed" was a quarter of a mile distant, and is now a farmhouse. Two hundred yards beyond the inn enter a branch road on the left; it ascends the high ground and passes through the Roman wall at a point where it has been rebuilt within the last few years to keep it in good preservation. The Crag Lough will be observed on the right at the base of some perpendicular crags. When over the ridge go through a gate on the right and follow a cart-track; the Crag Lough and the bold vertical cliffs, over which the Romans erected their wall, now present a picturesque appearance. Presently, on gaining the top of a slight elevation, the wide open district known as the Waste, appears in front, stretching away to the north, and close below are seen parts of the two sheets of water known as the Green Lee Lough and Brown Lee Lough, and there is observed a pleasant-looking house embowered in a small plantation, it being Sir Edward Blackett's shooting-box, near to which is a farmhouse, and the gamekeeper's cottage. The place has a lonely, rural and picturesque appearance, and on a fine day the stranger may while away an hour or two very pleasantly by sauntering about on the banks of the loughs. The visitor used to be able to obtain the loan of the rowing-boat on Green Lee Lough by applying to the gamekeeper, but this favour has been discontinued owing to some foolish people having done wilful damage to the boat.

Whilst the carriage is returning empty to "Twice Brewed," and thence to Housesteads, a distance of 5 miles, the visitor will walk 2½ miles from the lakes to the latter place. After crossing the ground in front of the ridge and proceeding through a gap in the wall, turn to the left and follow the course of the wall; it is here in a good state of preservation, and a mile castle will be observed before a small plantation is passed through, at the back of which is the fine station of Borcovicus or Housesteads. See page 203.

The journey home may be agreeably varied, and only a slight addition made to the distance, by following the road which leads past Haltwhistle, or by Chesterholm, Bardon Mill, and Haltwhistle. See pages 136 and 138.

A walk along the Roman Wall, over the Nine Nicks of Thirlwall.

A very pleasant 8 miles walk may be had by taking the train to Haltwhistle, and then strolling to the Roman wall, and tracing its course over the Nine Nicks of Thirlwall to Thirlwall Castle, and thence proceeding to Gilsland Hotel.

When through the town of Haltwhistle, take the road which branches to the left, close to Haltwhistle Burn, a streamlet that has its source in Green Lee Lough, one of the Northumberland lakes, and flows into the South Tyne. The road makes a steep ascent, commanding good retrospective views, and when the prospect opens to the north, the Nine Nicks of Thirlwall and the Roman wall appear. Another plan is to follow the footpath by the side of the burn; it is more romantic, but a trifle more circuitous. One mile and a half from Haltwhistle railway station, the military road is reached at the point where there is a small inn, called the Common House; here cross the turnpike and follow the road leading direct to the wall, which is seen a little less than half a mile distant, the Cawfield's mile station being also in sight.

When a few yards from the public-house, branch to the right to the mile castle, passing over the south ditch, which is here clearly traced, taking a direct line at the foot of the heights. The Cawfields mile castle is considered to be the most perfect structure of the kind known. See page 201. To the east of it the wall is almost perfect for nearly a mile.

Leaving the castle, the Haltwhistle burn is crossed close to the Burnhead farmhouse, which stands on the site of the wall. For the next 200 or 300 yards there are no remains, but the direction is clearly defined by the northern ditch. Presently in the stone fence a portion of the original wall appears, three or four courses of stones high; all traces then disappear until the next farmhouse, Great Chesters, is reached, which is situated upon the site of the wall and close to the camp or station of Æsica. The uninitiated might pass the latter without noticing any trace of its having been so important a place in former times, but on examining the spot more closely there is found to be a large square plot of land, 3 acres in extent, enclosed by high banks composed of stones overgrown with grass, and outside of which appears to have been a ditch, and inside are grass-covered heaps, where have evidently existed buildings.

To the next farmhouse, Cockmount Hill, distant a few hundred yards, there are only slight traces of the wall, but the present stone fence is a good guide, as it takes the same direction. A short distance to the left is a lead mine, which has been worked for the last seven years, but not much lead has yet been obtained. Just beyond the house the wall runs through a small plantation, and may be followed along a foot-track; it is overgrown with grass and shrubs, but in some places there may be observed three or four courses of facing stones. For the next half mile the only trace of the wall is a line of heaps of stone overgrown with ferns and grass, but by jumping over to the north side the stones are seen here and there neatly fixed in their original position. Here will be observed the remains of a mile castle entirely overgrown, and of the same shape and size as that at Cawfields, and distant from it about a mile. The wall then runs some distance tolerably perfect, being 7 feet, and on the north side 10 feet high, but without the ditch on the north, as the ground has a gentle slope in that direction.

Leaving a clump of trees and the farmhouse of Allolee on the left, the Nine Nicks of Thirlwall begin to be ascended, and the view opens out grandly to the west, whilst to the east is a long ridge of cliff-like hills, over which the wall can be traced, and at the foot of which lie the Northumberland lakes, one being visible from this point. To the north stretches for miles a wide tract of land gradually rising in the distance to slightly elevated ground, without a tree, and scarcely a farmhouse to be seen. To the south is a pleasantly wooded vale, watered by the South Tyne, and more distant heath-clad hills, terminating in Crossfell. Near at hand may be seen one or two houses, but the only denizens of the place appear to be innumerable sheep and black cattle, which constantly enliven the solitude.

The wall now almost disappears, but it may be traced by the grass-grown mound along the very summit of the cliffs, which present a sheer precipice of from 100 or 200 feet to the north, and gradually slope to the south. The walk along these tops is most enjoyable, the traveller being invigorated by a pure and healthy breeze, and having spread before him a glorious panorama stretching to the Solway Firth, with Skiddaw on the left, and Criffel on the right of that arm of the sea.

After leaving on the left, embosomed in trees, the farmhouse of Waltown, which was formerly a castellated tower, the property of a brother of Bishop Ridley, the martyr, the grass-grown remains of another mile castle are observed, and then a strip of the wall is found facing to the north, 5 feet high, and still perfect.

On descending from the crags close to a quarry of whinstone, worked for supplying paving-stones for the streets of Edinburgh, Newcastle, &c., the traveller reaches the farmhouse of Carvoran, and the site of the Roman camp *Magna*. For particulars respecting the camp, and the remaining part of the journey, see pages 117 and 118.

Gilsland to Bardon Mill, and thence to Chesterholm and Housesteads.

The finest Roman camp on the line of the wall is at Housesteads, and it may be visited either by taking the train to Bardon Mill or Haydon Bridge; the former is 3¼, and the latter 6 miles from the camp. Haydon Bridge being the larger place, and having plenty of posting accommodation, many strangers alight there from the train, but the route by Bardon Mill is not only the shortest but the most interesting, as it enables the tourist to visit the Roman camp of Chesterholm, where is standing the only remaining Roman milestone in Great Britain, except that in the wall of Saint Swithin's Church, Cannon Street, London.

Bardon Mill is a small old place, situated in a fertile district on the bank of the South Tyne River. On alighting at the station the traveller may follow the road either to right or left. Those who go to the left must take the first turn on the right and then ascend straight up the hill, avoiding a way leading north-west. If the opposite course be taken, the left-hand road must be entered at the last house through the village. After passing a row of cottages the road bends to the right, and continues to ascend the hill, with fine retrospective views across the vale to the summit of the high ground, southward. Half a mile might be saved by entering a footpath before arriving at the cottages. The path takes through the fields and conducts past some houses to the top of the hill in the direction of dark heath-covered ground. It is, however, not advisable to cut off this corner, as by so doing the camp of Chesterholm is not visited.

When on the top of the hill, leave the road, go through a gate on the left, and follow a way leading down to a small ravine planted with trees, and containing one or two houses; here on a slight eminence is the old Roman camp of Chesterholm. It is of the same shape and size as those situated close to the wall, and appears to have been on the line of a Roman road; close to it is a Roman milestone, a round solid block, 6 feet in circumference and 5 feet high, but without any inscription now visible. By following the lane 1 mile to west will be found the lower part of a similar milestone, lying loose on the ground, but we are told within a yard of the position it occupied when erect. The upper part has been broken off and split into pieces; the pieces are now used as gate-posts on the top of the field entering a cross road. At a neighbouring public-house on the military road, called "Twice Brewed," is also another portion of a similar stone, and we found a part of one used as a seat in the Robin Hood public-house, near Harlow Hill. Hodgson tells us that a few years since there were three successive milestones remaining west of Chesterholm, each in its proper place.

The camp at Chesterholm is well defined, the walls, and *débris* within, being overgrown with grass. It is supposed to have been the Roman station of Vindolana, and it has sometimes been called Little Chesters, The Bowers,* and Chester-in-the-Wood; and the adjoining stream goes by the name of Chineley Burn. The villa close by was formerly the residence of the Rev. Anthony Hedley, a zealous and warm-hearted antiquary. An old writer tells us of a temple having been found at the west end of the station "adorned with Doric pilasters and capitals," which, from the workmen's ignorance of the value of such antiquities, perished under their tools. Some years ago there was

---

* Hutchinson, in his 'History of Northumberland,' says that it was called The Bowers "on account of the trees which cover it."

discovered under a heap of rubbish, a few yards from the west wall of the station, a square room, *strongly vaulted above*, and paved with large square stones set in lime, and under this a lower room, whose roof was supported by rows of square pillars of about half a yard high. The upper room had two niches, like chimneys, on each side of every corner or square, which in all made the number sixteen. The pavement of this room, as well as its roof, was tinged with smoke, and the pillars were quite black with soot. It is supposed to have been a hypocaust, but the people residing hereabouts say that The Bowers, from the Roman age till within the last century, was the elysium of a colony of fairies, and this ruined bath the kitchen to one of their palaces, of which the soot among the stones was undeniable evidence; and confident belief affirmed that long passages led from this laboratory "of savoury messes" to subterraneous halls, that ever echoed to the festivities and music of the Queen of the Bowers and her aërial court.

On again entering the road the dark heath-clad height of Borcombe, crowned with a stone monument, is on the right, and at a little distance on the left is seen the ridge over which runs the Roman wall; bending to left and then entering the military way and continuing along it for a few hundred yards, the cluster of trees and shepherd's house are observed close to the camp at Housesteads. A rough cart-road must be entered, which proceeds through a few fields to the house. For a description of the camp see page 203.

From Housesteads the pedestrian might track the Roman wall to Cawfields mile station, and thence branch off to Haltwhistle. See page 136. Or he might go to Haydon Bridge, a distance of 6 miles by road, but reduced to 4 miles if he strikes across the fields, aiming first for the small sheet of water a little to the south of Housesteads, and then in a south-east direction. To reach Haydon Bridge by road the military way has to be followed to the east for 2 miles, and then the right-hand road entered, which runs southwards through a district bare of trees, and with only one or two houses, until the vale of the South Tyne is entered.

Willimontswyke Castle, the birthplace of Bishop Ridley, the Martyr.

Willimontswyke* Castle was the chief seat of the ancient family of the Ridleys, and is said to have been the birthplace of Bishop Ridley, the great Reformer, who was burnt at the stake in the days of Queen Mary. One of the towers of the old castle remains in ruins, and around it has been built a farmhouse and outbuildings. It is seen from the Bardon Mill railway station, being situated 1 mile distant on the bank of the South Tyne river. When the water is low it may be reached by crossing the stream at some stepping-stones close to the station, but at other times the opposite side can only be gained at a bridge 1½ miles farther down, close to Ridley Hall and the Allen River, thus increasing the distance from the station to the castle from 1 to 4 miles. The return journey might be varied by walking 4 miles along a cart-road on the south side of the river to Haltwhistle.

The farmyard is entered by an old archway, and the tower, which commands an extensive view, may be ascended by winding stone steps. Some time ago a cow got up these steps, and a hole had to be made in the wall before she could be got down. The building is now the property of Sir Edward Blackett, Bart.

Some persons will no doubt consider this tower the most interesting relic in the district, and few will visit it without dwelling with admiration on those brave and holy men who suffered patiently the most terrible of deaths rather than renounce the cause of the Reformation.

Nicholas Ridley was born in the beginning of the six-

* We give the spelling according to the Ordnance Maps, but have also seen the name spelt Wyllimountswick, Wilmontswick, Willymotswick, Willowmountswick, Willimoteswick, and Willowmontswick.
  The etymology of the word appears doubtful. One writer says, " Wick is a village or hamlet, and Willowmont in the Northumberland language signifies a wild duck, or duck of the rocks. This bird is called *Guillem* by the Welsh; *Guillemot*, or *Sea Hen*, in Northumberland and Durham; in the southern parts *Willocks*."

teenth century, but the exact date is not known.* His father was the third son of a very ancient family, which had been seated at Willimontswyke, through a long descent of knights for many generations; the second son was John, father to Dr. Lancelot Ridley, and a fourth son was Dr. Robert Ridley. The Ridleys appear to have had their full share in the disturbances so frequent in the border territory, and in works which treat on border history occur many instances both of their courage and their importance. A feud existed between the Ridleys and the Featherstonehaughs, another border family, which led on more than one occasion to fatal results. A passage in the 'Border Minstrelsy' mentions those branches of the Ridley family located at Willimontswyke, Hardriding, Hawden, and Waltown, the first of whom was probably the uncle of Nicholas Ridley, and father to the "Worshipful cousin of Willimountswick" addressed by the bishop in his last farewell, written in prison just before going to the stake.

Ridley received his school education at Newcastle-upon-Tyne, whence he was removed about the year 1518 to Pembroke College, Cambridge,† at the expense of his uncle, Dr. Robert Ridley, then a Fellow of Queen's College. His career at Cambridge was highly honourable and successful, and so great were the hopes excited by his learning and abilities, that a fellowship at University College, Oxford, was offered for his acceptance. This honour he thought it best to decline, preferring the prospects which his own university presented to him, and was accordingly the next year elected a Fellow of his own college, to the mastership of which he subsequently attained. Impelled by that thirst for knowledge which ever distinguished him, he went in the year 1527 to Paris, for the purpose of studying at the Sorbonne; and here doubtless he availed himself of every advantage presented to him by that then celebrated seat of learning. But the University of Paris was already in its decline, and Ridley has given a picture, by no means favourable, of the then

* We have seen it stated in a local newspaper that the date was 1493.

† There is a walk in the garden of Pembroke College still distinguished by the name of Ridley's Walk.

. BISHOP RIDLEY. 143

prevailing style of disputation among its members. His absence from England was not of long duration, for we find him, in 1530, junior treasurer of Pembroke Hall. He signed, as proctor, in 1534, the decree against the Pope's supremacy, and continued steadily rising in his university career. In 1538 he appeared in a new capacity, that of a parish priest. The vicarage of Herne, in Kent, was bestowed upon him; and with the intense but ·well-directed zeal which formed so essential a part of his character, he applied himself to the duties of his new situation. So successful was he as a preacher, that he attracted numbers who had hitherto altogether omitted the duty of attendance on the services of the church; nor was he less attentive to the other parts of his parochial duty.

In 1540 he was made chaplain to Henry VIII., and promoted in 1547 by Edward VI. to the Bishopric of Rochester; and from thence translated in 1550 to the Bishopric of London. He took an active part in the Reformation, and soon after the accession of Mary, in 1553, was committed to the Tower along with Cranmer, Archbishop of Canterbury, and Latimer, Bishop of Worcester, on a charge of heresy.

The following year the three were sent to Oxford to dispute with the divines there, that under the show of fair discussion the intended murder might be veiled. The disputation being ended, all were condemned. On the 16th October, 1555, Ridley and Latimer were burnt at the stake, near Baliol College;* Cranmer being spared for five months longer as he appeared to show signs of wavering. When at the stake, a kindled faggot having been laid at Ridley's feet, Latimer exclaimed, "Be of good comfort, Master Ridley, and play the man. We shall this day, by God's grace, light in England such a candle as I trust shall never be put out." Latimer died first, exclaiming, "'O Father of heaven, receive my soul." Ridley, after

* Lord Dacre offered ten thousand pounds to the queen if she would spare Ridley's life, but she refused. ˙ Perhaps one reason why this offer was made was that a cousin of Ridley's had married Mabel, a granddaughter of Lord Dacre. Another reason might be that Ridley's paternal grandmother was Mary, daughter of Thomas Curwen of Workington, and the Curwens were a very ancient and influential family.

much protracted suffering, expired, repeating the words,
"Lord, Lord, receive my spirit."

> "Read, in the progress of this blessed story,
> Rome's cursed cruelty and Ridley's glory:
> Rome's sirens sung, but Ridley's careless ear
> Was deaf: they charm'd, but Ridley would not hear.
> Rome sung preferment, but brave Ridley's tongue
> Condemned that false preferment which Rome sung.
> Rome whispered death; but Ridley (whose great gain
> Was godliness), he waived it with disdain.
> Rome threatened durance, but great Ridley's mind
> Was too, too strong for threats or chains to bind.
> Rome thundered death, but Ridley's dauntless eye
> Star'd in death's face, and scorn'd death standing by.
> In spite of Rome for England's faith he stood,
> And in the flames he sealed it with his blood."

Bishop Ridley complied with the apostolic maxim, "Let your moderation be known unto all men." The share which he took in the management of the Book of Common Prayer, and other ecclesiastical formularies, enables us to judge with some accuracy as to his correct views of Church government.* As a bishop, both at Rochester and in the more important see of London, his conduct was beyond all praise. A remarkable instance of the beneficial effect of Ridley's counsels is to be seen in the foundation of three institutions, in the reign of Edward VI., and which, in point of date, may be called the first-fruits of the Reformation. Both in the council chamber and the pulpit did this eminent prelate resist the sacrilegious spirit of his day, and though the young king was but partially able to oppose the tide of corruption, he yet founded, at the suggestion of Ridley, no less than sixteen grammar schools, and designed, had his life been spared, to erect twelve colleges for the education of youth. Shortly before his death he sent for the bishop, and thanking him for a sermon in which he strongly pressed the duty of providing for the poverty and ignorance of our fellow-men, asked by what particular actions he might in this way best discharge his duty. The bishop, who was not prepared for such a request, begged time to consider, and to

* The Book of Common Prayer having been sanctioned by Parliament, was first read by Bishop Ridley in St. Paul's Cathedral on the 1st of November, 1552.

consult with those who were more conversant with the condition of the poor. Having taken the advice of the Lord Mayor and aldermen of London, he shortly returned to the king, representing that there appeared to be three different classes of poor. Some were poor by impotency of nature, as young fatherless children, old decrepit persons, idiots, cripples, and such like, these required to be educated and maintained; for them, accordingly, the king gave up the Grey Friars' Church, near Newgate Market, now called Christ's Hospital. Others, he observed, were poor by faculty, as wounded soldiers, diseased and sick persons, who required to be cured and relieved; for their use the king gave St. Bartholomew's, near Smithfield. The third sort were poor by idleness or unthriftiness, as vagabonds, loiterers, &c., who should be chastised and reduced to good order; for these the king appointed his house at Bridewell, the ancient mansion of many English kings. The Hospital of St. Thomas, in Southwark, which had been erected and endowed the previous year, was also enlarged, and the grant confirmed. Many additions have since been made to those houses, and they have now risen to be amongst the noblest in Europe.

Although Ridley's biographers say he was born at Willimontswyke, the ancestral home of the family, Hodgson, in his 'History of Northumberland,' gives the honour to Unthank, a mansion between here and Haltwhistle, on the south bank of the river, and now the residence of the Rev. Dixon Brown.

Haydon Bridge.

Haydon Bridge, 15 miles east of Gilsland, is the place at which some tourists alight from the train, for a visit to Langley Castle, and the Roman Wall, and the Camp at Housesteads. Langley Castle is 1½ miles distant; Housesteads 6 miles. See pp. 151 and 203.

The village contains 907 inhabitants, and stands on both sides of the South Tyne river, which is crossed by a stone bridge of six arches. The church is a plain edifice, erected in 1796. The living is a curacy, in the presentation of W. B. Beaumont, Esq., M.P. There are also places of worship belonging to different denominations of Dissenters. In the neighbourhood are lead mines, one of which is supposed to have been worked in the time of the Romans. The manor of Haydon was formerly the property of Anthony Lord Lucy, of Cockermouth, who, in 1344, obtained a charter from Edward III., in which permission was granted to hold a weekly market and an annual fair. These privileges have been long disused. There is also a grammar school, which was founded by deed of the Rev. John Shaftoe, in 1685, and regulated by Acts of Parliament. It is governed by seven trustees, who have the right of appointing a master and an usher, the former of whom must be Master of Arts, and a clergyman in priest's orders. In addition to the grammar school, Mr. Shaftoe founded almshouses for twenty poor persons, each of whom received 3s. per week, with a supply of coals.

Haydon Bridge was the birthplace of the Rev. John Rotherham, the author of several works; John Tweddle, the Grecian traveller; and James Cunningham, Esq., who was mayor of Blackburn, 1859-60. Few travellers will pass the village unheeded when they learn that here also was born that distinguished artist,

JOHN MARTIN,

whom Bulwer denominates "the greatest, the most lofty, the most permanent, the most original genius of his age." He says: "I see in him ..... the presence of a spirit which is not of the world—the divine intoxication of a great soul lapped in majestic, unearthly dreams. .... Vastness is his sphere; he has chained and wielded it, and measured it, at his will: he has transfused its character into narrow limits; he has compassed the Infinite itself with a mathematical precision. He is not, it is true, a Raffaelle, delineating and varying human passion, or arresting the sympathy of passion itself in a profound and sacred calm; he is not a Michael Angelo, the creator of gigantic and preternatural powers—the Titans of the ideal heaven. But he is more original, more self-dependent than either; they perfected the style of others; ..... Martin has borrowed from none."

The house in which Martin was born is called East Land Ends, and is situated about half a mile from the railway station. The date of his birth was 19th July, 1789. He received the rudiments of his education at the grammar school of the village, and there gave evidence of his peculiar genius. He rarely left the school at play time, preferring to remain indoors and sketch upon his slate. He made several sketches upon the school-wall with a burnt stick, such as that of two schoolfellows fighting, and the master thrashing a boy over his knee, the latter being a most striking likeness of both master and boy. He often painted pictures upon coarse calico; and on one occasion, when there was great rejoicing in the village, the place being illuminated, young Martin had some pictures fastened to the end of some short poles, the other ends of which were stuck in the thatched roof, and they were greatly admired. At times he was known to go down to the river-side, to where a large quantity of fine sand lay, pour some water upon the sand, carefully smooth it, and commence sketching with a stick.

When he was fourteen years of age his parents removed to Newcastle, where he was apprenticed to a Mr. Wilson, coachmaker; but a dispute arising between them, the indentures were cancelled. When he first arrived in Newcastle he was much taken up with the variety of signboards, and would frequently leave the sports of his companions to withdraw to some spot where he could fix his attention upon a superior sign. Occasionally he traversed the town from end to end that he might compare the different paintings with each other, and then went home and arranged his rude materials for the purpose of sketching something of his own, which should surpass, and usually did surpass the best signs upon which he had been intent abroad.

After quitting the employ of Mr. Wilson, Martin was placed under an Italian master of great reputation in Newcastle, named Boniface Musso, the father of the celebrated enamel painter, Charles Muss. He remained under his instructions about a year, when Mr. C. Muss, who was settled in London, wished his father to go and reside with him, and Mr. Musso urged upon Martin's parents the advantage of young Martin accompanying him. After much cogitation, many misgivings on his mother's part, and solemn charges to their friend, it was ultimately agreed that he should join Mr. Musso in London, within a few months. He accordingly arrived in town at the beginning of September, 1806. Martin himself, in a letter to the 'Illustrated London News,' in 1849, says: "The treatment I received from Mr. C. Muss soon satisfied me that he conceived my means to be far more extended than they were; I therefore took an early opportunity of informing him that I had resolved never more to receive pecuniary assistance from my parents, who had already done enough in providing means for establishing me in London; that, as my present resources were not equal to a due recompense for his liberality, I thought it only right to tell him my position. He was pleased with my honourable candour, and saying that he would do all in his power to promote my laudable intentions, immediately undertook to employ me in his glass and china painting establishment, in a department where my facility in designing and painting landscape scenes would be very useful; and from this time I supported myself solely by my own exertions, and with advantage to my employers."

Martin married in 1809. Almost up to that time he had been in Mr. Muss' employ during the day, and had passed the nights until two or three o'clock in the morning acquiring that knowledge of perspective and architecture which proved so valuable to him in after life. Shortly before his marriage, Mr. Muss' establishment broke up, and those employed in it had the option of seeking independent employment, or following the fortunes of the different members of the firm. Martin accompanied his friend, Mr. Muss, and was subsequently engaged with him in the glass painting, carried on by Mr. Collins, in the Strand, occupying his evenings upon water-colour drawings, and contriving in odd hours to paint in oil the first picture he ever exhibited ("A Clytie"), which was sent to the Academy in 1810, and rejected for want of room, but not condemned. He sent it again in 1811, when it was hung in a good situation in the Great Room. At the beginning of the following year, having lost his employment at Collins's, it became necessary for him to work hard, and as he was ambitious of fame, he determined on painting a large picture, "Sadak," which was executed in a month. Mr. Martin himself said: "You may easily guess my feelings when I overheard the men who were placing it in the frame disputing as to which was the top of the picture!" The work, however, though hung in the ante-room of the Royal Academy, received, to Martin's great delight, a notice in the newspapers, and was eventually sold, under interesting circumstances, to the late Mr. Manning, for 50 guineas. The following year, 1813, he sent "The Expulsion" to the British Institution, and "Adam's first sight of Eve" to the Royal Academy, and was again given a place in the Great Room. His next painting was

"Clytie." In 1815 he sent the "Joshua" to the Royal Academy, but it was hidden in the ante-room. In 1817 he sent it to the British Institution, where it attracted great attention, and the painter was rewarded with the chief premium of the year, 100*l.*; but the picture was not sold till some years afterwards, when it went as a companion to the "Belshazzar." In 1818 he removed to a superior house, and had to devote his time mainly to executing some immediately profitable works; but in 1819, he produced the "Fall of Babylon," which was second only to the "Belshazzar" in the attention it excited. The following year came "Macbeth," one of his most successful landscapes. Then in 1821, "Belshazzar's Feast," an elaborate picture, which occupied a year in executing, and received the premium of 200*l.* from the British Institution. In the year 1822 appeared the "Destruction of Herculaneum," another elaborate work. In 1823, "The Seventh Plague," and "Paphian Bower;" in 1824, the "Creation;" in 1826, the "Deluge," and in 1828, the "Fall of Nineveh." In addition to the above he produced many other pictures, sketches, &c., but the most important of all was his acquiring the art of engraving, and producing the "Illustrations of Milton," designed on the plates, for which he received 2000 guineas: the "Belshazzar's Feast," the finest large steel plate ever engraved in mezzotinto; the "Joshua," and the "Deluge;" between the years 1823 and 1828. It will be seen that Martin's greatest works were produced within the eleven years immediately succeeding the first fair exhibition of his "Joshua." Only two of his pictures were exhibited abroad: the "Fall of Nineveh," at Brussels; and the "Deluge," in Paris. The first procured him the large medal of the exhibition, the Order of Leopold, and his election as a member of the Academy of Antwerp; the second, the gold medal, and a magnificent present of Sèvres from the King of the French. In his latter years Martin devoted much of his time to engineering subjects, as he felt a strong interest in the improvement of the condition of the people, and in the sanitary state of the country. He also produced three wonderful pictures. "Great Day of His Wrath," "Last Judgment," and "Plains of Heaven," which, having been exhibited in most of the large towns of Great Britain, are well known to the general public. One writer, speaking of them, says: "Martin was a poet of a high order, and with his pencil he painted the sublimest of epics. He is equally at home in scenes sublimely terrible, and the softest and most enchanting views which the mind of mortal can conceive. On the one hand, he gives us visions of gorgeous temples and palaces, built line over line up into the darkened heavens until they look as if mountains had been quarried into stately habitations by a world of giants, and these mountainous masses of masonry he depicts reeling with earthquake throes and toppling over in fearful ruin; while, on the other hand, he puts before you one of the sweetest, softest, and most entrancing visions of celestial felicity which ever the imaginations of the truest poets conceived. There is a Titanic grasp, a gigantesque power about all. John Martin had no equal."

Martin died at No. 4, Finch Road, Douglas, Isle of Man, on the 17th February, 1854, at the age of sixty-five, and was buried in the family vault of a relative in the cemetery at Kirk Braddan.

In 1754 there was born in Haydon Bridge a person known by the name of Ned Coulson, whose swiftness of foot and eccentricity of character made him quite a local celebrity. He could perform on the violin whilst he ran along the road with the instrument on his back. He could run with the greatest ease before a post-chaise, and has often alarmed travellers by passing them and then hiding himself, repassing, and at length bidding them a good night. He had a method of producing a sound somewhat resembling the report of a pistol, and this he mischievously employed to intimidate travellers. He has often been sitting in the inn at Haydon Bridge when travellers have arrived wet with perspiration, caused by the fright he had given them. He went 50 miles one stormy winter's night with a message, and returned next morning. On being asked by his master his reason for not going, he replied, "I have been, and here is the return message." He was not only swift, but strong, and courageous. He often walked on the parapet of the bridge in the village with a sack of corn upon his back. One day, after walking 65 miles, he reached home in time to take a successful part in some athletic sports. At Brampton races, Ned having said that he could run as fast as the horses, a wager was made, and he tried his speed against a certain horse, the distance being from Brampton to Glen Whelt. The rider of the horse gave in at Denton tollgate, saying he was matched against the devil, but Ned went to the end of the journey, and arrived back at Brampton before the horse and rider. Those who are apt to make too long a stay when visiting their friends or neighbours, will do well to remember one of Ned's mischievous tricks. Being good company and fond of fun, his house was a favourite resort, but when parties seemed inclined to stay too late at night, Ned took up his Bible and read the following: "Withdraw thy foot from thy neighbour's house; lest he be weary of thee, and so hate thee."—Proverbs xxv. 17. The bridge at Haydon Bridge having been taken away by a flood, Ned walked through the river, took a cold, and died December 27, 1807, aged fifty-four, and was interred at Bellingham.

Much of our information respecting Haydon Bridge was gleaned from a very intelligent and self-taught resident, Mr. Wm. Lee, who will be happy at all times to make himself equally useful to any visitor requiring information as to the topography, botany, and antiquities of the district.

Langley Castle.

Langley Castle is situated 1½ miles to the south of Haydon Bridge, and only three-quarters of a mile from Langley station, on the Allendale branch.

It stands on gradual rising ground, commanding a good view to the north-east. It is a large square keep, having had four towers with walls 8 feet thick. The outside masonry, which is high, is in such excellent condition, that if the few missing stones on the top were replaced it would appear as though it were a modern structure. The inside, however, is a complete ruin, its roof and internal fittings having been destroyed by fire at an early but unascertained period. The large banqueting room is entirely gone, and only defined by the windows and huge openings for the fireplaces. The spectator is enabled to gaze from the bottom upwards, right through the top of the towers, but there are no steps left by which to ascend.

A few small trees are on one side of the building, and on the other is a cottage, where the persons in charge reside, who show the building to visitors.

To the north-west are seen the heights over which runs the Roman wall, and the camp of Housesteads may be discerned by the practised eye. The grounds around are cultivated, and close by are a small dell and belts of trees, backed by rising ground covered with heath, so that from some points of view the building has a picturesque appearance.

Langley was the seat of the barons of Tindale, who held it by service of one knight's fee. Adam de Tindale possessed it in the reign of Henry I., and it continued in his male descendants till the time of Henry III., when the family inheritance was divided between two coheiresses, and this part came to Richard de Bolteby, by marriage of one of them. From the Boltebys, from like cause, it passed to the Lucys, barons of Egremont and Cockermouth, with whom it remained five descents, when issue male again failing it became the possession of Gilbert de Umfranvill, Earl of Anegos, by marriage of Maud, sister and heiress of Anthony Lord Lucy. On the demise of the Earl of Anegos, his widow married, in 1383, Henry Percy, Earl of Northumberland, a circumstance which united the large possessions of the Umfranvills and Lucys in the Percy family, with whom this castle and manor remained in 1567; but it afterwards became the property of the Ratcliffes, of Dilston, with whom it continued till it was forfeited by James, the last Earl of Derwentwater, in 1745. It was afterwards granted to the Commissioners of Greenwich Hospital, and is still in the hands of the Lords of the Admiralty.

Alston, and Allendale Town.

Alston is a market town, containing about 1500 inhabitants, situated near the sources of the South Tyne, on the confines of the Pennine mountain chain, and in the centre of an extensive lead mining district. It is 963 feet above the sea level, and is said to be the highest market town in England. Market on Saturdays. A branch line, 13 miles long, leaves the Newcastle and Carlisle Railway at Haltwhistle, and runs to Alston along a pleasant well-timbered vale, through which flows the South Tyne river.

Unless the visitor takes an interest in wild moorlands and mining operations, he will find little here to interest him, although the town contains one or two good inns, a few pleasant-looking houses, and a civil lot of people.

The market cross was erected by the Right Hon. Sir William Stephenson, who was born at Crosslands, in this parish, and elected Lord Mayor of London in 1764. Close to the railway station is a cascade, called the Low Nent Force, which has a fall of 30 feet over a ledge of limestone rock; and at a little distance is the High Nent Force, with a descent of 20 feet. Here also is the Nent Force Level, a stupendous work, begun in the year 1776, and designed and carried out by Smeaton, for the Commissioners and Governors of Greenwich Hospital (being part of the confiscated estates of James, Earl of Derwentwater), with the view of exploring the manor from Alston to Nenthead, a distance of upwards of 5 miles, and for the purpose of carrying off all the water from the mines without pumping. It commences beneath the scar limestone, and is driven under ground in the direction of the valley of the Nent. A rowing-boat is taken up it to the Nentsberry shaft, a distance of 4 miles, the voyage in those subterranean regions being in the highest degree romantic, reminding the traveller of some of the stories in the 'Arabian Nights Entertainments.' Strangers will be highly delighted with the excursion, especially if accompanied with music, when it is said to be grand beyond description. At one time the place was much frequented, but of late it appears to have been almost forgotten.

Another underground expedition, in character with this bleak and desolate district, will be found full of interest and romance to the majority of strangers. It is a cave in the limestone, and called *Tutman-hole*, being very similar to the caves in Yorkshire and Derbyshire. In Hutchinson's 'History of Cumberland,' published in 1794, we read: " There is a large cavern in Gildersdale fell, called Tutman-hole, which several persons have ventured to explore for a mile in length. At a place called Dunfell (which is in the limits of Westmorland), some miners were at work not long since, pursuing a vein of ore, when they opened into a spacious cavern. Some people, who have viewed this place, have found it expedient to adopt the contrivance of Dædalus in the labyrinth, and take a clue of thread with them, to guide them safely in their return, the chambers and passages are so intricate. The Rev. William Richardson was seven hours in examining this curious place: he describes the roof in some parts to resemble Gothic arches, in others a flat surface; that the windings are intricate; that he found in places the *stalactites*, and pieces of *rhomboidal spar*. He travelled near 2 miles in a right line, and discovered evident marks of some of the chambers having been filled with water, by the coating of mud on the sides. The greatest height of the vault was above 25 yards, and the breadth in some places about 150 yards. In other passages he could scarcely crawl. Other visitors have spoken of the astonishing lustre of the spar with which these vaults are encrusted, struck by light of the candles and flambeaux which they carried." Tutmanhole is 3 miles from Alston. It is reached by following the Penrith road for 2 miles to a farmhouse called the Bayles, whence a wire fence leads direct to the place. Some tourists may desire to proceed to Penrith, distant from Alston 18 miles. It is a pleasant journey, the road leading over the Hartside mountain pass, and then along the vale of the Eden, past the village of Melmerby, and Eden Hall.

At the hamlet of Nenthead, situated 5 miles east from Alston, there are extensive lead mines and smelting works, belonging to the London Lead Mining Company. Perhaps this is *par excellence* the model lead mining village in England. Baths, washhouses, reading-room, library, schools, and chapels, have all been provided by the company. It is a show place, and hundreds visit it every year.

Four miles south of Alston is the pretty village of Garrigill, situated at a height of 1124 feet above the sea level, on an alluvial terrace formed by the Tyne. Hereabouts is well displayed the gradual formation of valleys by river action. Strong stone embankments built in the last century, to prevent the river from washing away the land, are now in the centre of the meadows, while the bed of the river is worn down several feet below the old marks. From Garrigill to the source of the South Tyne is about 3 miles. The river rises in a peaty bog. The valley is narrow, and two long sweeping peat-covered slopes stretch to Bel Beaver on the east, and Noonstones on the west. On the top of Bel Beaver are some traces of an old camp. Crossfell mountain is to the west of Garrigill. It is about 7 miles from the village to its summit. The road is steep and rough, but on a clear day the view will amply repay the pedestrian for the labour of the ascent.

The inhabitants of these mining dales are very civil and

intelligent, but the stranger will sometimes receive a reply in an unknown tongue, unless his Celtic education has been attended to. Compulsory education is not new here. The London Lead Mining Company have always required their workmen to send their children both to day and Sunday school. The following extract from the Report of the Commissioners on Education, presented to Parliament in 1861, and originally taken from Forster's book on the lead miners of Alston Moor and Teesdale, clearly proves the good resulting from this system : "I prosecuted a pretty extensive house-to-house visitation, found everything clean, whole, and in its place; no trumpery little ornaments as in the collier cottages. Where there is a picture it is that of some favourite minister, such as Wesley ; or a copy of the ' Cottar's Saturday Night.' There are in almost every cottage some select Sunday books besides the Bible and hymn-book; an occasional volume of poetry, as Cowper, Milton, Burns, or some favourite local author, and not unfrequently some of the extensively illustrated books published by Fullarton, Black, or Blackie. I counted 19 copies of the Imperial Dictionary. There were no cheap periodicals or people's editions—they are not reckoned at all canny. The miners like everything good of its kind. Many of them have cows, and not a few of them have a pony also. The remarkable personal beauty of the children, as compared with those of the adjoining colliery districts, is, I presume, to be attributed to nothing but the transmitted and reflected intelligence which has resulted to the parents from their moral and religious cultivation. I saw nothing of a neglected brat ; no dirty or undarned stockings; no unblackened clogs or unwashed faces. The general character of the lead miners presents a striking contrast to that of the colliers. They consist of families who have lived for ages on the spot. . . . . A steady, provident, orderly, and industrious people. Engaged from year to year by the lead owners, and generally besides their work underground, cultivate a small farm, which in many cases is their own. A high-minded people they are, too, disdaining pauperism as the deepest degradation. They have been subject to very little or no mixture for ages past, as appears by their language . . . . . approximating to the dialect of the lowlands of Scotland. The lead miners are remarkably intelligent, and well educated. There are books in almost every cottage. Attendance on public worship is the rule, not the exception, and profane language is scarcely ever heard."

The rude old farmhouses are often very picturesque without, sheltered by a few aged beeches or sycamores, but within they bear testimony to a very rough way of life. They are generally built with a passage from the door right through the building, called the entry. Another passage, formed by a high screen, called a hallan, leads from the entry to the fireside. This second passage is called the heck. A passage turning to the other hand opens into the cowhouse. This was seldom the only entrance to the cowhouse, but it was so in some cases, as in a house at Loaning-head at the present time, the farmer and his cattle enter at the same door: the cattle turning off one way into the byre, and the farmer the other, into the kitchen. The kitchen is generally very low, with huge joists of undressed black oak.

"In days gone bye
The Hall of an Alston Moor squire
Was a lofthouse over the byre."

The hum of the spinning-wheel may still be occasionally heard, as the frugal housewife spins the self-grey wool into stockings, unequalled for comfort and wear. But these old houses are fast being altered or rebuilt, and many of the primitive customs of an hospitable race are passing away.

A pleasant drive of 18 miles, over a good road, will take the visitor from Alston to High Force, in Teesdale, generally considered the finest waterfall in England. About 5½ miles from Alston the road passes through the pretty and well-wooded estate of Ashgill, belonging to the London Lead Company. About five minutes' walk from the gamekeeper's house, on the roadside, is the Ashgill Force, a fall which is well worth seeing. The Ashgill burn here descends perpendicularly, about 50 feet, over the scar limestone, and a thick bed of shale beneath it. On account of the shale wearing away faster than the limestone, a passage is made behind the falling water and beneath the overhanging rocks. Below the waterfall is a charming little glen, where the parsley, oak, beech, and many other pretty ferns nestle in quiet nooks among the limestone rocks. The extensive plantations here contain a remarkably rich variety of wild flowers, and the meadows are in a high state of cultivation, forming a striking contrast to the wild heath-covered hills on either hand. After leaving Ashgill, the road gradually ascends for about 3 miles to the top of Yadmoss, 1946 feet above the sea. Here all trace of cultivation is left behind, and the barren moors stretch away for miles and miles in lovely, weird grandeur. Crossing Crookburn, the traveller leaves Cumberland and enters Durham. A stone by the roadside marks the boundary. The sources of the three great rivers of the north, the Tyne, Wear, and Tees, are within a very short walk from this point. The road here is often rendered impassable in winter by heavy falls of snow, and many persons have lost their lives through attempting to cross the fell in a storm.

The road now runs through the property of the Duke of Cleveland. Ashgill Head is the first house in Harwood after crossing the fell. Its elevation is 1794 feet, but Rumney's house on a hill to the left is marked on the Ordnance Map 1980 feet above the sea, and is probably the highest dwelling-house in England. Another at Ashgill, Priorsdale House, is 1766 feet. We had always understood that the inn at the top of the Kirkstone Pass, in Westmorland, which is 1475 feet high, laid claim to be considered the highest inhabited house in England; but the houses just mentioned, and many others, are several hundred feet higher. The road descends rapidly from this point. The character of the surrounding landscape is that of a wild, upland, pastoral district, surmounted by heather-clad mountains, gullied by ravines with rushing streams. At Langdon Beck, in the Forest, is a roadside inn, at which the traveller should put up his horse, and ask the way to Cauldron Snout, where the Tees flings itself down a rugged rock of 200 feet. No one who is ever in the neighbourhood, and cares for the wild and majestic in Nature, should fail to visit this place. The distance from Langdon is about 3 miles, through green meadows, and over rough bog. This part of the dale is called the Forest, but it is without trees; wild open tracts of land being in former times often known by that denomination. The visitor can either return to Langdon Beck, and drive down the road to High Force, or, if he does not object to a walk over rather rough ground, follow the river from Cauldron Snout down to the Force. He will find it a picturesque scene. Among the rugged cliffs of the Cronkly Scar the hardy juniper grows luxuriantly, and ferns and rare plants are to be met with in plenty. Below Cronkly the Blea Beck rushes down in pretty cascades from the summit of the hill, and then the Tees, after receiving a few small streams, plunges with a sullen roar down a fall of 70 feet into the black basin beneath. "Nothing can exceed the glowing grandeur of this scene; high rocky barriers shut in the waters; the wild fells stretch away and away beyond. . . . . . Tees High Force will seem to stand alone amongst the waterfalls, in the breadth of the fall; the passion of the swirling waters fretted and chafed by the rocks in the bed of the stream; the deep, sullen roar which all the year round greets the ear as one approaches the scene, and, above all, the sombre gloom of the surroundings." There is a comfortable inn at the Force, from which conveyances run every day, in the summer season, to the railway station at Middleton, 4 miles distant.

Two and a half miles north of Alston is a place called Whitley Castle, where are the remains of a Roman station. The form of the camp is peculiar, being that of a trapezoid, whereas the usual figure is that of a parallelogram. In another respect it differs from all other camps. It is surrounded by an extraordinary number of earthen entrenchments; and this fact, along with the comparative absence of Roman stones, renders it probable that the garrison trusted to breastworks of earth, rather than of masonry. Its whole area, including the entrenchments and ditches, amounts to nine acres.

Tourists who are fond of a moorland ramble will do well to walk the 12 miles from Alston to Allendale Town, and then catch the Allendale branch train to Hexham; or follow the course of the Allen river to the South Tyne, and catch the train at Bardon Mill.

The road leaves Alston close to the station, and after passing a tollgate, gradually ascends the fell; the hollow, down which flows the Ayle burn, being on the left. 1¾ miles out of the town, roads branch to right and left. Take the straight road: it crosses over the summit of the fell, and commands good views of the neighbouring hills, the Crossfell range being in the rear; and far away in the distance, to the east, are discerned the Cheviot Hills. A descent is made to a vale containing a few green fields, houses, and clumps of trees, through which flow the Mohope burn and the West Allen river.

ALLENDALE TOWN. 159

Near the source of the West Allen is the village of Coalcleugh, which is 1700 feet above the sea level, and said to be the highest inhabited village in England. Of late this village has decreased in size, owing to the poverty of the mines around.

Some distance farther down, the West Allen passes Whitfield Hall, and then runs for another mile or two through a beautiful vale, and joins the East Allen river near Staward-le-Peel, the two waters forming the Allen river, referred to at page 160.

The traveller might follow the stream past Whitfield Hall, and then to Staward-le-Peel, there gaining the train; or he might lengthen the journey 4½ miles, and follow the river to the South Tyne, and catch the train at Bardon Mill, thus travelling through a district exquisitely beautiful.

If he walks to Allendale Town he will cross the West Allen at the hamlet of Nine Banks, then go over another fell, and descending to the East Allen, walk up its banks for half a mile to Allendale Town, which is pleasantly situated, on high ground, directly above the stream. Here are extensive lead mines and some smelt mills. The level or tunnel of one mine is 7 miles long. The smelt mills are well worth a visit. Formerly the fumes from the furnaces were taken direct to the chimneys. As a good deal of lead in a volatilized state is brought away by the draught, much property was lost; deleterious matter was diffused in the air and deposited in the fields; and, as a necessary consequence, the health of the workmen was injured, and cattle and sheep were occasionally poisoned. Now, however, the vapours are taken along flues laid on the ground, and they eventually discharge themselves by a chimney planted upon the top of a hill, at the distance, it may be, of 2 or 3 miles from the works. The consequence of this arrangement is, that the metallic particles of the vapour are deposited before it reaches the outlet. The flues are swept once or twice a year, and sometimes produce a joyous harvest of hundreds or thousands of pounds.

Owing to the want of funds, the branch railway from Hexham, which it was intended to bring to Allendale Town, has been cut short, and ends at Catton Road, 1½ miles distant.

Staward-le-Peel, and the River Allen.

Before the river Allen enters the South Tyne, it flows for 4 or 5 miles through a deep wooded ravine, which is highly romantic and picturesque, and superior to anything of the kind in other parts of the district. It is comparatively unknown and little visited, but the few who have strolled up its exquisitely lovely banks pronounce it as beautiful as any of the far-famed streams of Derbyshire.

To reach it the tourist can take the train on the Allendale branch line to Staward. Half a mile from the station are the mines of Staward-le-Peel, on a wooded eminence, around the base of which, deep below, winds the river through a delightfully rocky and wooded ravine. The ruins are not extensive; only a small part of a tower and the base of an end wall remaining. The fortress was granted, in 1386, by Edward, Duke of York, to the friars of Hexham, to be held by the annual payment of five marks.

Paths lead down to the brink of the stream, where the tourist will be perfectly secluded, and at every step have charming views of the Glen, with high crags and woods on either hand. It is a place " ' to sit on rocks, and muse o'er flood and fell,' for the voice of Nature is heard in these woodland solitudes; the waving breeze of summer stirs the forest leaves; the notes of the feathered tribe make vocal the greenwood glade; the stream is heard here gently rippling on its shore, there, murmuring over rocks that oppose its even flow, or in the distance falling over the weir with a monotonous but soothing sound; and the influences on every hand are such as tranquillize and exalt the mind."

As the waters of the Allen flow into the South Tyne river, close to Ridley Hall, 1½ miles from Bardon Mill station, some tourists will first make their acquaintance with the stream from that point. If the Tyne be crossed at some stepping stones near the station, the distance to the Hall is reduced to 1 mile, and the traveller passes Beltingham Church, a small edifice, containing a number of tablets, and in the graveyard of which are an ancient cross and three venerable yew trees. Ridley Hall is a modern mansion, the residence of Mrs. Davidson. In 1567 the estates were in the possession of the Ridleys, of

Willimontswyke Castle. For 2 miles up the river the grounds on each side belong to Mrs. Davidson, and the tourist cannot proceed close to the stream without obtaining permission, but if the public road, which passes the Hall, be followed for 2 miles, the river may be reached by a footpath which passes two or three farmhouses and descends to a chain swing-bridge leading over the water at a house known as Plankey Mill, and from thence a walk of 1 mile by the river's bank conducts to Staward-le-Peel.

The scenery all along the brink of the river is, however, so extremely beautiful, that the stranger ought to ask permission to stroll by the pleasant grassy path-like grove which runs from the Hall for 2 miles through the woods, close to the stream.

Hexham.

Hexham is a picturesque old town standing on the south bank of the Tyne, at the point of its junction with the brooks Hextol and Halgut. It contains a population of 5331. Market day, Tuesday. It is supposed by some to have been a Roman station, and during the dark and unsettled times of the Saxon Heptarchy it was a place of considerable importance.

A church was erected here in 674, by St. Wilfrid, which is said to have been in those days the finest building on this side of the Alps. Four years later Hexham was raised to the dignity of an episcopal see, an honour which it retained, under a succession of twelve bishops, until A.D. 821. In 860 it was united to the see of Lindisfarn, and twenty-three years later the seat of the bishopric was removed from Lindisfarn to Chester-le-Street, and afterwards to Durham. Henry I. being offended with the conduct of Flambard, Bishop of Durham, gave Hexham to the see of York, and the connection continued until the early part of the present century, when it was severed, and Hexham again united to Durham.

St. Wilfrid was an extraordinary personage, and one of the principal churchmen of those times. He was a Northumbrian by birth, of honourable parentage, educated as a monk in the convent of Lindisfarn, and had, by travelling to France and Rome, acquired the learning of that age, and a particular acquaintance with the rites and canons of the Roman Church. He also acquired a high relish for the riches, pomp, and splendour he had seen in the foreign churches. This education concurring with a haughty, ambitious, and intractable spirit, rendered him a most notorious troubler of the peace of the English Church, and a principal instrument of subjecting it to the usurpations of the Roman pontiffs. He was one of the chief disputants at the Conference, held by the Northumbrian king at Whitby in 664, respecting the observance of Easter. Being consecrated Bishop of Northumberland, which then included all the district between the Humber and the Firth of Forth, he fixed the seat of his diocese at York, made great additions to the cathedral there, the roof of which he covered with lead, and glazed the windows; he also built the cathedral at Ripon, and employed the most skilful artists he could procure from France and Italy. He had the government of nine abbeys; in his family the sons of many of the Northumbrian nobles resided for their education; his attendants were numerous; his fortune splendid; and at his table he is said to have been served on gold. His principal patroness was the queen of the Northumbrian king. From her he received Hexham and the adjacent lands, said to have been lands of her own dowry, for the support of the convent and of the magnificent church built by him in that town. When the queen took the veil and retired into the abbey of Coldingham, Wilfrid lost favour at court. His enemies persuaded the king to divide his immense diocese into two provinces, the see of one bishopric being fixed at York, and the other at Hexham. Wilfrid went to Rome to obtain redress, and got a favourable decision. On his return the king committed him to prison, alleging that he had used bribes at Rome. After remaining prisoner about a year, the bishop was set free upon condition that he should abandon the Northumbrian dominions. He retired to the Isle of Wight, and there employed his time in preaching until the death of the king, when he returned to his native country. Upon his return he was reinstated in the see of Hexham, and is said to have been afterwards restored to that of York, and to have obtained possession of his monastery of Ripon; once more he offended the court, was expelled from his diocese, and obliged to seek refuge in the neighbouring kingdom of Mercia, where he was appointed to the see of Leicester.

He again appealed to Rome, and made a journey to that city at the age of seventy. An agreement was concluded, and he was restored to the monasteries of Hexham and Ripon, and soon afterwards the famous St. John of Beverley, who was then Bishop of Hexham, being translated to York, Wilfrid regained his diocese of Hexham, and four years afterwards, in 709, died in peace at his monastery of Oundle, and was buried in the church of St. Peter at Ripon. St. Wilfrid was contemporary with St. Cuthbert, and with Bede the historian.

The church at Hexham was laid in ruins by the Danes in 875, and after continuing in a dilapidated state for more than 200 years was restored in the early part of the twelfth century, and a second time doomed to partial destruction, inasmuch as a Scottish army burnt down the nave in 1296. At the same time 200 boys were burnt alive in the Grammar School, such was the savage barbarity of the times. The choir, and the north and south transepts remain, with a part of the chapter house, but the dormitories are entirely gone. The building is said to form a very text-book of the early English period of pointed church architecture. In it are comprised every distinctive feature that marks the style, combining a simplicity and grandeur of effect not excelled by any other structure in the kingdom.

On entering the south door, indeed the only door, the visitor is struck with the effect of the beautifully proportioned pillars, and the noble arches that sustain the tower, and form the divisions of the cross. In the entrance are to be seen two Roman altars which were dug out of the earth near the door, one about thirty, and the other about seventeen years ago. There are also several gravestones of the old canons of Hexham, which were found in the chapter house some years since. The eastern aisle of the south transept contains a curiously carved Saxon tombstone; and a shrine, generally supposed to be that of Prior Richard, who died in 1190, and whose manuscript history of the times is still extant. On this shrine are carved grotesque figures of St. George, the fox clothed in the garb of a monk preaching to the geese, the thumb screw, the nightmare, &c. The upper part is rich flamboyant tracery in woodwork. Within this oratory stands a stone altar with five small crosses; above are three paintings of St. Peter with the keys, St. Andrew holding the cross, and St. Paul with the sword; beneath are represented the sufferings of Christ. The Saviour is in the centre, with his hands crossed before him and tied, crowned with thorns, &c., but much obliterated. In a niche below the altar slab sits an ape, having taken possession of the seat of sanctuary, shutting out the weary pilgrim, as he appears by the appropriate costume of the cockleshell in front of the cap, with scrip and staff. Opposite the ape is a hare, the meaning of which is, that security from our enemies must be had by flight and speed. The interest of this altar is great, in consequence of the rarity of such in the ancient churches. Passing on to the choir, we next come to a large slab of stone which has been inlaid with brass, the only remaining portion simply bearing the inscription, "Robertus Ogle, who died in 1410." Immediately adjoining this are the remnants of the monks' stalls, but unfortunately the canopies are all destroyed. Each seat is a chair with elbows or arms quaintly carved, and the bottom made to be occasionally turned up, when the under face displays a grotesque mask, flowers, or other ornament.

On the north side of the choir, within 3 or 4 feet of the communion rails, stands the Freed-stool or sanctuary chair. In ancient times St. Wilfrid procured for this church the privilege of sanctuary, a right confirmed by the highest authority, viz. the papal see, archbishops and bishops, kings and princes, Scotch as well as English. The sanctuary extended in various directions to some distance from the church. One writer says: "The stone seat is called the Freed-stool, that is, the chair of peace, to which if any one flying for safety cometh, he shall be altogether secure." There is a similar stone chair or Freed-stool in the cathedral at Beverley, in Yorkshire. Speaking of Hexham, another writer tells us: "There were four crosses set up at a certain distance from the church, in the four ways leading thereunto; now if any malefactor flying for refuge to that church, was taken or apprehended within the crosses, the party that took or laid hold of him there, did forfeit two hundredth. If he took him within the town, then he forfeited four hundredth; if within the church, then twelve hundredth; if within the doors of the quire, then eighteen hundredth, besides penance as in case of sacrilege; but if he presumed to take him out of the stone chair, near the altar, called Freed-stool, or from amongst the holy relics behind the altar, the offence was not redeemable with any sum, and nothing but the utmost severity of the offended Church was to be expected by a dreadful excommunication, besides what the secular power would impose for the presumptuous misdemeanour." These and other privileges were diminished in 1413, on account of the place being an asylum to outlaws and robbers; and were finally abrogated in the 28th Henry VIII., when the Archbishop of York and his temporal chancellor were made justices of the peace for the *shire* of Hexham, which district, in the 14th of Elizabeth, was annexed to the county of Northumberland. One writer, when speaking of the Freed-stool, says: "I have no doubt whatever that this is the 'Cathedra' of the Saxon bishops of Hexham;" and another tells us: "It is very probably the seat on which the bishops of the see were consecrated, and perhaps even that in which the kings of Northumbria were crowned."

Passing from the choir into the transept, northwards we see the beautiful rood-screen, of the flamboyant style of architecture, with numerous paintings, much obliterated. On the four centre panels at the top is a remnant of the "Dance of Death," beginning with the cardinal, monarch, bishop, and pope, and monograms below. Continuing on to the north transept we come to a most beautiful and somewhat singular monumental arch. It is thought to be the tomb of Elfwold, a king of Northumbria, who was slain in the vicinity of Hexham by one of his nobles on the 21st September, 788. The monks went in solemn procession and brought the body to the church and honourably interred it. A miraculous light is said to have often been seen over the place where Elfwold was killed, but the exact place cannot now be ascertained. On the stone that covers the shrine there is carved a richly floriated cross. Adjoining this tomb are also two recumbent figures, the one a female, of whom nothing is known; the other a knight, supposed to be Galfred-de-Ayden. Beyond is another figure, that of a knight templar, Umfraville by name, who died in 1227. Above the arcades of this aisle is to be seen some beautiful foliage carved in the stone, also rich corbels and bosses. The next thing to be noticed is the baptismal font, of a date coeval with the building. Immediately below the font is the subterraneous crypt, an appendage to the ancient cathedral of St. Wilfrid. There is a similar crypt in the cathedral at Ripon, also built by St. Wilfrid. These are the only Saxon crypts in the country. The crypt at Hexham, concealed for many centuries beneath the *débris* of the nave, was only discovered as recently as 1726, in digging for a buttress to support the west side of the tower. Here it may be noted, the crypt is nearly, if not entirely, built of Roman stone, chiselled in a curious manner. In it are two Roman inscriptions, one sadly cut away, the other almost complete. The more perfect of the two is of great historical interest, owing to the name of the Emperor Geta having evidently been designedly erased with a tool, which was done by order of Caracalla to all similar monuments after the murder of his brother Geta. The visitor is fully repaid by descending into this ancient place of devotion. Emerging from the crypt, we next notice the stair, which originally led to the dormitories; it is quite unique in structure, not being found in any other of our home churches, though the same feature is frequent in continental churches. This stair leads to the belfry. There is a fine peal of bells, eight in number; the original peal, six in number, was cast in 1404, but recast into eight in 1742. From the belfry the visitor can ascend by the ladder to the top of the tower, the view from which is very fine. On the west side of the church stands the Seal, what would once be the open cloister of the monks, now a park or recreation ground for the public. Several monumental windows adorn the church, but they are all of recent date.

On the west side of the north transept was found, in 1832, a small copper vessel containing about 8000 Saxon coins, the principal bulk of which are now in the British Museum.

On the dissolution of the monastery in 1536, the prior, whose name was Jay, was hanged at his own gate for having instigated the people to resist the action of government. The gate may still be seen in the Cow Garth.

Many other old buildings—remains of the priory—stand in the immediate neighbourhood of the church. The cloisters, enclosed on the north by the south wall of the nave, still 20 feet in height, and in excellent condition, with the lavatory of remarkable beauty on the west side, and the chapter house on the east, will well repay a visit. Over the ancient refectory, which yet exists in good condition, there is an extensive suite of rooms of modern construction, now used as county court and magistrates' rooms. Leading from the market there is an archway, and tower, called the Moot Hall, where a court is still occasionally held; the principal part of the rooms are now occupied as dwellings.

A large and distinct block of building—square in shape—seems to have been the stronghold of the place. Its walls are 9 feet thick, and it has vaulted dungeons. The projecting corbels on the summit, for supporting platform, have a fine effect. It is now disused, but seven years ago it contained a bank, and the office of the lord of the manor. In this building is preserved an oak beam covered with quaint early English inscriptions, which it has baffled many an antiquary to decipher: it was formerly the lintel over a fireplace which was removed to make way for one of more modern description.

Dilston Castle.

The ruins of this castle stand in a commanding position, on the east side of the brook called Devilswater, half a mile from Corbridge railway station, and 4 miles from Hexham.

It is not known at what precise period the castle was first built, but it is supposed to have originally belonged to the family of D'Eivill, of whom we have a record as far back in history as the reign of Henry I., and in the reign of Henry II. we find a family seated here of the name of Dyvelston. Their possessions appear to have been extensive, and Dyvelston is mentioned as having manorial privileges. One of the family, Sir Thomas, was sheriff of Northumberland in the ninth year of the reign of Edward I.; he was interred in Hexham Abbey. Leaving no issue, his barony and possessions were inherited by his cousin, William-de-Tynedale, lord of the neighbouring barony of Langley. The last member of the direct line of the family died in 1416, and their estates were settled on Sir William Caxton, a collateral descendant on the female side; and the barony seems to have acquired by this time the name of Dilston. On the failure of male issue a co-heiress became lady of Dilston, and married John Cartington, a Northumberland esquire. Some time about 1494, Sir Edward Radcliffe, Knight, came into possession of Dilston by marriage with Anne, daughter and heiress of the above-named John Cartington. This Sir Edward, who held the office of high sheriff of Northumberland, in the 17th Henry VII., was the third son of Sir Thomas Radcliffe, of Derwentwater.

The Radcliffes were a noted Lancashire family, of Saxon origin, who had their name from the village of Radcliffe, near Bury, and their pedigree assumes a De Radcliffe anterior to the reign of Henry II. In the time of Henry V. Sir Nicholas Radcliffe married Margaret, daughter and heiress of Sir John de Derwentwater.

The early history of the Derwentwaters is shrouded in obscurity, but as far back as the reign of King John the family occurs as possessed of lands in the northern counties, being lords of the manor of Bolton, in Westmorland, and having estates around the Derwent Lake, in Cumberland, and in other places. In the 48th and 50th Edward III., and 1st and 4th Richard II., Sir John de Derwentwater, above mentioned, was sheriff of Cumberland, and he was twice, viz. 2nd and 11th Richard II., returned to Parliament as a knight of the shire. His son-in-law, Sir Nicholas Radcliffe, was sheriff of Cumberland in 1422. The next in descent, Sir Thomas Radcliffe, knight, married Margaret, daughter of Sir William Parr, of Kendal Castle, an ancestor of the last queen of Henry VIII. It was Sir Edward, the third son of this Sir Thomas, that won the lady of Dilston for his bride.

The eldest son, John, succeeded to the Cumberland estates, and he appears to have lived at the house on Lord's Island, Derwentwater, for there he made his will in 1527, and the following year was interred in Crosthwaite Church, where there is his effigy and that of his wife, and a memorial in brass, with a black letter inscription. He was a person of eminence in his day, and was many times selected for the important office of sheriff of Cumberland, under Henry VII. and Henry VIII. He likewise several times held the commission to treat with his warlike, predatory neighbours, the Scots, touching peace and other matters affecting the realm. He died without issue, and the Cumberland estates then descended to Sir Cuthbert Radcliffe, of Dilston, the son of Sir Edward Radcliffe.

Sir Cuthbert was high sheriff of Northumberland in the 19th Henry VIII.; in 1514 he married Margaret, daughter of Henry, Lord Clifford. One of his successors, Sir Edward

Radcliffe, was a distinguished loyalist in the time of Charles I., and his estate was confiscated by the Commonwealth. He appears to have been reinstated on the accession of Charles II., for he died in 1663, aged seventy-five, and was interred in the family vault below the chapel adjoining Dilston Castle. He was succeeded by his only surviving son and heir, Sir Francis, who was born in 1624, and created Baron Dilston, Viscount Langley, and Earl of Derwentwater by James II., in March 1688, only nine months before the king was compelled to flee the kingdom. In the previous year, Edward, the eldest son of Sir Francis, had espoused Lady Mary Tudor, youngest natural daughter of King Charles II., who was, at the time of her marriage, only fourteen years of age. The Earl departed this life in 1697, aged seventy-two, and was interred at Dilston. He was succeeded in his dignities and estates by his eldest son, Edward, who thus became second earl. The latter had issue, James, his eldest son and heir, born in London, June 28, 1689; Lady Mary Tudor Radcliffe, his only daughter, who, after 1720, married William Petre, of Stamford Rivers, and died without leaving issue surviving; Francis, who died unmarried in 1715; and Charles, who survived his brother, the third earl, for thirty years, and then, in 1746, went to the scaffold on a sentence of treason passed in 1716.

The second Earl and Countess entered into a deed of separation, dated the 6th February, 1700, and in less than five years they were parted finally by the death of the Earl, which occurred on the 20th April, 1705. His youthful relict did not long remain a widow, for she married in 1705 Henry Graham, Esq., of Levens, son of Colonel James Graham, of Levens, Privy Purse to James II., and so nephew to Richard Graham, Viscount Preston, elder brother to the colonel, but he too departed this life in the following year; and in August of 1707 she contracted a third matrimonial engagement. Her third husband was James Rooke, whom also she survived, as well as her illustrious son, James, the third and last earl, and his countess, and even the dynasty of her royal father's house, for she departed this life at Paris, on the 5th November, 1726, in the fifty-fourth year of her age.

James Radcliffe, the third and last possessor of the transient earldom of Derwentwater, was only sixteen years of age when his father died. Early in childhood his parents took him to France, where they helped to swell the court of the exiled monarch James II. of England, and the boy was educated in company with young Charles Stuart, afterwards called "The Pretender," being both about the same age. The whole period of the young Earl's minority was thus spent on the Continent, and he did not visit his ancestral home until 1710, when he was in his twenty-firsst year. On the 10th July, 1712, he married Anna Maria, eldest daughter of Sir John Webb, Bart., their acquaintance having begun when both were receiving education in the French capital. On the morning of the 6th of October, 1715, he left Dilston, in company with his friends and servants, to join in the rising in favour of "The Pretender;" on the 14th November following the invading force was defeated at Preston, and the whole made prisoners. The Earl was committed to the Tower of London; on the 9th February, 1716, his peers found him guilty of high treason, and on the 24th of the same month he was beheaded on Tower Hill. His remains were interred in the family vault at Dilston. His Countess died in 1723, and their only son met with his death by accident in 1731, when in his nineteenth year. Their only daughter was married in 1732, in the seventeenth year of her age, to Robert James, eighth Lord Petre, whose descendants still survive. The Hon. Charles Radcliffe, the only brother of the unfortunate earl, was beheaded for treason, as before stated, in 1746, having been taken prisoner on board a French vessel, when on his way, as it was supposed, to join in the rebellion of the previous year. During his residence in France, after his escape from England in 1715, he married the Countess of Newburgh. The Countess was a widow, and it is said Charles urged his suit sixteen times. His last proposal was urged after adopting the novel expedient of coming down the chimney, when the Countess, half alarmed and partly pleased at his perseverance, received her daring suitor graciously. They had issue three sons and four daughters. The eldest son, the third Earl of Newburgh, claimed the reversion in the Derwentwater estates, but he afterwards seems to have acquiesced in an Act of Parliament, passed in 1749, settling those estates upon Greenwich Hospital; for, having no other means of subsistence, he accepted 24,000*l*. as a relief for his support, and consented that his title under the settlement should be extinguished. On the fifth Earl of Newburgh petitioning Parliament in 1788, a bill was passed granting 2500*l.* a year to his lordship. He died without issue, November 29, 1814, and his widow had an allowance of 1000*l.* a year after his death. She died in 1861. The Cumberland estates were sold by the Commissioners of Greenwich Hospital about the year 1832, to Mr. Marshall, of Leeds, and on the 13th October, 1874, the estates in the county of Northumberland were put up to auction. The principal lot, including Dilston Castle, was purchased by William Beaumont, Esq., the owner of extensive adjacent estates, for the sum of 231,000*l.* Prior, however, to the sale taking place, the vault beneath the old chapel at Dilston was entered, and six coffins reverently removed. The first five contained the ashes of Francis, the first earl, who died 1796; of Edward, the second earl, who died 1705; of Mr. Francis Radcliffe, who died in 1704; and of the Ladies Barbara and Mary Radcliffe, whose decease took place respectively in 1696 and in 1726. These five coffins were carried to the cemetery of the Catholic church at Hexham, there to be reinterred. The sixth coffin, which contained the remains of James, third and last Earl of Derwentwater, was removed to Thorndon, in Essex, there to be reinterred in the family vault of Lord Petre. So ends what has been aptly denominated the Derwentwater romance.

ROMAN WALL SECTION.

A WALK ALONG THE ROMAN WALL, FROM COAST TO COAST.*

ALMOST everyone is taught at school that the Emperor Severus erected a wall between the Solway Firth near Carlisle and the river Tyne near Newcastle, as a barrier against the incursions of the Picts and Scots who dwelt in the more northern region of Caledonia; and in after life the wall dwells in the imagination, but how few persons have any intelligible idea of the vastness of the original work, or of the state of the remains as they exist at the present day.

No better method, we venture to think, can be adopted of obtaining an accurate idea, not only of the present state of the wall, but also of its original condition, than by actually walking along it, and tracing out its whole course from sea to sea, and obtaining as much information as possible from the inhabitants of the district; supplementing this with a perusal of the works written on the subject, but especially of the book entitled 'The Roman Wall,' produced within the last few years by Dr. Bruce, of Newcastle. This plan we adopted, first taking a pedestrian excursion along the route of the wall from Bowness to Wallsend, then, after perusing Bruce and other writers, again strolling along the whole length of the wall, for the purpose of correcting and increasing our knowledge of the great work by the help of the light obtained from books and maps. These labours have led the writer to take a deeper interest than hitherto in the history of Rome, and in that of the ancient inhabitants of his own country; he ventures therefore to hope that his readers will also have their interest awakened, and that thus they will obtain a thorough appreciation of the wonderful work accomplished

---

* We recommend the walk to be taken from west to east. By doing so the traveller moves from the less remains to the greater, and his interest grows.

in this island by those ancient conquerors of the world. As Dr. Bruce remarks: "The casual wanderer by the relics of the Vallum and the Wall may not succeed in culling facts that are new to the historian, but he will probably get those vivid glances into Roman character, and acquire that personal interest in Roman story, which will give to the prosaic records of chroniclers a reality and a charm which they did not before possess." Truly, no person can traverse the course of the ruins from coast to coast without obtaining a hundredfold more insight into British and Roman history than by the study of books; neither can he do so without a feeling of enthusiasm or a certain expansion of mind as he contemplates a work which Sir Walter Scott, in 'Guy Mannering,' speaks of in the following terms: "And this, then, is the Roman wall. What a people! Whose labours, even at this extremity of their empire, comprehended such space, and were executed upon a scale of such grandeur! In future ages when the science of war shall have been changed, how few traces will exist of the labours of Vauban and Coehorn, while this wonderful people's remains will even then continue to interest and astonish posterity! Their fortifications, their aqueducts, their theatres, their fountains, all their public works, bear the grave, solid, and majestic character of their language; while our modern labours, like our modern tongues, seem but constructed out of their fragments."

The wall was not less than 75 miles long, and extended over hill and dale in an almost straight line from Bowness on the Solway to Wallsend on the Tyne. Its breadth, though varying a little according to the nature of the ground, is thought to have been generally nearly 8 feet, and about 9 feet at the base, this breadth reaching to a height of 14 feet; being crowned on the north side with a parapet 4 feet high, thus making the height of the wall 18 feet. It must have presented a solid and unadorned, but neat and uniform appearance, the outside stones being composed of regularly shaped and well-dressed freestone, from 15 to 20 inches long, 10 inches broad, and 8 inches thick, which would sometimes be obtained from the adjoining quarries, but must often have been carried long distances. Most of the stones have a wedge shape, tapering towards the end, which is set into the wall. Dr. Bruce thinks stones of this shape would be conveniently carried on the backs of "poor enslaved Britons;" and the present inhabitants along the line of the wall tell us they were conveyed in the apron of an old woman, and the wall was built in one night. Both these modes of conveyance, we venture to think, are too romantic for the practical Romans, who were not unacquainted with horses and carts.

The inside part of the wall consists of rubble stone, similar to that found in the massive walls of our old castles, and not unlike the concrete which we are beginning to use so extensively at the present day. These stones are of all kinds and shapes, both large and small, evidently picked up on the spot, and they are cemented as firm as the solid rock, by lime, which, when fresh and mixed with sand and gravel, has been poured in amongst them, and filled every crevice. Occasionally, however, the lime has been put on with the trowel, but where this plan is adopted the rubble stones are often laid upon their edges in a slanting position, somewhat in the fashion of herring-bone masonry. The Romans had evidently some better method of preparing the lime than that with which we are acquainted at the present day, for after standing sixteen centuries it is as hard as stone. When travelling along the wall, in places where the outside stones still remain, the lime is generally not visible, apparently having been removed from the exposed parts by the action of rain, and by the plants and herbs which have grown upon it. The whole construction is so massive and so well put together, that it would in all likelihood have stood almost perfect until now had it not been for the destroying agency of vegetable growth, and still more the destruction caused by the inhabitants of the district, who have used the wall as a quarry whence they might obtain stones for their fences, houses, and castles. Considering the destructive agencies which have been at work for many centuries, the wonder is that so much of the structure remains.

The front of the outside stones of the wall is often found to be roughly scabbled with the pick, the markings taking various shapes, such as a cross, waved lines, or small squares; the diamond broaching being most common. Perhaps these marks denoted by what legion or body of workmen the stones were prepared, or on what parts of the building they were to be used.

At regular intervals of about 4 miles, fortified camps or stations were erected, there being, it is supposed, seventeen or eighteen of these on the line of the wall, each having contained from 600 to 1000 soldiers, horse or foot as the case might be. They were generally close to the wall on the southern side, and appear, from the remains existing, to have formed almost a square, containing from 3 to 6 acres, surrounded by high, thick walls, provided with four gateways, and laid out in streets, barracks, temples, baths, &c., some of the buildings having massive and occasionally beautiful sculptured stones. Outside these stations are heaps of grass-grown rubbish, from which it is inferred that there also existed suburbs, where dwelt natives and camp followers.

The 'Notitia Imperii,' a document which was compiled about the year 403, or a few years later,* and may be considered as a kind of army list of the Roman empire, gives a list of the prefects and tribunes, and the stations at which they were located along the line of the Roman wall. The stations now no longer bear their Roman names, but from this list, coupled with inscriptions found on the spot, it is thought many of the names of the stations have been ascertained with tolerable certainty; but as to the correct names of some of the other stations antiquaries are yet undecided.

In addition to the stations on the line of the wall there were others situated at different places to the north and south of it, the whole being connected by a system of roads enabling the soldiers to be amassed at any point attacked. To the north were supporting stations at High Rochester, Risingham, Bewcastle, Netherby, Middleby, &c. To the south, at Shields, Jarrow, Wardley, Corbridge, Hexham, Chesterholm, Whitley Castle, Old Penrith, Old Carlisle, Ellenborough, Moresby, Papcastle, (probably Keswick), and many other places.

We are inclined to think that the wall would naturally be continued past Wallsend to Tynemouth, and that consequently our antiquaries are entirely in the wrong as to the names given to the different stations. In the Notitia the first entry along the line of the wall is the following: "The tribune of the fourth cohort of the Lingones at Segedunum." There was undoubtedly a Roman station at Tynemouth, and it was a place of some importance, for an inscribed stone, dug up some time ago, states that a

* Hodgson says, "From internal evidence Pincirollus thought this work was written about the end of the reign of Theodosius the younger, who died in 450." If this date be correct, the Romans must have remained in Britain longer than is generally supposed. In another part of his history Hodgson curiously enough adopts the year 450 as the date of the Notitia, without any comment.

temple was erected there in the reign of the Emperor Severus, and it is a remarkable fact that an altar was found there in 1783, which reads as follows: " To Jupiter the best and greatest, Œlius Rufus, the Prefect of Cohort the fourth of the Lingones." This inscription would bear out the supposition that Tynemouth is the station of Segedunum; and in all probability Pons Ælii would be Wallsend, for a wall went down there to the brink of the stream, and it is natural to expect a bridge to cross the river at that point for communication with the station at Wardley, which was directly opposite, and a road would run thence to the stations at Jarrow and South Shields. An old writer tells us " he had frequently, after high tides, observed large well-wrought ashlar stones, lying on the side of the river at the foot of the field on which the station stood—the scattered ruins probably of a quay." Hodgson, in his 'History of Northumberland,' places Segedunum at Wallsend, but appears to bear out our supposition, for he says: " Mention is made of the Blackchesters in the fields of East Chirton, in a deed in 1320, and lines of ancient Roman earthworks still remain there, and in other places between Tynemouth and Wallsend, on the north side of the Tyne. Indeed, in fortifying the isthmus between this place and the Solway Firth, it was very unlikely that the Romans, at any period of their occupation of the country, would leave either side of the entrance of the Tyne without defence: and that the Saxons founded some part of their monastic buildings here as in many other places, with Roman remains, is evident from the discovery of two stones bearing inscriptions, which are now in the possession of the Society of Antiquaries in London. They both formed foundation stones, at the depth of 6 feet from the surface, of some ancient building on the north side of Tinmouth Castle."

Many other facts have helped to convince us that antiquaries are by no means correct in the names they assigned to the different stations on the line of the wall. It has been taken for granted that where a station produced an inscription bearing the name of a cohort mentioned in the Notitia, its real position had been ascertained, especially if inscriptions in like manner satisfactory had been found in neighbouring stations; but this method is based on the supposition that the same cohort occupied the same station for centuries, which can hardly be admitted when we remember that the soldiers were not natives of Britain, but were brought from all parts of the Roman empire, and would be changed and moved about in a manner similar to the plan adopted in the British army at the present day. We are supported in this objection by Hutchinson, in his 'History of Cumberland,' for he says he cannot admit that cohorts would remain stationary for long periods. Inscriptions by the same cohort are found in more than one station, and at the same station are often discovered inscriptions by various cohorts, clearly proving they were not stationary; and, as Hodgson remarks, "Many circumstances might occasion a cohort to erect an altar where it was not stationed." In order to make facts agree with theory, it is amusing to notice what unlikely suppositions are resorted to. We give one instance: Netherby was a Roman station, situated 10 miles north of Carlisle, far away from the wall, and altars having been found there bearing inscriptions by the same tribune as others found at Birdoswald, Hodgson says they were probably carried from Birdoswald to Netherby, which is a distance of 20 miles. Far more likely is it to suppose that the same tribune occupied both stations at different times, than that the altars have since been carried from one place to the other. If Newcastle had been the Pons Ælii of the Romans a station would naturally have been looked for at Gateshead on the opposite bank of the river, as at Carlisle on the Eden, but no traces of such have ever been found. If Tynemouth be Segedunum, and Wallsend Pons Ælii, and the order of the stations then agree with the Notitia as far as Birdoswald (not including, as some do, Chesterholm, which is some distance from the wall), then Housesteads would be *Æsica*, and Great Chesters, *Magna*, and this is supported by the derivations of the names given by Hodgson. Speaking of Æsica, or Great Chesters, he says: "This station was seated at a short distance from the right bank of Haltwhistle burn, and thus might have its name from being upon, or near the *esc*, or water." Now, if Æsica has its name from being near the water, it is very suitable for the station of Housesteads, which is near to, and overlooks the large sheets of water known as the Northumberland Lakes; but not at all applicable to Great Chesters, which is some distance from the tiny stream of Haltwhistle burn. Speaking of Magna, that is Carvoran, Hodgson says, very significantly: "That Carvoran was the Magna of the Notitia, I have been unable to find better evidence than the order of that work. Should the name Magna have Castra understood after it, and thus mean The Great Chesters?" If Housesteads be the Roman Æsica, as we suppose, then Great Chesters, being next in order, would be Magna. To the west of Birdoswald it is acknowledged that there has not yet been produced an inscription to corroborate the order of the Notitia. Although only one station, viz. that at Castlesteads, is visible over the 16 miles of ground from Birdoswald to Stanwix, it is almost certain that there would be one at or near the hamlet of Banks as stated at page 88, and another near either Old Wall or Walby. It is generally acknowledged that there was a station at Stanwix, and another at Carlisle, on the opposite bank of the river Eden, and the latter is thought to have been Luguvallum; but although admitting it is highly probable there was a station on each bank of the river, we cannot reconcile the names given to these with the fact that Luguvallum is not mentioned in the Notitia as on the line of the wall—for any station at Carlisle would clearly be on the line of that barrier.

Between each station were castella or mile castles, about a mile apart, for the protection of the batches of soldiers while guarding the wall. They were about 60 feet square, and attached to the south side of the wall, and were protected by the same kind of masonry as the wall, and of the same height and thickness. In each there is a gateway to the south and to the north, and though the castles generally were a mile apart they were not invariably that distance, but placed in positions where the wall required extra protection, and where roads led through the barrier to the north. As there was a gateway leading to the north at each of the stations and castles, numbering in all perhaps nearly 100, the territory north of the wall cannot have been given up to the enemy, and the wall itself could not be looked upon as a mere boundary fence, but as a base of military operations, and a line of safe retreat in case of defeat, an intrenched camp, in fact, stretching across the island. In some of the mile castles the foundation of an inside wall has been found, parallel with the outside wall, and a little distance from it; thus leading to the supposition that between the two had been buildings for the lodgment of the soldiers. Dr. Bruce, speaking of the mile castles, says: " Against their massive stone walls buildings of a comparatively slight structure were placed, each with a sloping roof, whilst a considerable space in the centre was left unoccupied and uncovered."

In each of the spaces between the mile castles were four stone turrets or watch-towers, used as sentry-boxes, and placed about 350 yards apart, thus allowing the sentinels to be within call of one another, so that communication could be kept up along the whole length of the wall, without having recourse to a sounding trumpet, or pipes laid under ground, which the inhabitants of the district tell the stranger was the case. Unfortunately none of these turrets remain, but old writers speak of some of them as existing in their day.

Along the wall, with the exception of a few places where it is on the summit of steep precipices, the Romans added to its height and strength by making a ditch close below, on its north side. This ditch was generally about 36 feet wide, and 15 feet deep. It is now easily traced from sea to sea, along almost the whole of the line, and is a good guide in places where the wall has been entirely destroyed. As it follows the course of the wall over hill and dale, it must have been intended as a dry ditch, and not to be filled with water. In making it the solid rock has in many places had to be excavated, and the stone thus obtained would no doubt be used to assist in the building of the wall. Occasionally the soil dug out of it has been deposited on its northern bank, thus adding to its depth.

To the south of the stone wall, at a distance perpetually varying, in some places being only a few yards, and in others almost half a mile apart, but generally 60 or 80 yards distant, is a vallum or earthwork, apparently consisting, where most perfect, of three ramparts and a fosse, but in many places only the fosse is now to be seen, and in others both ramparts and fosse have disappeared. Dr. Bruce says it fell short of the stone wall by about 3 miles at each end, but we think that in this he is mistaken, for we had not walked along the line of the wall many yards from Bowness before we observed a parallel ridge a few yards to the south, and a resident in the district, who accompanied us, said that it must have been the foundation of another wall, as it contained so many stones. Not knowing of the vallum at the time, this circumstance appeared very puzzling, but believing as we now do that the vallum was the Roman road, and would be continued to the end of the wall both at Bowness and Wallsend, we are fully convinced the ridge referred to was the remains of the vallum.

Various have been the conjectures as to the origin and use of the vallum. Some have thought it was made by Hadrian, and not being found a sufficient barrier, that Severus afterwards erected the stone wall. Horsley appears to have been the only antiquary who has looked upon the vallum as a road. He conceived that the stations were built by Agricola, and that the north agger of the vallum was constructed by him as a military way to communicate with them. He thinks the ditch of the vallum and the mounds on each side of it were constructed by Hadrian, as his defence against the Caledonians, and that he availed himself of the previously existing road and stations of Agricola. He is further of opinion that the wall, with its castles, turrets, and military way, are to be ascribed to Severus. Dr. Bruce, along with Hodgson, the historian of Northumberland, thinks it was made at the same time as the wall, and was part of the same engineering scheme, and that it was for protection from the south. He says: "A careful examination of the country over which the wall runs almost necessarily leads to the conclusion that whilst the wall undertook the harder duty of warding off the openly hostile tribes of Caledonia, the vallum was intended as a protection against sudden surprise from the south. The natives of the country on the south side of the wall, though conquered, were not to be depended upon. In the event of their kinsmen in the north gaining an advantage they would be ready to avail themselves of it. The Romans knew this, and with characteristic prudence made themselves secure on both sides." No one can walk along the wall from end to end without being fully convinced that Dr. Bruce is right in considering the whole, viz. north fosse, wall, stations, and vallum, as one engineering scheme, and made at the same time; but, although agreeing with him in this, we cannot allow that his solution of the use of the vallum is in any way satisfactory to us. After much thought, personal observation, and inquiry on the subject, we are convinced that the vallum has been the ancient Roman road, and on stating our belief to a farmer living on the line of the wall at, or near, the station of Great Chesters, we were agreeably surprised to find that this view was supported by the high authority of the men engaged on the Ordnance survey, for some of them had told him they thought it must have been made with that object. We had come to this conclusion, independently, by observing that it could have been little or no protection from either the north or the south, but that it followed the exact track which a road would naturally take if accompanying the wall, and such a road would be required by the Romans for the conveyance of the soldiers, horses, provisions, and war material; and this view was confirmed by husbandmen in different parts of the route, who stated that they dug up the foundation of a road on the line of the vallum. Dr. Bruce says no such foundation had been met with, but in this he must be mistaken, for the Rev. Mr. Wright, the vicar of Gilsland and Upper Denton, states that when digging for the foundation of the new schools, close to the vicarage, which is on the site of the vallum, they came upon the pavement of a road 14 feet broad. A few yards distant, where the vallum or road would have to cross the Poltross burn, we observed a bit of Roman masonry, which was discovered by the men when quarrying close by, and it appears to have been part of the abutment of a bridge. Dr. Bruce cannot have observed this, for he remarks, there are no traces of a bridge over the Poltross. Many other facts might be adduced which have helped to convince us that the vallum was the road. The blacksmith living between Birdoswald and Banks Head told us that he had often heard old people say they remembered the time when the vallum was the only road used between those two places. Now the lines of the vallum exist there in a most perfect state, but the road is on the very site of the wall. To the east of Sewingshields the modern military way has in some places been made along the vallum, and Horsley, who thought he could in some places trace the old Roman road on the vallum, says: "When the two are united they make a military way very beautiful and magnificent." Dr. Bruce admits the absolute necessity of a road near the line of the wall; and it is worthy of note that he states the vallum and wall never part company, and that he never finds any trace of the road except along the sloping sides of the heights between Carvoran and Sewingshields. The vallum runs for miles in a straight line, at the very foot of these hills, and in the exact position that we should have expected a road to take; in fact the modern military road is parallel with it all the way, and only a few yards distant. The wall, stations, and mile castles here being so high up the hill, the main road naturally would be carried below, whilst smaller branch roads would lead from it to the stations, and along the side of the hill, winding from castle to castle, in an up and down course, from one high point to the other. Another fact, clearly proving that the vallum was the road and not for defence, is, that whenever possible it avoids eminences, running to the north or south of them, and would be commanded by an enemy on the higher ground. This is seen at the Pike near Banks Head; between the Poltross and the Tipalt; below Great Chesters; at Harlow Hill; Carr Hill; Craggle Hill; and Hare Hill, &c., &c. The stations being generally attached to the south side of the wall, a road would be required to come to the southern gateway, and we find the vallum almost always takes that course; in fact the only stations that it does not touch are those of Housesteads and Great Chesters, which are situated a few hundred yards distant, on the hillside, and are approached by diverging lines. At Carvoran and Castlesteads it was found more convenient to take the vallum between the wall and the station, so that it was clearly not for defence from the south. Just as the vallum, being a road, had to come close up to the different stations, so, when crossing a river, it approached close to the wall, the two then being as it were thrown into one, a circumstance which of itself is, we think, a clear proof that the vallum was a road and not a fortification. This is clearly seen near Chollerford, where the North Tyne is crossed. Hodgson says that there the murus and the vallum came close up to the bridge on each side of the river, and that at the bridges on other rivers the barriers also closed in the same way. Another fact which militates against the vallum being a fortification is, that there are no apparent paths of egress through it to the south. Hodgson, quoting from Horsley, gives a fact which clearly proves that the military road and the vallum were not distinct works. He says: "Near the second castellum from Harlow Hill the military road seemed to cross the north agger, or rather to run upon it, there not being sufficient room for it between that agger and the castellum;" and he makes the same remark about a castellum to the west of Welton. We noticed many other places where the vallum was not more than 20 or 30 yards from the wall, too near to allow of a road between when passing the mile castles. Had the vallum and the road not been one and the same, sufficient room would undoubtedly have been left for the latter. Another difficulty cannot be overcome by those who suppose that the vallum was meant to guard against attacks from the south. They cannot explain the object of the small rampart on the south edge of the fosse. Dr. Bruce gives what appears to us a far-fetched supposition. He says: "Possibly it may have been intended as a foothold for the soldiers when fighting on this platform against the revolted Britons south of the barrier."

It is advisable, when discussing this subject, to compare the line of barrier between the Solway and the Tyne with other similar works constructed by the Romans. We have two such. One the Scotch, or Graham's Dike, 40 miles in length, between the Firth of Forth and Firth of Clyde; and the other the Devil's wall in Germany, which extended for 200 miles along the Danube, where that river was not broad and deep enough to be itself a sufficient protection. The Scotch dike was erected in the year 140, by Antoninus Pius, the successor of Hadrian, and consisted of a deep ditch, with a rampart of earth intermingled with stone on its southern side, and behind these a military way, a regular causewayed road, 20 feet wide, which kept by the course of the wall or mound, at irregular distances, approaching in some instances to within a few yards, and in others receding to a considerable extent. There were also numerous stations and watch towers. The Devil's wall in Germany consisted of a deep ditch with a high stone wall on its south side, and behind these, roads and camps were formed. Gibbon observes: "Its scattered ruins, universally ascribed to the power of the demon, now serve only to excite the wonder of the Swabean peasant." It will be seen that both these works corresponded with the barrier running across the north of England, and in both instances roads ran near to and in a line with the wall on the south side, but there was no vallum for protection from the south.

Similar barriers were erected by the Romans in other parts of their vast empire, and in this they were only following the plan adopted by the still older nations of Greece, Persia, and China; for we find remains of walls across the isthmus of Corinth; the north of Greece near

Thermopylæ; in the Crimea between the Black Sea and
the Sea of Azof; between the Euxine and the Caspian; in
one or two places in Syria; from the Euphrates to the
Tigris near ancient Babylon; but the greatest mural fortification in the world is that in China, which is 1500 miles
long, 20 feet high, and 11 feet broad, built of stones and
bricks, with inside filled with earth—it passes over ridges
attaining a height of more than 5000 feet above the sea
level, and was commenced 215 years before the time of
Christ, and finished in five years, being the most astonishing production of human labour and industry to be met
with on the face of the whole earth.

Although the Roman wall between the Solway and the
Tyne is popularly ascribed to Severus, many antiquaries
are disposed to confer the honour on Hadrian, and on this
disputed point there has been much learned disquisition.
Dr. Bruce, the highest living authority on the subject,
throws his weight into the scale of Hadrian, but the
information on the subject is so meagre that no solution
satisfactory to all parties is likely to be attained.

Spartian, a Roman historian, who wrote about eighty
years after the death of Severus, in speaking of Hadrian,
says: " He first drew a wall for 80 miles to separate the
Romans from the barbarians;" and then he mystifies us
by saying that Severus "fortified Britain with a murus
drawn across the island, and ending on each side at the
sea, which was the chief glory of his reign, and for which
he received the name of Britannicus." The historians
Herodian and Dion Cassius, who were contemporaries of
Severus, and wrote copiously on his reign, never mention
a word about any wall or other fortification that he
erected on this island, but they were not ignorant that
the island was crossed by a great wall, for Herodian tells
us that " the two most considerable bodies of the people of
that island, and to which almost all the rest relate, are
the Caledonians and the Meatæ. The latter dwell near
the Great Wall that separates the island in two parts: the
Caledonians lived beyond them." Bede and other later
historians endeavoured to reconcile Spartian's accounts by
attributing the vallum or earthwork to Hadrian, and the
murus or stone wall to Severus.

We are inclined to agree with Dr. Bruce that the whole
works belong to the reign of Hadrian, for in the absence
of satisfactory information handed down by historians, he

founds his opinion on the best of guides, the inscribed slabs and altars found at the stations and castles on the line of the wall, and most of these undoubtedly belong to the reign of Hadrian. Dr. Bruce's view is also confirmed by the fact that most of the coins found are those of Hadrian, from which it appears that Roman legions received their pay at the wall in his reign. This renowned emperor came to Britain in the year 119, but we are not aware how long he remained. Most of the island had been conquered by Agricola during the years 78, 79, and 80, and he had erected forts as far north as the Firths of Clyde and Forth,* but the natives being now in revolt, and Hadrian being anxious to visit every part of his dominions, he came over, quickly subdued the insurgents, and then erected the wall, mounds, ditches, and stations we are now considering, and of which Hodgson writes: "Through the whole line there is unity of design very skilfully adapted to the purpose for which the whole was formed, and to the nature of the ground over which it had to pass." The Britons being again in revolt in the reign of Severus, that emperor came over in person in the year 208, and remained until 211, when he died at York. He conducted successful campaigns against the northern inhabitants of the island, and caused the stone wall and the camps to be repaired. As is well known, the Romans remained in Britain until the dissolution of the empire at the beginning of the fifth century. On their departure the inhabitants of the northern part of the island broke through and began to demolish the stone wall, and ever since then its destruction has been in progress.

Those who desire to walk along the wall from the west to the east coast, can go from Carlisle by the Silloth line, as far as Drumburgh station, a distance of 9 miles; and thence by a vehicle called a "Dandy," drawn by a horse along a branch line, for 2½ miles to Port Carlisle, on the shores of the Solway Firth.

Port Carlisle, anciently called Fisher's Cross, is now a small dull place, of one street, the resort of a few summer visitors. The Earl of Lonsdale owns most of the property

* Horsley and some other antiquaries were of opinion that Agricola erected the stations which are on the line of the wall, and that the wall was built afterwards; but in this they are clearly mistaken, for no inscriptions mentioning the name of Agricola have been found at any of those places.

around, and in 1819 an attempt was made to constitute it the port for Carlisle city. A canal between the two places was opened in 1823, but in 1854 it was filled up and a railway made on its site, which was continued in 1856 from Drumburgh to Silloth, 12 miles farther down the estuary. Previous to the opening of the canal, vessels sailed up the Firth to Fisher's Cross, where the larger ships unloaded, but smaller craft, of perhaps forty or fifty tons burthen, came to the mouth of the Eden at Sandsfield and Rockcliff, whence carts transported their cargoes, chiefly of timber, to Carlisle. Port Carlisle being found unsuitable as a place for shipping, owing to the harbour constantly filling with sand and mud, large docks were constructed at Silloth, the foundation stone being laid by Sir James Graham, on the 18th August, 1857. But although steamers in connection with the North British Railway still sail from the latter place regularly to Liverpool, Dublin, Isle of Man, &c., it is found to be far from a prosperous seaport. The ground around Silloth is composed chiefly of small sandhills, upon which have been erected a number of houses and hotels, and the place is considered to be a healthy summer resort. The breadth of the Firth, which at Port Carlisle is only 1 mile, is here increased to 12 miles.

After walking along the shore from Port Carlisle for a mile, the traveller finds himself at Bowness, a small quiet old village, composed of a few farmsteads, lodging-houses, and fishermen's cottages; but containing few traces of the Roman city which once existed here. The inhabitants appear to know little of the old Romans, but they are well informed as to the Salmon Fisheries Act, and can argue ably and with feeling on the injustice of allowing the standing engines and nets to be used on the Scotch side, and within sight, whilst they are deprived of them. We cannot but sympathise with them, for such an anomaly certainly seems unfair.

Prying about amongst the houses, we find two or three small altars and inscribed stones in the walls of the buildings; and around the old church is an ancient coffin lid, a stone effigy, and other relics worthy of notice. The camp, the ramparts of which are not easily traced, appears to have been situated just to the north of the site of the church, and to have contained 5½ acres. There is no satisfactory account of the wall being continued past

Bowness, but old people point out a spot 200 or 300 yards distant where it appears to have entered the sea, as a quantity of stones were dug out of the beach there not many years since. Camden tells us that here was an ancient harbour, which is now filled with mud and sand, and that a paved causeway is said to have gone along the shore from Bowness to the Roman station at Ellenborough, near Maryport, and from thence a wall was built for 4 miles along the coast to Workington. At the present day a small strip of what appears to have been the wall is standing near Workington, and we are sometimes led to think that it might possibly have been continued all the way to Bowness, which supposition is supported by the fact that some Roman historians say the wall was 132 miles long. A Roman road is said to have run from Bowness all along the Cumberland coast, and crossed the estuary of the Dudden into Cartmell, and then across Morecambe Bay. At first sight it will strike the stranger that there was no necessity for a wall at Bowness, the Solway, which is here 1 mile wide, being a sufficient protection; but he presently finds that in this he is mistaken, for to the east of this point the sands may be crossed at low tide to the Scotch side, but such is impossible farther to the west. Many an inroad was made into the English border by chieftains crossing the Solway from the Scotch side, and we are told of a battle fought on foot in the estuary when the tide was out, and then continued on the return of the water by men on horseback and in ships. From the promontory is a view of the Cumberland hills, Skiddaw, and others; and on the Scotch side is the coast of Dumfries and Criffel range of heights; whilst half a mile down the Solway Firth there is seen, stretching for 1¼ miles from coast to coast, a viaduct conducting the Solway Junction Railway across.

Between Bowness and Port Carlisle the wall and vallum may be traced through the fields by the slightly elevated lines, upon which the herbage has a stunted and discoloured appearance; and in one place there is yet standing, in the midst of a thickly-grown fence, a part of the wall, a few feet high, consisting of cemented rubble stone, but without the facing stones. Also in the bottom of a drain, in one place, are observed some flags, which have been the foundation of the wall; the groundwork having often been formed in that manner. A few years since a strip of the wall existed here in a tolerably perfect state, but was then removed for building purposes. This appears to have been its fate for long distances. When stones have been scarce, the inhabitants have resorted to the wall for material for every kind of building, and the traveller, owing to the uniformity of shape of the Roman stones, is soon able to distinguish them in edifices miles distant.

From Port Carlisle to Drumburgh, a distance of 2 miles, its course has to be traced by the slight ridge and sickly herbage. It is cut by the railway, ascends a small height, then again is cut by the railway, and attains the top of the hill upon which is situated the village and castle of Drumburgh. The castle is occupied as a farmhouse, and has the appearance of a private residence. The inside has a very ancient look, the walls are very thick, the rooms large, with wide open chimneys, old oak beams, and wainscoting; and steps lead to the top of the roof, which, however, is not now turreted. A royal licence to fortify the mansion was granted in 1307, and Leland, writing in 1539, says: "At Drumburgh the Lord Dacre's father builded upon old ruines a pretty pyle for defence of the country. The stones of the Pict wall were pulled down to build it." Extensive alterations were made upon it in the reign of Henry VIII. It now belongs to Lord Lonsdale. In front of the building is a Roman altar, and another in the garden wall in the rear of the house.

Many of the houses in the village are built of clay (called clay dubbins), and will be examined with curiosity by most visitors. Such erections appear to have been very common in these parts until within recent years. An old lady told us that when she was a girl, clay houses were often built. The clay having been got ready, the neighbours assembled on what was called a "Watering day," and they set to work and mixed the clay and water together, the young people of both sexes having fine fun by sprinkling each other with water. The clay was often mixed by treading with the feet, and it was not unusual to get this work done by cattle, confining the animals in a round space containing the clay and water. When the clay was ready, poles were fixed a few yards apart, and having made a foundation of loose stones to protect the house from rats and to keep it dry, the clay walls were made about 2 or 3 feet thick, a layer of straw being placed about every 3 inches. These houses are said to be very warm and comfortable. At the back of the village are some mounds, supposed to be the ruins of a small Roman camp about three-quarters of an acre in extent; and also a Roman well. The proprietor of the adjoining house says, that in digging for repairs, traces of the wall were met with. Milestones have been found here, and there is observed, built into a wall, part of an ancient baptismal font curiously figured with flowers.

From Drumburgh to Burgh-by-Sands is a broad flat marsh, containing about 1500 acres of pasture land. Generally it is tenanted by many thousands of cattle and sheep, which are looked after by two or three herdsmen. Some of it is common land, and other parts of it belong to Lord Lonsdale, the neighbouring farmers having the right of pasturage according to the acreage of their farms. The whole waste is supposed to be divided into so many imaginary plots, called stints, upon which are allowed a certain number of cattle or sheep, and these stints are put up, on a certain day in each year, to public competition. On a fine day the cattle present a picturesque appearance. In the summer of 1307 the marsh presented a scene of another description, for here was encamped a large army under Edward I., waiting for a favourable opportunity to cross the Solway Firth, and enter Scotland. On the 7th July, before the army had moved, Edward, who had been ill some time, died in his tent. On the spot where he breathed his last, 1½ miles from Burgh-by-Sands, has been erected a monument, which is seen for many miles round. The original, a square column 9½ yards high, with a Latin inscription, was placed there in 1685 by the Duke of Norfolk, but it fell in 1795, and was rebuilt in 1803 by the Earl of Lonsdale. Previous to the erection of the first monument a heap of stones marked the spot. The country people say that Edward had been warned in a dream that he would die at Brough, and consequently had avoided a place of that name in Yorkshire; and on arriving here and asking an old woman the name of the place, was surprised to hear the ill-fated word. Sometimes when there are high tides and stormy weather, the sea overflows most of the marsh, and within a recent period the currents have washed away hundreds of acres of land. The currents in the Firth are constantly changing their course.

Around St. Bees, and at other places on the coast, may be seen, at low water, stumps, *in situ*, and prostrate trunks of trees, the remains of ancient forests; thus showing that the sea is gradually but constantly overflowing and receding from the land. Here also has been a similar submerged forest, for on cutting a canal a short distance to the east of Port Carlisle, a prostrate forest of considerable extent was met with. "Although the precise period when the forest fell is not ascertainable, there is positive proof that it must have been prior to the building of the wall, because the foundations of the wall passed obliquely over it, and lay 3 or 4 feet above the level of the trees." Much of the timber was sound; some of it was used in forming the jetty at Port Carlisle. Camden says: "That the figure of the coast hereabouts has been altered, appears plainly from roots of trees covered with sand at a good distance from the shore, which are commonly discovered when the tide is driven back by the violence of the winds. I know not whether it be worth the while to observe that the inhabitants tell you of *subterranean* trees, without boughs, they very commonly dig up; discovering them by the dew which never lyes upon the ground that covers them." Similar trees are mentioned in Todd's manuscript history of Carlisle, written about 1685. Speaking of the time prior to the Norman conquest, he says: "There was no face or appearance of a city, but the very foundations were so buried in the earth that it is said large oaks grew upon them, so that it looked more like a forest than a place of civil government. And this is not only attested by our historians, but also made out by some discoveries that had been lately made of large unknown oak trees, buried 10 or 12 yards in the ground, one of which was found lately by Mr. Robert Jackson, alderman, in digging for a well; which rude timber can be no other than some of those old monumental oaks that stood upon the walls as marks and witnesses of its utter ruin and destruction."

After descending the hill at Drumburgh all trace of the line of the wall disappears until we arrive at Dykesfield, on the opposite side of the marsh. It is a direct line across the marsh from one point to the other, and some think the wall would follow that course, and that it has since been washed away, not leaving a trace behind. Others think it highly improbable that the Romans would build a wall within the reach of the sea, and conclude it has gone round the edge of the marsh by Easton and Boustead Hill. The latter supposition we think the most probable, but antiquaries ought to be able to set the matter at rest by ascertaining where the foundations of the wall were cut when the Canal and the Silloth Railway, were made. A resident at Easton told us that it was not met with when the canal was made near Drumburgh, therefore it could not cross the marsh. On examining the map it is clear that if it came by Easton it ought to have been cut by the Silloth line near the junction at Drumburgh, and again near Dykesfield by the canal. In all probability a record would be kept, for Hodgson, in his 'History of Northumberland,' tells us that William Chapman, Esq., the engineer of the canal, paid great attention to antiquities, and offered a high price to his workmen for all they found.

At Easton we met with what appeared a portion of the foundation of the wall and the ditch, and were told that here had been found some altars or inscribed stones that had been taken away to Lowther Castle. The buildings here are undoubtedly composed of Roman stones from the wall. Between Easton and Boustead Hill another lettered stone had been found and carried away.

As there are no quarries hereabouts the stones for the wall must have been brought long distances. Some of the inhabitants think they must have come from Hawrigg quarry, about 12 miles distant. Others think they might be got from Rockcliff quarry, on the opposite side of the marsh; or at Lazonby or Kirk Oswald, also far away; the lime also must have been carried long distances rather hard work for Dr. Bruce's " poor enslaved Britons."

From Dykesfield to Burgh the site of the wall may be satisfactorily traced, and stones are being constantly turned up by the plough. The vallum here appears; and it has been taken for granted that it ended here, but we think it highly probable it was continued through to Bowness, in close companionship with the wall.

Burgh-by-Sands is situated in a commanding position, and is thought to be the site of a Roman station of about 3 acres in extent. Hardly any traces of the ramparts remain. The church, which is supposed to be within the eastern boundary, is an ancient, picturesque object. The ivy-covered tower on the western side is a massive castellated structure, which must have been originally a castle or peel house, the walls being 7 feet thick. The church might be a later addition. This supposition is borne out by the fact that until 1704 there was another tower at the east end of the building. In a paper written by Mr. Cory, and published in the 'Transactions of the Archæological Institute' in 1859, the church of Burgh is described as a fortified church, and classed with those of Newton Arlosh and Great Salkeld, in Cumberland, and Annan, in Scotland. The towers were made capable of standing a short siege, and cut off from the rest of the building by an iron door. The second tower at Burgh was probably the vicar's residence. The cockpit was at the beginning of this century in the churchyard. If the tourist wind by the dark stone staircase to the top of the turret, he will have an extensive prospect. In the vicarage garden and the churchyard are pieces of Samian ware, querns, and other relics.

The barony of Burgh has often changed owners, and by female inheritance has passed through six great families. In the year 1685 it was purchased by Sir John Lowther from the representatives of Mary Dacre, wife of Thomas Howard, Earl of Suffolk, son of the Duke of Norfolk, and is now the property of the Earl of Lonsdale. It has often been stated in local histories that the barony, during the time of Henry II., was in the possession of a Sir Hugh Morvill, one of the four knights who assassinated Thomas-à-Becket; and by way of atonement he is said to have given the rectory of Burgh to the abbey of Holm Cultram, and it was appropriated to the monks by the Bishop of Carlisle. This story has, however, been utterly exploded by Mr. Hodgson Hinde, in a paper read before the Archæological Institute in 1859. The murderer of Becket was Sir Hugh Morvill, lord of Kirk Oswald and Brough, in Westmorland—quite a different personage.

From Burgh the wall ran in a straight line for 1½ miles to the village of Beaumont, and close by the church, which stands on an eminence formerly occupied, in all probability, by a mile castle. In the burial-ground are some curious old incised monumental slabs. Two or three hundred yards from the mount, the wall crossed the Beaumont beck, and gained the high bank of the river Eden. On each side of the beck, the north fosse is deep and well defined. Keeping on the cliffs overhanging the river, we presently reach Kirkandrews; the vicarage house, the graveyard, and the well of St. Andrew are there, but the church was pulled down some centuries since, and the parish joined to that of Beaumont in 1692. Formerly a church is said, but on doubtful authority, to have existed a mile distant to the south, at a place called Kirksteads. At the latter place were found some curiously carved stones, a quern, and a large Roman altar, which are now in a garden at Kirkandrews. On the altar is part of an inscription, thus translated by Dr. Bruce: "Lucius Junius Victorinus and Caius Ælianus, Augustal Legates, (belonging) to the sixth legion, (styled) the victorious, the dutiful, and the faithful, (erected this altar) on account of achievements prosperously performed beyond the Wall." The vallum is thought to have run in a straight line from this village to Burgh, thus avoiding the high ground around Beaumont. After crossing the fields to Grinsdale, we again reach the cliffs above the river, and continue by a footpath along the site of the wall. In one or two places the lines of the vallum may be seen, but all traces disappear before arriving at Carlisle. When the great main sewer of the city was made, both wall and vallum were cut across, and it was then ascertained that the wall went direct from near the castle over the river to Hyssop Holm Well and Stanwix, but the vallum took a bend, and crossed the green south of the castle, thus including the castle hill between it and the wall. Carlisle is supposed to have been a Roman station, which, in all probability, existed on the site of the present castle. Roman coins, jewels, baths, a theatre, and inscribed stones, have at various times been found when excavating in different parts of the city. Camden tells us that "the wall passed the river over against the castle, where in the very channel the remains of it, namely, great stones, appear to this day." None of these great stones are now to be seen, but, without doubt, such would exist there in former times, and since Camden wrote his history the bed of the river may have considerably changed its course, for in old maps it is placed much nearer the castle than at present.

There is said to have been a Roman station at Stanwix, but no traces remain. Part of its site is occupied by the church and graveyard. Great numbers of Roman remains were found during the rebuilding of the church, particularly a fine figure of Victory. The site commands an excellent view of Carlisle, and the castle, Skiddaw mountain, and Tindale fell; and to the east and north a wide, level, cultivated tract of country.

o

In one place the ditch is yet quite distinct between the church and the river, near Hyssop Holm Well, and we were told that five years ago the foundation of the wall, 13 feet broad, was cut through when making the sewers for St. George's Terrace, and many cartloads of stones were removed.

For about 10 miles from Stanwix little of the wall remains visible above the ground, but farmers constantly plough up parts of its foundation; stones are therefore strewn about it, and its course may be traced by the ridge-like form of the ground, the barren nature of the soil, or the peculiar coloured vegetation; almost invariably a footpath or lane runs along it, being the remains of the old drive, or packhorse road between Carlisle and Newcastle. The north ditch or fosse can nearly always be traced: it shows as a slack in the ground; when viewed from a distance, it can easily be followed by noting the depressions in the hedges. The vallum here and there appears a few yards to the south.

From Stanwix church follow a footpath which runs along the wall for half a mile, to the hamlet of Tarraby, and then go along a grass-grown lane and past two or three fields, until the road leading from Carlisle to Houghton is met at right angles. Here proceed across the opposite fields, or follow the road to right for a few hundred yards, until the turnpike-road from Carlisle to Brampton and Newcastle is entered, and by the side of it, 2 miles from Carlisle, is Drawdykes Castle, a farmhouse, strongly built, but not castellated. It is on the site of a very old castle, the last vestige of which was destroyed about the middle of the eighteenth century, and had been the ancestral home of the Aglionby family for many generations. It now belongs to Charles Featherstonehaugh, Esq., of Staffield Hall, he having married one of the Aglionbys. On the parapet are three large heads carved in stone, said by the residents to be originally from the Roman wall, which ran only 200 yards distant in front of the house. The figures, however, when closely inspected, are clearly not Roman. Others say they represent Major Aglionby, his attorney, and his Satanic majesty. The stranger is allowed to ascend by the old oaken stairs to the parapet and leaden roof. Here is a capital view of Carlisle, the Cathedral, and Skiddaw range of hills; also Crossfell, Castle Carrock, Tindale, and Talkin fells. Over the doorway of one of the rooms is some lettering, and in the garden wall at the back of the house is a Roman monumental stone, supposed to have been originally brought from Stanwix, which Dr. Bruce reads: "To the Divine Manes of Marcus Trojanus Augustinius; his beloved wife, Œlia Amella Lusima, caused this tomb to be erected."

Half a mile from Drawdykes is Linstock Castle, which was, up to about 1300, the residence of the Bishops of Carlisle, having been granted to that see by Henry I.; but the situation, so exposed to Scottish attacks, compelled the bishops to move to Rose. At Linstock, about the year 1293, was entertained the Archbishop of York, who remained for a considerable time whilst on his visitation. The present building is not turreted, but merely a tall, massive dwelling-house, with walls 7½ feet thick, and built of stones from the Roman wall—a fine sample of the strongholds known as Peels, which were common in all the Border district in the mosstrooper days. At night the cattle belonging to the farmer were secured in the apartment below, whilst he and his family barricaded themselves in the room above. This upper room was generally floored with stone flags, resting upon heavy oak beams, which would long resist the action of fire. The slates of the roof were pinned down with sheep's shanks. Arrow loops were placed in various parts of the building, so as to expose an enemy to the utmost disadvantage.

At many of the farmhouses in the neighbourhood of Alston may be observed relics of the strange customs of an uncivilized age. The byres (cowhouses) are below the dwellings, access being had to the latter by stone ladders. In one house at Lonning Head, near Garrigill, the farmer and his cattle enter at the same door, the cattle turning off into the byre, and the farmer into the kitchen. Irthington vicarage was so until four years ago, when it was altered. Macaulay, in his 'History of England,' referring to those times, says: "Before the union of the two Crowns, and long after that union, there was as great difference between Middlesex and Cumberland as there now is between Massachusetts and the settlements of those squatters who, far to the west of the Mississippi, administer a rude justice with the rifle and the dagger. The magistrates of Cumberland and Northumberland were authorized to raise bands of armed men for the defence of property and order, and provision was made for meeting the expense of those levies by local taxation. The parishes were required to keep bloodhounds for the purpose of hunting the freebooters. Many old men who were living in the middle of the eighteenth century could well remember the time when these ferocious dogs were common. Yet even with such auxiliaries it was often found impossible to track the robbers to their retreats among the hills and morasses; for the geography of that wild country was very imperfectly known. . . . . The seats of the gentry and the larger farmhouses were fortified. Oxen were penned at night beneath the overhanging battlements of the residence, which was known by the name of the Peel. The inmates slept with arms at their sides. Huge stones and boiling water were in readiness to crush and scald the plunderer who might venture to assail the little garrison. No traveller ventured into that country without making his will. . . . . The irregular rigour with which criminal justice was administered shocked observers whose life had been passed in more tranquil districts. Juries, animated by hatred and by a sense of common danger, convicted housebreakers and cattle-stealers with the promptitude of a court martial in a mutiny; and the convicts were hurried by scores to the gallows."

Returning to the north side of the Brampton road, in front of Linstock Castle, a lane is entered which runs along the site of the Roman wall, past Walby and Wallhead, and here and there are distinct traces of both the vallum and north ditch.

Scaleby Castle is about a mile to the north, and worth a visit. The road to it leads past the Highfield Moor farm. Though the castle is in a flat situation, it appears to have been a place of more than ordinary strength. Parts of the massive old walls are standing, in a dilapidated state, overgrown by ivy and shrubs, and surrounded by trees, and a deep moat; presenting a scene of utter desolation. One portion of the building has been renovated, and occupied by the owners of the estate, and close by is a large farmhouse. The manor was given by Henry I. to Richard Tilliol, whose issue male failing in the reign of Edward IV. his possessions were divided between his two heiresses. The estates, thus separated, passed afterwards by purchase into various hands.

Resuming the stroll along the Roman wall, the farmhouse of Bleatarn is reached. Here the north fosse runs in front of the building, and just behind are slight traces of the vallum. Three quarters of a mile farther is Old

Wall, a hamlet evidently built entirely of stones from the wall. The ditch now becomes very distinct. It passes through the gardens, and is wide and deep for hundreds of yards. In one place it is planted with trees, and will act as a guide to the stranger after the lane ends, and until a few fields are crossed to the road at the hamlet of White Flat. The vallum is also observed about 30 yards to the south. At White Flat the ditch is distinct, and the stones of the wall are seen in the bottom of the fence. Passing close to the south side of Newtown of Irthington, the road is crossed which leads to Brampton, situated 2 miles to the south, whence the Written Crags on the Gelt may be visited. (See page 57.) The wall now passes the farmhouses of Headswood, Beck, and Cambeck-hill. The north ditch and vallum are seen in two or three places; and when crossing the streamlet at Beck some of the stones of the wall are observed in the fence. On the west side of the Cambeck river the fosse of the wall has been cut deeply into the red sandstone rock. The river may be crossed by a footbridge after a pleasant walk of a few hundred yards up the bank of the stream. There are no visible remains of the Roman bridge which would undoubtedly cross the river somewhere near the ford. On the opposite bank the wall went in the direction of the fence. A few hundred yards to the south is Castlesteads, the beautiful residence of G. J. Johnson, Esq. The gardens, a little way from the mansion, occupy the site of a Roman station, supposed to be "Petriana," which was to the south of both wall and vallum, and in this respect unlike most of the stations, for they were generally attached to the wall and between it and the vallum. Many altars and other antiquities have been found here, most of which are preserved on the spot, but beyond these there are few signs of Roman occupation. In all probability there would be one or two stations between Stanwix and Castlesteads, but no traces of them are now to be met with. We are inclined to think that Walby is the most likely spot. The farmhouse of Sandysike is passed, and then we arrive at the village of Walton, where is a charming view of Naworth Castle and Lanercost Priory, the vale of the Irthing, and Skiddaw in the distance.

After crossing King Water, the roads must be forsaken, and the fields entered. The wall passes to the north of the farmhouses of Dovecote, Low Wall, and How Gill, and may be traced here and there in the fences. In the rear of the latter building is a rude inscription, of which Dr. Bruce says: "It seems to record the achievements of a British tribe, the Catuvellauni. Tacitus tells us that Agricola took southern Britons with him to the battle of the Grampians; Hadrian and Severus may have been similarly accompanied in their expeditions." At the Garthside farm, just before ascending Craggle hill, up which the ditch is well defined, there are pieces of the wall in the hedge five feet high—the most promising patch seen since leaving Port Carlisle. From Craggle hill the Solway is seen. On the next height, Hare hill, the ditch is well defined, and there is a large strip of the wall in good preservation. This point commands a glorious prospect, including Carlisle, the Solway, Skiddaw, Blencathara, Tindale, Talkin, and Castle Carrock fells. To the north the view extends past the Beacon and Bewcastle district right into Scotland. Close at hand are Naworth Castle, and Lanercost Priory, looking extremely beautiful. The wall is here 4 or 5 feet high, and in places half hid by the overgrowth of the fence. The vallum runs through the wood a few yards to the south, and is better defined than it has hitherto been during the whole of its course, giving evidence of an approach to a more perfect state farther east. A resident, with whom we had a chat, seemed very concerned that the Earl of Carlisle should think so much of this old wall as to let it remain, when the stones could have been used, instead of bricks, in building a house which was then being erected not many yards distant. Would that in former days there had been such earls to astonish the simple-minded rustics by similar care of this ancient monument.

After a steep descent, a small strip of the wall is met with, 9 feet 10 inches high—higher than in any other place. It is stripped of the facing stones, and exhibits layers of stones put in edgeways and cemented with lime. Hutton says: "I viewed this relic with admiration. I saw no part higher."

After crossing the hollow down which flows Banksburn, the road is entered which ascends the hill to the Banks hamlet and inn, and then continues for 3 miles on the site of the wall to Birdoswald. The north ditch is close to on the left, and a few yards distant on the right may be traced the vallum now and again, and it becomes exceedingly well defined a little farther on, the mounds of earth being very large. After passing the hollow where are the inscriptions on the Coome crags, a long stretch of the wall in excellent preservation is passed, and then the station of Birdoswald is reached, which is considered one of the most perfect camps on the line. Birdoswald, Coome crags, and the wall and ditches as far west as Banks Head, having been described at pages 82, 84, and 87, we have purposely avoided giving them here more than a passing notice.

From Birdoswald the wall is traced by the present stone fence for a few yards to the edge of the cliff overhanging the Irthing. Here, on the very top of the precipice, is a part of the foundation well preserved. Antiquaries are undecided as to how the wall descended to the stream. Traces of it are met with directly opposite on the farther side of the river. Although now the cliff is very steep, it might in former times have a gradual descent, and have since been worn by the action of the weather. An old lady residing at Willowford, the farm below, told us that fifty years since there was a tolerably easy footpath from the river's brink to the top of the cliffs, which are now quite precipitous and impossible to ascend. Camden says, "The wall crossed the river Irthing by an arched bridge," but he does not tell us whether any visible traces remained in his day. Dr. Bruce merely says: "How the wall crossed the river, and ascended the cliff which bounds its western bank, no remains are left to show. Usually in the summer season passengers may cross the river dryshod." Feeling confident that here would exist the foundation of a bridge similar in character to the wonderful remains to be seen on the banks of the North Tyne at Chollerford, we paid many visits to the place, and came to the conclusion that such would be met with if the accumulation of sand on the banks of the stream were removed. Fortunately, on our last visit, we met at Birdoswald with Mr. John Armstrong, a master mason, residing at Gilsland, and he assured us that when the old Peel house at Willowford was pulled down, thirty-six years since, and the present farmhouse built, the foundation of the bridge was visible, and a great number of very large stones, beautifully shaped, and with the luis holes in them, were taken from the bank of the river, close to where the wall evidently crossed, and were broken and used in building the house. From the quality of the stones it was evident they had come from the Lodges Quarry, near the Low Row railway station. He was also of opinion that they only got a part of the stones, and that many more would be found in their original positions if the sand were removed. We hope that ere long so valuable a relic may be divested of its covering. It would be most interesting, not only to the historian and the antiquary, but to the architect and the general public, and a great source of attraction to all who visit Gilsland.

From the river to Gilsland vicarage and railway station the wall is easily traced, and fully described at page 79; therefore we pass along, and commence on the Northumberland side of the Poltross burn, bidding farewell to the Cumberland portion of this great Roman work.

Between Gilsland railway station and Thirlwall Castle, a distance of 2 miles, no portion of the wall remains, although some of it was standing a few years since; but the north fosse and the vallum are very distinct, and here and there in an excellent state of preservation. They run parallel with the railway on higher ground, a few yards distant to the south. This is perhaps the most exposed part of the whole line of the wall, owing to its being on the comparatively level tract between the two rivers, Irthing and South Tyne, and it was here, at the farmhouse called the Gap, that the barrier is said to have been first broken through by the Picts and Scots. The Romans appear to have been aware of its weak state, for a short distance farther south we find, on the high ground, traces of a line of small square camps or earthworks. After crossing the railway, a little to the west of Greenhead, the barriers went over the level ground direct to Thirlwall Castle and the Tipalt streamlet; and the fosse and vallum are distinctly seen ascending the opposite heights in a parallel and straight course.

The wall presently attains the summit of a range of hills, which, at a mean height of 700 feet above the sea level, stretches in an almost continuous line for 12 miles to the east, presenting to the north a bold cliff-like ridge of perpendicular rock, from 100 to 200 feet high; overlooking in that direction a vast extent of plain, called the "Waste," which is covered with short grass, and here and there a patch of heather, but without a single tree, shrub, or fence of any description to break the line of vision, and hardly a house to be seen. To the south the ridge has a gentle green slope, and at its feet the vallum is traced for miles following a perfectly straight course. Near the

CAWFIELD MILE CASTLE. 201

vallum is the modern military road between Carlisle and Newcastle, and 2 miles farther south, over high ground, is the railway, and also the South Tyne river.

Ascending from Thirlwall Castle, the Roman station of Carvoran is passed, where the Roman road, known as Maiden Way, is supposed to have crossed from south to north, and then the wall runs along the very edge of the cliffs, called the Nine Nicks of Thirlwall, following in an undeviating line the ups and downs of the crags. A pure pleasant breeze comes over these heights, and fine views are had whilst the traveller wends along and inspects the ruin which is here and there standing a few feet high, but generally laid prostrate and overgrown. Vestiges of two or three mile castles will be observed, and then the station of Great Chesters will be passed, all of which will be found described at page 136, where is included the part of the wall running for 5 miles between Thirlwall Castle and the Cawfield Mile Castle.

After crossing the streamlet, called to the south of the wall Haltwhistle burn, and to the north, Cawburn, we again begin ascending, and at once meet with the Cawfield Mile Castle. As this castle is considered to be one of the best specimens of that kind of building, it will be as well to examine it thoroughly. The site was covered with earth until about twenty-four years ago, when the proprietor, Mr. John Clayton, of Chesters, near Chollerford, who fortunately owns the property through which the wall here runs, caused it to be opened out. This gentleman is well known for the interest he takes in the Roman remains, and for his liberality in preserving them in their present state. The castle stands on the slope to the south of the wall, the wall forming its northern side, and it contains an area of about 360 square yards, being 20 yards long by 18 yards broad, inside measurement. Its walls are 7 feet thick, and now about 4 or 5 feet high, the south-west and south-east corners being rounded on the outside. There is a large opening for a gateway in the centre of the south wall, and a similar one directly opposite in the north wall, consisting of massive blocks of freestone. It is impossible to say what were the internal arrangements, but it is supposed there would be an open space in the centre, and buildings on each side for the accommodation of the soldiers on guard.

Beyond the castle the wall is in excellent preservation

for about 600 yards, running on the edge of the precipices, and apparently varying a little in thickness according to the nature of the ground. The north ditch vanishes when the wall runs over these steep heights, but again invariably appears when a gap has to be passed over, even if only a few yards across. A mile from the last castle appear the grass-covered mounds of another, a foot or so high; and 200 yards farther are the stones, 1 foot high, of a tiny building, which might be taken for a turret, but is in all probability modern. Then the wall for half a mile is 5 feet high, and in an excellent state, perhaps better than in any other part of its course.

Arrived on the summit of Winshields fell, which is 1230 feet above the sea level, and half way between the two coasts, and the highest point attained by the wall, the traveller will do well to rest a few minutes and enjoy the prospect which it commands, for he must presently make a slight descent, and will lose much of the grand panorama that has been in view ever since ascending these cliff-like heights from Thirlwall Castle. To the west, on a clear day, the sea around the Solway is visible, and the heights of Criffel and Burnswark. To the north, the wild waste stretches like a vast plain, with the exception of very slight undulations, to the Cheviot Hills, which now begin to appear in the distance. Near at hand, to the north-east, are the sheets of water known as the Northumberland lakes; and to the east the eye ranges a long distance over an undulating tract covered here and there with patches of trees; whilst to the south are low hills; and farther away others reaching to the summit of Crossfell and Tindale fell. One or two farmhouses are in the hollows on each side of the wall, but, with these exceptions, few habitations are visible.

Continuing eastwards much of the wall remains, and runs in an up-and-down course on the brink of precipices, reminding the overlooker of the familiar pictures of the Great Wall of China. Passing over Peel crag, a mile castle is observed, with walls 6 feet high and 6 feet broad, and gateways to north and south, and then the wall mounts Lough crag, a grand perpendicular ridge of rock directly overhanging one of the lakes. Some fine peeps are obtained down the wild rocks to the sheet of water. Leaving the cliffs and lake, the north ditch appears; and after passing Hot Bank farmhouse, another steep ascent is made. The wall, after a break of a few yards, again appears 5 feet high, and continues so for about a mile, where there is another castle similar to the preceding ones. It then runs through a small plantation, in a dilapidated condition, overgrown by long grass, nettles, and trees. Emerging from the plantation it appears almost perfect, and the stranger will be startled on finding that he has come suddenly upon the wonderful remains of the Roman station of Borcovicus, or Housesteads.

The situation is wild and solitary, but the ruins are so extensive, and give evidence of such massiveness and grandeur, that the stranger, when wandering alone amongst the scattered broken columns, will feel that he is in a city of the dead, and he will be reminded of Pompeii or Babylon, or of Scipio amongst the ruins of Carthage. On every hand, over a large area, are pedestals, carved stones, huge and well-shaped blocks of freestone, and the foundations and remains of the walls of edifices, or mounds of *débris* overgrown with grass, evidently the relics of beautiful stately buildings. A more striking example of the power of that wonderful people is perhaps not to be met with in the British Isles. The spot is more interesting and suggestive than any ruined abbey or castle. Here the traveller may muse alone amongst those huge remains, being disturbed only by a few sheep or cattle, or the cry of the lapwing; and while contemplating in amazement and admiration the singular scene presented by these relics of an ancient and mighty nation, the thought must occur to every reflecting mind that all these walls, columns, and chambers were ancient ruins before any existing castles, or abbeys, or churches were built in this land.

The area of the station is nearly 5 acres, but outside the walls there have been at one time extensive suburbs, probably occupied by natives and camp followers. The boundary walls are in a good state of preservation, being about 10 feet high and 7 feet broad, and forming almost a square. They stand on sloping ground close to the south side of the great wall, the latter forming the northern fence of the camp. The south-east and south-west corners of the walls are rounded. In the middle of the walls, to the north, east, south, and west are openings, about 10 yards wide, the remains of double portals formed of massive blocks of stone, and presenting a noble appearance. Streets running crosswise from gate to gate met in the centre of the camp, and other narrower streets ran parallel with these. In this way the whole of the interior of the camp was divided into parallelograms of greater or less size. Ruts, thought to be caused by the action of chariot-wheels, are said to be observed in the stone threshold of the gateways.

Many antiquities have been found in the station, such as altars, statues, Samian ware, glass, millstones, boars' tusks, horns of deer, and coins; also gold signet-ring, and gold pendant for the ear, both figured. Many relics found here and at other stations on the line of the wall have been removed to the Museum at Newcastle, and to other museums and private mansions. In one of the guard-rooms a heap of coal was found; but although the Romans probably obtained coal from different parts of the district, these may have been brought here for the use of some mosstrooper, who would undoubtedly be the occasional occupant of so favourable a situation. It is, however, almost certain that the Romans used coal, for some has also been found at the stations of Ellenborough and Bewcastle. In front of the station, to the south and south-west, the ground descends a bank in terraces, which appear to have been cultivated. Upon them are foundations of streets and houses, so that the approach to the camp would probably have a noble and beautiful appearance. At present, the only building near the site is a shepherd's house; but previous to its erection a farm-house, which has been removed, stood near the south gateway.

Leaving Housesteads, the wall is traced for the next mile or two over a continuation of the ridge of cliffs, but little of it is standing, and it is often distinguished by nothing but a line of grass-grown rubbish, and one or two faint traces of mile castles. The views are, however, very fine, especially to the west, the lakes being visible, and the cliffs along which the traveller has come stand out picturesquely for miles. Although there are few traces of the wall as the traveller proceeds, the associations connected with this portion of the ground will by many be considered supremely interesting.

Not far from Sewingshields, the farmhouse standing on the east end of the cliffs, is the site of the castle referred to by Sir Walter Scott, in the sixth canto of "Harold the

Dauntless," under the denomination of the Castle of the Seven Shields. Too truly he says:

> .... "No towers are seen
> On the wild heath, but those that Fancy builds;
> And, save a fosse that tracks the moor with green,
> Is nought remains to tell of what may there have been."

Though no part of the building remains to please the eye, the imagination may dwell pleasingly on the following story:

"Immemorial tradition has asserted that King Arthur, his queen, Guenever, his court of lords and ladies, and his hounds, were enchanted in some cave of the crags, or in a hall below the Castle of Sewingshields, and would continue entranced there till some one should first blow a bugle-horn that lay on a table near the entrance of the hall, and then with 'the sword of the stone' cut a garter, also placed there beside it. But none had ever heard where the entrance to this enchanted hall was, till the farmer at Sewingshields, about fifty years since, was sitting knitting on the ruins of the castle, and his clew fell, and ran downwards through a rush of briars and nettles, as he supposed, into a deep subterranean passage. Full in the faith that the entrance into King Arthur's Hall was now discovered, he cleared a vaulted passage, followed, in his darkling way, the thread of his clew. The floor was infested with toads and lizards, and the dark wings of bats, disturbed by his unhallowed intrusion, flitted fearfully around him. At length his sinking courage was strengthened by a dim, distant light, which, as he advanced, grew gradually brighter, till, all at once, he entered a vast and vaulted hall, in the centre of which a fire without fuel, from a broad crevice in the floor, blazed with a high and lambent flame, that showed all the carved walls and fretted roof, and the monarch and his queen and court reposing around in a theatre of thrones and costly couches. On the floor, beyond the fire, lay the faithful and deep-toned pack of thirty couple of hounds; and on a table before it the spell-dissolving horn, sword, and garter. The farmer reverently, but firmly, grasped the sword, and as he drew it leisurely from its rusty scabbard, the eyes of the monarch and his courtiers began to open, and they rose till they sat upright. He cut the garter; and as the sword was being slowly sheathed the spell assumed its ancient power, and they all gradually sunk to rest, but not before the monarch had lifted up his eyes and hands, and exclaimed:

"'O, woe betide that evil day
On which this witless wight was born,
Who drew the sword, the garter cut,
But never blew the bugle-horn.'

Terror brought on loss of memory, and the farmer was unable to give any correct account of his adventure, or to find again the entrance to the enchanted hall."

We are also told: " To the north of Sewingshields, two strata of sandstone crop out to the day; the highest points of each ledge are called the King and Queen's Crag, from the following legend: King Arthur, seated on the farthest rock, was talking with his queen, who, meanwhile, was engaged in arranging her 'back hair.' Some expression of the queen having offended his majesty, he seized a rock which lay near him, and, with an exertion of strength for which the Picts were proverbial, threw it at her, a distance of about a quarter of a mile. The queen, with great dexterity, caught it upon her comb, and thus warded off the blow. The stone fell between them, where it lies to this very day, with the marks of the comb upon it, to attest the truth of the story. It probably weighs about twenty tons."

A little to the west of Sewingshields, the Black Dike, a ditch and earthwork of unknown antiquity, ran through a gap crossed by the wall. It is supposed to have been the boundary line between the kingdoms of Northumbria and Cumbria, and is said to stretch from the borders of Scotland through Northumberland and Durham into Yorkshire.

The part of the country around Sewingshields appears to have had a bad reputation in former times. One depression on the ridge was so much frequented by the freebooters of the middle ages that it was called Busy Gap, and a "Busygap rogue" was a well-known name of reproach. Camden, writing in 1599, says, " that he dare not proceed into those parts from Carvoran, being afraid of the rank robbers hereabouts." Another ancient writer, speaking of the "Waste" to the north of the wall, says: "It would be impossible for a man to live there even half an hour. Vipers and serpents innumerable, with all other kinds of wild beasts, infest that place, and, what is most strange, the natives affirm that if any one should pass the wall he would die immediately, unable to endure the unwholesomeness of the atmosphere. Death also, attacking such beasts as go thither, forthwith destroys them . . . . . They say that the souls of men departed are always conducted to this place, but in what manner I will explain immediately, having frequently heard it from men of that region relating it most seriously, although I would rather ascribe their asseverations to a certain dreamy faculty which possesses them."

Bidding adieu to Sewingshields and its traditionary lore, the traveller will enter the military road running from Carlisle to Newcastle, at the point close to an earthen camp called "Brown Dikes." A long tract of comparatively level country is now traversed, where little of the wall remains; but the north ditch, vallum, and modern military road run close together, and parallel with each other for about 6 miles, the road for most of the distance being upon the very foundation of the wall. Here, for 4 or 5 miles, the vallum will be the principal object of attraction, for its proportions are truly formidable, the ditches being deep and the mounds high. Hodgson, speaking of this part, says: "Over Tepper-moor, for a long way, all the works of the vallum are remarkably bold and distinct. The ditches of both works dug out of a strong substratum of basalt, and with huge masses of that rock strewn by their side, form one of the boldest and most remarkable features of the whole line of the wall . . . . One block of basalt, lying on the north side of the fosse, now 'split,' probably by the 'winter's frost,' into three pieces, which, from the parallel positions they lie in, have evidently been raised in one mass, measures not less than 165 cubic feet, and weighs more than 13 tons. Was it raised by levers and burs on rollers, up an inclined plane ? or by a crane, in a rope or chain ? It has no mortise in it for a luis."

After having travelled on the road 3 miles from Sewingshields, some desolate looking heaps of overgrown rubbish are observed on the ground on the right, the remains of a Roman station, supposed to be "Procolitia," now called Carrowburgh. Some distance farther the road leaves the wall for a few yards; and a portion of the latter, about 100 yards in extent, is observed on the left, in a very promising state, and also the remains of a mile castle. The aspect of the country now gradually changes. The wild moorland tract on either side, over which fly a host of plovers, screeching as though resenting the intrusion of the stranger, gives way to enclosures, cultivated fields, and farmsteads clothed with trees; and the scenery in advance improves at every step, until the whole country becomes most beautiful with well-timbered rising ground in the distance. Presently the traveller reaches Walwick, and is agreeably surprised to find that he has entered a beautiful and well-wooded valley, through which flows the North Tyne. The trees around Chesters, the mansion of Mr. Clayton, are so large and thickly studded as to remind one of the grand homes of the English aristocracy. When the river is reached, where the road crosses the stream by a handsome stone bridge, the inn is seen close by, on the left; a large, well-managed house, where every comfort can be had; and on the opposite side of the river is Chollerford Railway station, on the Border Counties Railway.

Whilst at Chollerford the tourist should make a slight détour and visit Swinburne and Chipchase Castles, which are only 2 or 3 miles distant, to the north.

Before crossing the river and proceeding on the journey, the Roman station of Cilurnum must be seen. It is situated five minutes' walk from the inn, in the Chesters park, on the west side of the stream. Some of the walls, gateways, and buildings have been laid bare within the last few years, and present features of special interest; among them are a vaulted chamber and remains of baths. Several important inscriptions, sculptures, and other relics found in the station are preserved in the adjoining mansion.

After proceeding from the inn for half a mile along a footpath, through a plantation by the east side of the river, a sight is presented to the stranger which will probably impress him more with the magnificence of Imperial Rome than any other remains in Great Britain. It having been suspected that here was the foundation of a bridge on the line of the wall, the accumulated earth was cleared away at the bidding of the owner, Mr. Clayton. The result was that hundreds of large blocks of well-shaped freestone were exposed to view, placed in the exact position they originally occupied, and forming a massive abutment for what must have been a large and beautiful bridge.

The masonry is superb, the stone being neatly dressed, and fitting closely to each other; the burying of the abutment under silt having preserved it in astonishing freshness. The facing stones are tastefully ornamented with feathered tooling. All have been placed by the aid of the luis, and have been bound together by rods of iron imbedded in lead, the grooves for the rods, and in some places the lead, remaining. In the northern part there are still five courses of facing stones, giving a height above the foundation course of 6 feet. The face of the abutment, from which the roadway of the bridge would spring, is parallel with the stream, and about 22 feet long; but the sides are bevelled off so as the better to resist the thrust and the eventual recoil of the waters. The extant northern bevelled edge is about 53 feet in length; the southern about 80. The river has retired from the eastern side, with this effect, that the eastern abutment stands now high and dry, whilst the western foundations are submerged and in far less complete a state of preservation. Imbedded in the centre of the abutment is a piece of masonry of the exact form of a pier. It is supposed that this pier once stood in the river (which has always shown a tendency to trend westward), and formed one of the piers of the original bridge. Several stones among the *débris* will repay minute examination. Amongst them is one about 4 feet in length, resembling an axle-tree. It has orifices as if for receiving handspikes. Its use is not known. There is also a circular shaft, about 9 feet long and 2 feet in diameter, which has several peculiarities. The platform of the bridge was carried over three water piers, two of which, under certain lights and in favourable condition of the river, can be seen in its bed. One lies now buried on the eastern bank. The western abutment has been of the same form and construction as the other, but is now quite submerged. Mr. Clayton, in a paper in the 'Archæologia Æliana,' says: "Those who have seen the magnificent remains of the Pont du Gard (justly the pride of Gallia Narbonensis) lighted by the glorious sun of Languedoc, may think lightly of these meagre relics of the bridge of Cilurnum, under the darker skies of Northumberland; but it may be safely affirmed that the bridge over the Gardon does not span a lovelier stream than the North Tyne, and that so much as remains of the masonry of the bridge of Cilurnum leads to the conclusion that

P

this bridge, as originally constructed, was not inferior in solidity of material and excellence of workmanship to the mighty structure reared by Roman hands in Gaul."

When clearing the rubbish from the abutment of the bridge a portion of the wall was laid bare. It is 6 feet 4 inches thick, and 8 feet 8 inches high; a piece 10 or 12 feet long being exposed. This terminates in a square castle or tower, standing on the abutment of the bridge, and now about 8 feet high.

Leaving the bridge, the direction of the wall eastwards may be traced through the adjoining field by slightly elevated ground. When over the railway two or three fields have to be crossed, and then the grounds of Brunton, the residence of Major Waddilove, are entered. Here a portion of the north fosse is boldly developed, and a few yards of the wall, 7 feet high, and presenting nine courses of facing stones. Leaning against the wall are two Roman altars, one 5 feet long. In front of the house the military way is entered, and on the top of the ground the north ditch and a small portion of the wall are visible on the right. Presently the ditch crosses to the left-hand side of the road, and becomes very wide and deep.

Somewhere in this neighbourhood, Cadwallo, a king of the Britons, was defeated, about the year 633, by Oswald, King of Northumberland. Oswald was a convert to Christianity, and established a bishopric on Lindisfarn, or Holy Island. He erected many churches and convents, and after his death was looked upon as a saint. It is said that when the battle was about to commence, Oswald erected the sign of the holy cross, and on his knees prayed to God that He would assist His worshippers in their great distress. The cross being made in haste, and the hole dug in which it was to be fixed, the King himself, full of faith, laid hold of it, and held it with both his hands till it was set fast by throwing in the earth; and this done, raising his voice, he cried to his army: "Let us all kneel, and jointly beseech the true and living God Almighty, in His mercy, to defend us from the haughty and fierce enemy, for He knows we have undertaken a just war for the safety of our nation." All did as he had commanded, and accordingly, advancing towards the enemy, they obtained the victory.

The distance from Chollerford to Newcastle is 21 miles, and during almost the whole of the way the road runs on the very site of the wall in a straight undeviating course over hill and dale; traces of the north fosse being close to on the left, and the vallum on the right, most of the way. The foundation stones of the wall are often visible under the traveller's feet, but the only places in which it is observed standing above ground are at Heddon-on-the-Wall, 7 miles from Newcastle, where it is in the bottom of a thorn fence for 15 or 20 yards; at Dean House, 2 miles farther east, in the garden close to the main road, are parts of the wall and gateway of a mile castle; and at Denton Burn, 3½ miles from Newcastle, is a strip, about 8 yards long and 3 or 4 feet high, which is now enclosed by some wooden railing.

There are slight traces of Roman stations at Halton Chesters (Hunnum); Rutchester (Vindobala); and Benwell (Condercum); and another station would probably exist at Harlow hill. At Halton Chesters, Watling Street is supposed to have crossed the line of the wall. It was the main eastern road running from England to Scotland.

Although there are few traces of the wall after leaving Chollerford, the vallum and north ditch are often in a very perfect state; and the walk is very enjoyable—good views being obtained over a wide extent of cultivated country. About 6 miles from Newcastle the colliery district is entered; other collieries have been passed a short distance farther back, but they have been out of sight in the vale on the right, through which flows the Tyne, and where is the railway. The traveller is now passing near the birthplace of the Stephensons, and after dwelling so long on the Roman antiquities his mind will naturally revert to the wonderful nineteenth century, and the mighty effects likely to be brought about by the agency of steam and railways.

In the busy streets of Newcastle, and amidst the shipping, the collieries, and the engineering and chemical works along the Tyne, he will feel rather out of place when busy with his antiquarian researches.

Newcastle is supposed to have been the Roman station of Pons Ælii, but few traces remain. A bridge is supposed to have crossed the Tyne here. A considerable portion of the old town wall remains, and some of it appears to have been built of Roman stones, perhaps upon the site of the old Roman walls. At the bottom of Clayton Street, not far from the castle, and only two minutes' walk from the railway station, is a long high strip; and close to the central station is another portion, said to be Roman, and which can be seen from the entrance gates of the railway.

Wallsend, which stands on the Tynemouth line of rails, is about 4 miles from Newcastle, farther down the north bank of the river, and there the wall is said to have ended. About fifty years ago remains of the wall could be traced the whole of this distance, but now it has vanished, and only the north ditch is indistinctly traced from Byker Hill to Carville Hall, or Cousin's House, at Wallsend. The station is supposed to be Segedunum, and to have been where is now a Methodist chapel, and an old colliery, and the wall is thought to have stretched down to the brink of the river. The coast at Tynemouth is 6 miles distant.

LOCAL NAMES.

The place-names of the district treated of in this book are principally derived from the Celtic or Ancient British, the Roman, Saxon, Danish, Norse or Icelandic, and Norman languages. Though, to the general reader, the nomenclature of a country may seem at first sight to present but few attractions as a subject of study, yet the pursuit is not without a fascination of its own for those whose leisure and inclination lead them to enter upon it; while its importance in an ethnological point of view cannot be overlooked by the historian. Place-names may be regarded as pages of history embroidered with the borders of romance. Celtic names people our imagination with the stately Druid, and the free-limbed, fierce, fantastically painted warrior. Roman names appeal to our constructive faculties, and call before the mind's eye disciplined armies and massive buildings. Saxon names excite our rural tastes, and wrap us in dreams of waving corn-fields, flowery meadows, and forest glades; while Danish and Norwegian names present us with pictures of daring enterprise and ruthless bloodshed. Instead of indulging in fancies such as these, however, the student must turn to the fountain-heads of history—place-names—and endeavour to convert these stagnant pools into rippling streams of etymology. The Celts were a prehistoric race who had settled in Britain at a period long anterior to its invasion by the Romans nearly 2000 years ago. Cæsar, in his Commentaries, furnishes us with scattered notices of their habits of life, dress, customs, and modes of warfare. They themselves are silent, except that they have bequeathed to us valuable fragments of history in the names of our rivers, glens, and mountains. A careful study of these, the oldest place-names in Britain, has revealed to us much that must otherwise have remained unknown in the psychological and mental characteristics of the race; for these names are, as it were, their fossilized thoughts, ideas, and impressions. They were not satisfied with giving to rivers, mountains, and glens, names merely to be identified by, but they embodied in these names the physical characteristics of each mountain and glen, and the character and habits of the streams. The mountains still retain their nomenclatural distinguishing features; and though the glens by the march of modern agricultural progress may have lost something of the poetry of their names, the streams still retain in their names the rudiments of Celtic song. They are sluggish, rapid, or winding, as they were thousands of years ago. What a freshness and fragrance have these Celtic names about them, and what pictures do they present to us of primitive nomadic life! From our imperfect knowledge of the original elements and structure of the Celtic tongue, as well as from the attrition it has undergone by the lapse of time, the names bequeathed to us by these early settlers may often seem obscure and partially unintelligible, but where they have been successfully broken up and analyzed, they have been found to contain the elements of poetry, history, and striking topographical word-painting.

Our next name-givers were the Romans, but they came and left as conquerors, and there scarcely remains a single name-record on the physical features of the country they subdued to attest the truth of history as to their lengthened occupancy. Imperial Rome simply intersected our island with a war-trail of names, which we find in the remains of the marvellous works they left behind them—their stations, fortresses, walls, bridges, aqueducts, and roads.

Then came the bold adventurous Anglo-Saxons to conquer, colonize, absorb, and name. They seized upon the country and made for themselves a new home; they enclosed the *Ham*, and called it by their name; they did not merely give their homes a name, but they embalmed that sacred name in their hearts, as a shrine of family happiness; they did not merely enclose fields, but they also introduced the sacred principle of property. Judging from the names of its towns, villages, and single homesteads, Northumberland is pre-eminently the land of Saxon settlements. The purely Saxon suffixes, *ham*, *haugh*, *ing*, *law*, *ley*, *shaw*, *ton*, and *wick* alone are found in more than one-half the names furnished by a modern directory of the county, and a closer comparison would probably show that fully two-thirds are of Saxon origin. Taylor remarks that the universal prevalence throughout England of names containing the word *ham* gives us the clue to the real strength of the Anglo-Saxon character.

" The grand old *homes* of England,
How beautiful they stand."

But the time came when the Saxons in turn had to fight for the sanctity of their homes with another fierce and warlike race of invaders, pirates, and plunderers—the Danes. And here again we are not only able to follow the track of the invaders, but to mark their permanent settlements in the land. Though the part of the country under notice was repeatedly subject to the incursions of the Danes, being laid waste, we learn, as far west as Carlisle, in the year 875, and though Northumberland especially, still retains strong Scandinavian traces, both in the physical characteristics of its people and in its dialect, yet comparatively few place-names exist to bear out and confirm the facts of history. This may probably be accounted for by the fact that the country was thickly peopled before the Danes appeared on the scene, as well as that the two contending races, being originally of the same stock, and speaking kindred languages, would the sooner coalesce and become welded into one people. Wherever a Danish name does occur it seems rather to point to a village settlement than to an isolated homestead, as if they were obliged to keep together in order to hold what they had seized amid a hostile settlement. To the Danes we are indebted for one hallowed term in our nomenclature round which all hearts can gather—Kirk; and if they were not the inventors of secret writing—the Runes—they at least perfected and used them down to the time of the Conquest, as is proved by the Runic pillar at Bewcastle. The Scandinavian pirates—Old Norse Vikings—the Norwegians, came at last like an inundation; they were not content with living among a hostile race on sufferance, but fought, conquered, and took possession of the soil, and imprinted their own nomenclature on the geographical features of the district which they had seized upon. By the time of the tenth century they had effected various settlements among the Western islands and headlands of Scotland, and pushing southward had established their headquarters in the Isle of Man. One stream seems to have been diverted thence from the main channel eastward, and to have overrun Cumberland and Westmorland, where, judging by the prevailing place-names in that portion of these two counties known as the Lake District, they must have permanently settled down. Curiously enough, as far as we can be guided by the evidence of place-names, they seem not to have overlapped into Northumberland, for there is a sharp philological demarcation at the county boundary. The Norwegian test-words, *force, garth, thwaite,* &c., which are so abundant in Cumberland, occur only in a very few instances on the Northumberland side of the border. This brings us to the last but most important conquest in our national history, that of the Normans. At this eventful period this part of England appears to have been so completely filled in with place-names, that no space was left to imprint their nomenclature upon the soil. We find a few names referable to Norman sources, but these chiefly designate either the stronghold of the baron or the richly endowed monastery.

To summarize our notes, it may be observed that Celtic names are mostly to be found in the names of our rivers, glens, and mountains: Roman, in those of the walls, fortresses, bridges, and roads; Anglo-Saxon, in homesteads and enclosures; Danish and Norwegian, in towns, villages, and forest clearings; and Norman, in castles and abbeys. Except through the medium of place-names, we have no means of tracing the settlements of these different peoples, especially now that they have become blended into a homogeneous race, and speak a common language which has already made for itself a home in every quarter of the globe.

ALPHABETICAL LIST OF THE PRINCIPAL ROOTS FOUND IN THE NAMES OF PLACES IN NORTHUMBERLAND AND CUMBERLAND.

ABBREVIATIONS.—C., *Celtic*; A.S., *Anglo-Saxon*; D., *Danish*; N., *Norse.*

All, C., white, and Aon, a contraction of Afon, C., water. Irish, Abhainn, pronounced Avan; Manx, Awin; and modern English, Avon. The Allen, a tributary of the Tyne; the Aln, as in Alnwick; and the Ellen, in Cumberland, all signify the white or clear river.

Beck, D., a stream, a river. The term beck for river is almost of universal application in Cumberland; in Northumberland *beck* is generally supplanted by A.S. *burn*,—as Cald*beck*, Hartley*burn*.

Brough, burgh, burg, bury, A.S., a fortified place, a stronghold; derived from A.S. beorgan, to shelter or hide; hence to bury. Brough, in Westmorland; Burgh-on-Sands.

But, N., a boundary. Garbut Hill; the But-of-the-Bog. In a fierce contest about a boundary between two lords, a commissioner from London settled the meaning of this word.

By, D., a dwelling, village, or town. Icelandic, byr, an abode. Scotby, Bywell, Byershall.

Cam, C., crooked or bending. Cambeck, in Cumberland; Borcam, Northumberland.

Car or *Caer*, C., a fortress. Carlisle, Carvoran (the great fortress), Carlatton.

Carr, D., marshy ground. Thornhope Carr, War Carr, Prestwick Carr, &c.

Cath, C., a strife, battle, contest. Catstairs on the Roman Wall; Catstones, North Tyne; Catlan Beacon, in Allendale.

Chester, the Anglicized Latin castra, a station, camp, or fortress. The Roman stations on the Northumberland portion of the Wall are called chesters; those on the Cumberland portion take the name of castle. Compare Bew *castle* with Black *chesters*.

Crag; Scotch, *craig*; and Irish, *carrig*, a rock, as in Carrick Fergus, Castle Carrock, Craighead, Croglin (the rocky stream). *See* Linn.

Den, A.S., a deep-wooded valley, a dean; as Denton, Denwick.

Dodd, N., primarily a member, a limb; hence applied to a lesser mountain. Humble Dodd, Dodd Rig.

Drum, C., a ridge; Irish, *druim*; Manx, dreem. Drumburgh is either the fortified place, or, according to the old spelling, Drumbogh, simply the ridge along the marsh.

Dun, Don, C., a hill fort. Haydon Bridge, Wardon.

Dwr, C., water; Gaelic and Erse, dur, water. Enters largely as a component into river names throughout Europe. Gild*er*dale.

Fell, N., a moor, hill, or mountain. The term is used throughout both counties to signify hilly or mountainous ground. Tindale Fell, Cross Fell.

Force, N., a waterfall; Icelandic, forsa, to rush furiously. In the Lake District a waterfall is termed a force, as Scale Force, Nent Force, Ashgill Force, Alston. In Norway the waterfalls are known as fosses. Wordsworth revived the use of this and a few other old expressive words peculiar to the north of England.

Ford, A.S., a river passage. Slaggyford, Chollerford. Ford as a suffix in towns on the sea-coast is of Norse origin, and signifies an arm of the sea; a frith, a passage; as Deptford, Wexford, &c.

Garth, N., primarily a fence or hedge, thence an enclosure. A garden is a place enclosed or guarded. Wraygarth. The Anglo-Saxon form is yard, or geard.

Gate, D. gata, a street or road. Picts-gate or Maidenway. The Anglo-Saxon *geat* means a gate. A common saying among the peasantry of Cumberland is, "I've been a weary *gate*," signifying a long tiresome journey.

Gill, N., a ravine. *Gil*sland, Gelderdale, gil, dur, C., water, dale, N.

Glen, C., a narrow valley; Welsh, glyn; Manx, glione. Glendue, the black or dark valley.

Graf, N., a grave. Thorngrafton, probably, the dwelling or village by the burial-place of some person of distinction called Thorn.

Hag, A.S., that which is hedged in; a coppice, a wood; as Moss Hag, Haggwood, Strand's Hagg. Hay and haigh (*infra*) are different forms, with wider significations, of the same root.

Ham, A.S., a home, a dwelling, village, town. "In Anglo-Saxon charters this suffix is frequently combined with names of families, never with the names of individuals" (*Taylor*). Beltingham, Addingham.

Haugh, Northumberland; holm, Cumberland; A.S. holm; a river island; a green plot of ground environed with water or lying along the winding banks of a river. The *holms* of Cumberland assume the name of *haughs* in Northumberland. In the latter county, along the banks of the North and South Tyne and their tributaries, a synonymous term, *eal* or *isle*, is very common. Midgeholme, Ashholme, Rotheryhaugh, Weydon Eals.

Hay, Haigh, A.S. *haga*, a hedge, a place enclosed or surrounded with a hedge. The hay was generally the chase, park, or place enclosed for hunting. Haydon Bridge.

Heugh or *sceugh*, N., a low hill, probably from N., haugr, and therefore identical with the Lake District *how;* a mound. Brokenheugh, Collarheugh Crag, Haresceugh, Northsceugh.

Hoe, N., a sepulchral mound. Icelandic, haug(r), a mound. Compare heugh, sceugh. Prudhoe in Knarsdale; Presthoe near Poltrossburn.

Hope, N., a place of refuge, a narrow valley between two hills. Birdhope, Blenkinshope, Snowhope, Hartsop.

Hurst, a thick wood. Taylor remarks, " The *hursts* and *charts* were the denser parts of the forest; the *leys* were the open forest glades where the cattle love to lie, and the *dens* were the deep-wooded valleys, and the *fields* were little patches of felled trees or land cleared in the midst of the surrounding forest." Hardhurst, Longhurst.

Ing, A.S., a meadow. *Ing* is also a Saxon patronymic denoting " the son of." In this latter sense it enters largely into the place - names of Northumberland. The Directory contains seventy-five such names. In Cumberland it occurs only two or three times. Killingworth, Bavington, &c.

Keld, D. kilde, a fountain; A.S. kild, a well; allied to " cool"; Danish, kulde, chilliness. Keldwell, source of the Glendue; Threlkeld.

Kemp, A.S., camp, combat; *cempa*, a soldier, warrior. Kempshaw Rigg, near Cardrew. The primary meaning is an open field or plain. This root is found in all the Teutonic dialects, and signifies a combat. German, kampf, a combatant; English, champion.

Kirk, D., a church. Very common in the parts of England settled by the Danes; seldom or never found in the purely Anglo-Saxon districts. Kirkhaugh, Kirkhouse, Kirkbride.

Knot, A.S., a rocky hill; as Knotwood, at Castle Carrock.

Law, A.S. hlœw, hlaw, a grave or barrow; a tract of gently-rising ground. Blakelaw, Merelaw, Butterlaw.

Ley, A.S. leah, an open place in a wood, a glade. Frequent in Northumberland place-names. Upwards of forty. Ridley, Headley, Lambley.

Lough, C., a sheet of water, a tarn, lake, &c. Welsh, *llwch*; Gaelic, loch; Erse, lough. Crag Lough, Coanwood Lough.

Man or *mœn*, C., a district; as Triermain Castle.

Nab, A.S., a beak, nose, neb; hence applied to a projecting rock. Weydon Nab, Nab Scar.

Nent, C., a valley. Nenthead.

Peel, C., a stronghold. Staward-le-Peel, Peel Craig. " While the Lords of the Marches reared for themselves castles like Langley, the commonalty took refuge in a class of fortified dwellings called peel houses" (*Bruce's* ' *Wallet Book* ').

Pen, ben, C., a head; hence, a hill, a mountain. Penpeugh, Benwell, Penrith.

Raise, cairn of stones, a tumulus. Hespeck Raise; the Raise, Alston; Dunmail Raise.

Rew, C., a moor. Wardrew, Cumrew.

Rigg, A.S., the back, the ridge, a long hill. The ridges of low fells in both Cumberland and Northumberland are termed riggs. To the north of Gilsland we have Peat Rigg, Burnt Rigg, White Rigg, Black Rigg.

Ross, C., a promontory. Rosehill. This bold promontory, on which were the remains of an ancient camp, was ruthlessly reduced by the railway company on the construction of the Newcastle and Carlisle Railway.

Shaw, A.S. sceaga, a shady place, a wood, a brake. The Shaw's Hotel, Bradshaw (brad, broad), Birkshaw, Stagshaw.

Shield, A.S. scyld, a shield, shelter, protection. In Cumberland the *shield* takes the form of *scale*, and across the Scotch border it passes into *shealing*. These different forms of the word are from the same root and are of the same import. Like the shields in Northumberland, the scales of Cumberland are numerous; both were originally shepherd's or herdsmen's huts, erected for the shelter of both men and cattle in the outlying districts. Scaleby, Skelgill, Carrshields, Shilbottle, Winter Shields, Shield-in-the-Wall, Sewing Shields.

Stoke, A.S., a place surrounded with stocks or piles, i.e. stockaded. Stocksfield, Stokeld Burn, Stockbridge, Greystoke.

Syke, A.S. sich, a furrow, gutter, watercourse. The term is applied to a marshy or boggy watercourse liable to be dried up in summer, and is allied to "soak" and "suck." Several places on the Moors are known as "Candlesieve Sykes," showing they were resorted to for the sieves or rushes, the pith of which was used for rushlights. Wylie Syke.

Tain or *tian*, C., running water, a river. Hence the name of several British rivers. Tynes in Northumberland, Tyne in Haddington, Teign in Devon.

Tarn, N., a small lake; Icelandic, *tiorn*, from taaren to trickle, allied to "*tear.*" The Northumberland lakelets are all termed *loughs*. Blea (blue) Tarn, Redtarn, Talkin Tarn, Tindale Tarn, Tarn Wadling, in Cumberland. Crag Lough, Broomlee Lough.

Ton, A.S. tynan, to hedge; tun or ton, a hedge, an enclosed place, a dwelling, then a village or town. In Scotland a simple farmstead is still called a "*toun.*" Brampton, Angerton.

Tre or *tri*, C., a house or village. Trewick, Triermain.

Whelt, C., to beat. A word still common in the dialect. "Give him a whelt." Glenwhelt.

Wick, A.S. wic, a suffix denoting a station or dwelling; then a village, a town. As in the case of ford and gate, there is a characteristic difference in the meaning of this term as applied by the Anglo-Saxons and the Norsemen. With the latter the *wick* was a station for ships, hence a bay or harbour. The names of towns on the sea-coast containing this suffix are of Norwegian or Danish origin. So of *gate;* with the Danes the gate was the road or passage along a place; with the Anglo-Saxons, a passage through a place, e. g. the town wall. See also the difference between Norse and Anglo-Saxon ford.

Worth, A.S., a close, field, or place warded or protected; of the same import with "ton." Taylor observes, " probably an enclosed homestead for the churls subordinate to the 'tun.'" Naworth, Warkworth.

Yard, A.S. gard, a hedge, enclosure, or place *girded* round. This is another term of the same import with garth, ton, and worth; all conveying the idea of protection.

RIVER NAMES AND PLACE-NAMES.

With the help of the foregoing general terms it is apprehended that our readers will have little difficulty in understanding the meanings of the greatest portion of the more common place-names, which it would be too tedious to enumerate in these pages. A short list of those of less obvious significance, gleaned from various sources, is subjoined. The pages of Hodgson, Nicholson, Burn, and Hutchinson furnish abundant etymologies of the two counties, but later researches based upon more correct philological principles show many of these to be too strained or fanciful to stand the test of criticism. In the preparation of this list of place-names the later and more reliable authorities, Taylor, Ferguson, and Sullivan, have been consulted.

River Names.

Allen, Ellen and *Aln*, all signify 'white water, or clear river.

Croglin, Crag (Linn, a deep pool), a waterfall. The rocky river.

Eden, of unsettled origin.

Esk, C. uisque, water. A common name for rivers in England and Scotland.

Gelt, C., loud sounding.

Gilderdale. Gill; dur, water; dale, a valley.

Hartleyburn. Sax. hart, a deer; ley, a glade; burn, a rivulet.

Irthing, C.; the twisting, wandering, or erring burn.

Knar, C., clear.

Tippal, C. ti, pwl, pool; spreading out.

Tyne, C. tain; rapid or hasty.

VALLEYS, ENCLOSURES, DWELLINGS, &c.

Allendale. The valley of the white river.

Alston, anciently Aldenston. A.S.

Barhaugh, formerly *Berehalgh*. A.S. bere, barley. Barleyholm.

Bewcastle. The Castle of Bueth, who was lord of the district before the time of the Conquest.

Birdoswald, properly *Burdoswald*. A.S. burh. The borough or town of Oswald.

Blenkinsopp. A.S. hope. The hope or valley of the Blenkings.

Cargo. C. carrig, and how, a hill.

Carraws, Carraburgh. C. carrig, a rock.

Coanwood, formerly *Collingwood*. C. collen, the hazel tree.

Corbridge stands at the confluence of the Cor with the Tyne. Possibly from C. cwr, steep, precipitous.

Cramel Linn, pron. Crau-mel-lin: crau, the softened form of crag; mool, mel, a fell; and linn, a waterfall.

Featherstone. Difference of opinions exists among etymologists respecting the origin of this name. Fader's-ton, provincially feyther's, i. e. father's town—or from Feadar, a proper name, has found most acceptance. The following note in MS. by the late Lord Wallace was found in a copy of Hodgson's 'History of Northumberland': " Two persons are mentioned in the Saxon Chronicles; one a military leader, by whom all the country now called Alston Moor was held under the name of Feuerstein, which means Firestone. It next appears as Fethirstane. When arms were first taken they took the Feather, and it is probable that this afterwards introduced Feather, which has led to the confusion in the name and its origin."

Haltwhistle. In all the early authorities the orthography is Hautwysel, Hautwisel, or Hautwycsell. The derivation of this name still remains a puzzle to etymologists. In its modern form it would seem to imply the "high boundary." Hodgson adopts a Norman derivation—haut, high; wes, watch; and hill—the high watch-hill or beacon. A more probable explanation has been suggested. The earliest mention of the name occurs in a deed of the date 1307. It is there written Altewis. This would refer to a Celtic source—alt, high; uisque, water; with the later addition by the Saxons of selig, blessed, contracted to sel or sill—i. e. the sacred place or hill on the high water.

Hexham, in ancient documents Hextoldham and Hextoldesham. Hext, A.S. for hehst, highest, as next, for nighest. This would give, the highest, old, ham; or, the home by the brook Hextol (height of source).

Kella and *Kelsick.* Cold Law, or hill, and Cold Syke.

Kirkaugh receives its name from the situation of the church on the haugh or river-formed land.

Kirklinton. D. kirk; A.S. ton; and Line, the name of the local stream.

Lanercost. Welsh, llan, a church. Llanerch originally signified a glade in a forest.

Maidenway. C. maiden, raised, elevated. The raised or high way. Near Keswick one of the mountains is called Maiden Moor.

Midgeholme. A.S. myge, mygge, a small gnat.

Naworth. Ger. neu, new; A.S. worth, which see. Sullivan remarks that Naworth and Newark have precisely the same meaning.

Netherby. A.S. nyther, lower, comparative of neath; D. by. Compare, Upper*by,* and Middle*by* across the Solway.

Pada burn, from padda, a frog.

Pen peugh. C. pen, a hill; pou, a district.

Ridley. A.S., the ridded lea, i. e. land cleared of wood and stones.

Stapleton. A.S. stapul, a stake, that which is fixed; secondary meaning, a place to which merchants agreed to carry their commodities for sale or barter. A fair or market. Hence market town.

Walton, Wallhouses, Walbottle. A.S. botl (an abode), Walwick, Wallend. Walby, Wall, Wallbours, Wallshiels, Walltoun, Wallmill, Wallfoot, Wallhead, Welton, Benwell. Thirlwall, Oldwall, Wallknoll, and Heddon-on-the-Wall, all owe their names to their position along the course of the Roman Wall.

J. CLARK, Haltwhistle.
P. HARRISON, Keswick.

GEOLOGY.

LIKE steam and electricity, the science of geology was little known before the present century, and, like them also, it has had a wonderful influence in bringing about several great and rapid changes with regard to political, religious, social, and scientific subjects. Although the science is still in its infancy, it has numbered amongst its professors many eminent men, and theory after theory has been advanced and has then rapidly given way to others more consistent with ascertained facts. At one time all fossil deposits, and past changes in the earth's crust, were referred to our Biblical Deluge. This idea having to be discarded, was succeeded by theories of awful universal cataclysms and catastrophes. Then the formation of valleys and hills came to be explained by the shrinking of different parts of the earth during the time when it was supposed to be cooling from an original molten state. To account for the different strata and the fossils they contained, it was supposed that there had been vast epochs, during which time there were deposited over the whole globe particular rocks containing fossils of living beings peculiarly adapted to the state of the earth at each era. In this way, we were told, the whole surface was alternately covered with coal, lime, chalk, slate, sandstone, &c. At the present day it is universally acknowledged by our greatest geologists, and is considered a fundamental axiom of the science, that different portions of vast continents have been in the past, and are still gradually rising and sinking by the force of internal heat, and in this way only, they say, can they explain the deposition of the different strata, and the irregularity of the earth's crust. In my Guides to the Lake District and the Isle of Man, I ventured to regard this hypothesis as being as absurd as any of the others; and after much study I am still convinced that my theory, which maintains the stability of the land and the instability of the sea, is the only true basis upon which to build the science of geology.

The following extracts from my Lake Guide will enable the reader to see in what way I explain that the sea level changes, and brings about the irregularities on the earth's surface, by a never-ceasing movement similar to what is now daily taking place in every part of the globe.

"It would seem that although the ocean currents might, by scooping out the bed of the sea, and depositing the matter in other parts, alter the relative level of earth and water, they could not alter the original level of the sea, and no mountains or continents could appear. But when we take into account the all-important fact that the earth is a round body, we presently find that we might have mountains and continents as high as those at present existing. Whilst reasoning on this subject we must not forget that relatively the greatest irregularities on the earth's surface are not more than the speck on an orange.

"For the sake of illustration let us suppose the outer crust of the globe perfectly smooth, and covered with an ocean 1000 feet deep. It is clear that the heat from the sun would cause currents in the water which would scoop out from one part of the bed and deposit in other parts. If the whole of the ocean in the southern hemisphere were, from this cause, to become 2000 feet deep, the earthy matter thus removed would be deposited in the northern hemisphere, and the whole of the latter half of the globe would be dry land. The water would first leave the north pole and gradually sink to the equator. If, during this operation, currents also existed in the northern hemisphere, mountains and valleys would be left; and here and there inland seas might exist, apparently below the sea level. In this way we should have all the inequalities that we find on the surface of the globe; deep valleys and high mountains in the sea corresponding with those on land. A never-ceasing change going on throughout the globe, the water gradually leaving one continent and overflowing another. When land appeared above the water it would have all the irregularities of surface caused by currents, tides, and innumerable other agencies. In fact, given a globe, an ocean, heat from the sun, and immeasurable periods of time, almost everything revealed by geology is easily and quite naturally explained.

"It thus appears that the principal irregularities on the surface of the earth may have been caused without the agency of subterranean heat; but it is necessary, in order to establish the theory, to show that the contortions of strata do not require for their origin any upheaving force.

"It is obvious that if the Lake District were now to be sunk under the sea, with mountain precipices and slopes of every imaginable shape, and after having deposited upon it volcanic matter, lime, chalk, sandstone, or any other material, the waters should again subside, after currents had in places washed away and formed precipices in the new deposit, the geologist would observe that the new strata would be infinitely contorted, and lie at every possible angle. Supposing a deposit of sandstone on Skiddaw and in the Derwent valley, it would slope down the mountain side at every angle, from one degree to 90. In the valley and near the foot of the mountain it would be horizontal. If the whole valley were filled up to the height of the highest part of Skiddaw, it would then also lie over the summit in a horizontal layer. Supposing that the top of the mountain was again exposed to view by part of the deposit being washed away, it would appear as though the mountain had been upheaved and thrust through the sandstone, and the latter would show signs of having been tilted by that apparent movement, although in reality it was tranquilly deposited on the side of the mountain. In this way, by taking into account an infinite variety of changes, may the inclination of strata be explained without requiring the agency of an upheaving force."

It must not be supposed from the above that I overlook the fact that there are internal fires, the origin of volcanoes and earthquakes, which have in various places, and at different periods of the earth's history, emitted lava and ash that have overspread large tracts of country. What I maintain is that these are mere rivers of fire which here and there shake, or make way through, the crust of the globe, but whose effect is infinitesimal when compared with the changes brought about by the unceasing currents, tides, and waves of the ocean.

Some persons will jump to the conclusion, that whether the changes are brought about by fire or by water, the result is the same; but such is not the case. By fire we should have primitive unstratified rocks pushed up from the interior, and the stratified resting upon them; whereas by the agency of water we know of no primitive unstratified rock; but beneath the oldest rocks known to us we must expect there exists another series of still older stratified rocks. By this reasoning, if we could pierce through our Silurian slate mountains, we might meet with layers of sand, lime, and coal, and all strata known to us; and therefore, if this theory be correct, it is of vast importance that it should be understood and acknowledged.

Once having admitted the possibility of a change of sea level, it is astonishing how simplified the study of geology becomes, and with what ease it is explained how, by a never-ceasing process extended over an immeasurable period of time, the different rocks have been deposited in regular strata from the lowest known depths to the tops of the highest mountains, and this, as a rule, without the agency of internal fires.

The presence of granite will by many be considered to militate against this theory; but it must be borne in mind that although it has been almost the universal belief of geologists that granite is the most primitive rock on the globe, and that it has been pushed through the superincumbent strata by the force of subterranean fires, this theory appears likely soon to be exploded, and to be superseded by one which accounts for the formation of the granites principally by water and crystallization, and to take from that rock the proud pre-eminence of being the most ancient and the parent of all others.

Geology being a science of modern origin, and having been studied principally in the British Isles, our first geologists naturally fell into the error of supposing that the order of superposition which was met with in the strata of Great Britain would be applicable to the whole crust of the globe; and finding granite in places beneath the oldest British strata, the Cambrian and Silurian, they at once jumped to the conclusion that it was at one time the only rock existing on the globe, and now underlies all others.

A wider experience has shown that this is not the case, and that with time and strata in geology, just as with distances and stars in astronomy, it is utterly impossible for us to arrive at the beginning. The oldest rocks at present known, the Laurentian, are found to be composed principally of limestone, and to contain fossils, so that it was undoubtedly formed in an ocean which teemed with life, and was probably surrounded by continents covered with vegetation and tenanted by innumerable kinds of animals. The quiet and never-ceasing operations of nature were undoubtedly the same then as now, and the continents, like those existing at the present day, had been formed at the bottom of an ocean by the disintegration of others previously existing.

Whether man has lived on the globe during these innumerable ages we may perhaps never ascertain, for as almost all rocks have been formed under the sea, the preservation of the bones of animals is very rare; but nothing that we know would preclude the possibility of his having existed during those far-off times, since in recent years his remains have been found in strata which must have been formed hundreds of thousands of years.

Another false idea which is still largely believed in by geologists is that the same kind of strata which is found in different parts of the globe was all deposited at the same epoch, and contains fossils of fishes, plants, or animals which became extinct after each particular era. Changes exactly similar to those of the present day have no doubt been taking place on the earth as far back as man will ever be able to penetrate; and in different tracts of the globe, but mostly under the ocean, are now being deposited every kind of strata with which we are familiar, and, in all probability, in many of them are now being imbedded plants and animals which have been thought to be extinct, and which we are acquainted with merely from our knowledge of geological fossil specimens. When we meet with a limestone, sandstone, chalk, slate, coal, or other strata, in distant parts of the earth, say Australia, similar to those in England, that is no proof that they are of the same age, even though they contain the same kind of fossils. It must be admitted that many species of animals, plants, and fishes found in a fossil state, now no longer live on our globe; but this must be expected when we see around us so many gradually disappearing from the face of the earth at the present day. Looking at geology in this light, we are compelled to admit that, whether or not the Darwinian theory of the origin of species be correct, the longest cycle in the past history of the earth that we can penetrate brings us no nearer to facts by which that theory can be proved or disproved than are to be met with in the life of the globe at the present day. In like manner our vistas into the past bring us no nearer the beginning of the actual history of the globe than the glance of the astronomer into the immensities of space enables him to approach either with telescope or in imagination the innumerable worlds that lie beyond his ken.

We have dwelt thus long on the broad general facts of geology, because we believe that no person can obtain a just appreciation of the geological structure and history of any portion of the earth's crust, without previously freeing his mind from those narrow views which too many entertain, who see in every elevation or mountain the result of the upheaving forces and subterranean fires, instead of the denuding effects of water resulting in the formation of the valleys. The following extracts from two eminent practical mining engineers, authors of standard books on the mines of the Alston Moor district, lend support to the remarks I have advanced. Westgarth Forster, speaking of the Newcastle coal-field, says: "The inequality of the surface does not affect the dip or inclination of the coal measures, and when they are interrupted, or cut off, by the intervention of a valley, they will be found on the sides of the opposite hills, at the same levels as if the beds had been continuous. . . . . . The conclusion is obvious, that the present irregularity of hill and dale has been occasioned by the partial destruction and dispersion of the uppermost rocky masses, which constitute the coal formation."

Mr. William Wallace says: "That the stratum which outcrops on one side of a valley, and is found on the contrary side, occupying its exact position between other layers of strata, was at some former period a continuous and unbroken sheet, no one who has paid attention to the subject doubts for one moment." Referring to the value of theory, he writes: "It is only in the school of Bacon that the mind can be properly disciplined for inquiries into the most difficult problems of geology and mineralogy. Habits of close observation must be combined with the intellectual power of conducting rigorous processes of inductive and deductive reasoning; and this power is only attained by profound study and reflection; by a long course of philosophic cultivation and logical habits of thinking. It may be safely affirmed that few working miners possess the requisite time and means for prosecuting such studies. Hence while the *art* of mining has attained great perfection, the *science* of mining scarcely exists, and the opinions of practical men on the subject are based upon an empiricism of the lowest order. . . . . I am convinced of the folly of pursuing such inquiries in the mazes of experience, without any theory, or guiding principle of causation." In the northern part of England treated on in this book, we see exemplified the false ideas entertained by many eminent geologists. The Pennine mountain chain, including Tindale Fell and Crossfell, they denominate the Pennine fault, and take for granted the erroneous theory that it was pushed up by heat above the surrounding country, whereas it is undoubtedly merely the relic of a vast tract which was much higher than the highest point now remaining; and the present irregularities of hills and valleys are the result of the denuding effect of water, in all probability occasioned principally when the land was beneath the ocean and subject to its currents.

Crossfell, and perhaps the whole of the Pennine mountain chain, rests conformably on the old red sandstone and conglomerate lying in the denuded hollows of the lower Silurian or Skiddaw slate rocks, the latter being visible in many of the valleys on the side of the mountain, especially to the west, in the direction of Penrith. The slate rocks are well developed in the Lake Country, and appear again in the Cheviot Hills, in Scotland, but they are not to be found in any part of the district around Carlisle or Gilsland, or the country traversed by the Roman wall. The old red sandstone is found in one or two small patches near the Ullswater Lake and at the base of Crossfell, but nearer than this we have no trace of it in the tract under our consideration. The fact that it lies in the hollows of the slate rock proves that the latter had undergone great denudation before the sandstone conglomerate was deposited.

The Pennine mountain chain, including the heights of Crossfell and Tindale Fell, the district around Alston Moor and Haltwhistle, and the country about Gilsland watered by the Irthing and the Tipalt, are composed of the strata known as the mountain or carboniferous limestone, which consists of different layers of limestone, sandstone, shale, and coal. In many places on the Pennine chain and around Alston it is covered with the millstone grit, which is composed of sandstone, shale, and two or three thin beds of coal. The sandstone being occasionally used for millstones explains the origin of the denomination of the group. The coal in the mountain limestone is worked in many places by horizontal shafts, but it is often of inferior quality, locally termed crow coal. In some places, however, deep pits are sunk, and a superior coal obtained. This is especially the case at Fourstones, Haltwhistle, Blenkinsop, and to the north of Tindale Fell, on the west side of Hartley Burn. In the Alston Moor district it is rich in veins of lead ore, and apparently ever since the time of the Romans it has been one of the principal mining districts in England. The mining operations have enabled the strata around Alston to be minutely studied, and practical and scientific mining engineers, such as Westgarth Forster and William Wallace, have written treatises on the subject. Forster gives a general section of the strata, including two hundred and forty different layers. Of these thirty are coal, with a total thickness of 50 feet. Wallace in his sections names sixty-four layers, and gives 1133 feet as sandstone, 1181 feet plate or shale, and 480 feet lime; but of course in no single spot are all these strata to be met with. Separate names, now well known in the district, are given to the different strata, such as Great Limestone, Melmerby Scar Limestone, Jew Limestone, Tynebottom Limestone, &c.; and mining engineers, when working in one of these, know of course what to expect below, and thus benefit by the past experience of others.

What are known by geologists as the true coal measures lie above the millstone grit. They branch inland from Newcastle in a narrow belt stretching as far as Lambley, at the north-eastern base of Tindale Fell. In some places near the east coast they are overspread by the magnesian limestone.

On the west side of the Pennine chain, the new red sandstone abuts against the carboniferous series, and stretches past Carlisle to the coast. It occupies the vale of the Eden, and is well developed on the banks of that river, and along the Caldew, Petteril, Esk, Cambeck, Gelt, and the Irthing as far as a point a short distance above Lanercost. Around the Solway Firth it is covered with sand, gravel, and peat.

In the midst of the strata of the carboniferous series there is said to be a layer of whinstone, and also a dyke of the same rock; and a great cliff-like ridge of whin runs from the river Tipalt to beyond Sewingshields, with the Roman wall on the top of it for about 10 or 12 miles. It is generally thought to be a basaltic rock, and various have been the conjectures as to its origin. My knowledge of it is very limited, but I have great doubts as to its being a basalt. The term *whin* is in this district often applied to hard sandstone, and wherever the true whin may be found, I imagine it will not have been pushed up, but be the remains of an ancient uneven surface of that rock, upon which the limestone and other strata have been regularly deposited. If it be of volcanic origin, it has probably been spread over an ancient sea bottom during the time of the deposition of the layers of carboniferous lime, coal, and sandstone. Mr. W. Wallace says: "The whin dyke causes no displacement of the strata, and with the exception of this dyke there are no indications that the district under consideration has ever been subjected to volcanic agency of a violent or spasmodic character." In a note in Westgarth Forster's book we read: "The author of the article 'Mine,' in Brewster's 'Encyclopædia,' says, in the sections which have been made of the Newcastle coal-field, the term *whin* is applied to many of the strata; these strata so named are, however, not *whin*, but are sandstones of the hardest kind. The misapplication of the name *whin* (or greenstone) has led mineralogists to wrong conclusions as to the coal formation of that district." In another part of Mr. Forster's book, when treating of a rock supposed to occupy among the carboniferous strata of Derbyshire the same position as the whin of Northumberland, and which is known by the name of toadstone, as it has the appearance of the back of a toad, it is stated in a note that it has never received the name of basalt, though it occasionally assumes its character and hardness.

Our doubts as to the volcanic origin of the *whin* also extend to the 90-fathom dyke, which is one of the principal geological phenomena of the Newcastle coal-field. Mr. Wallace tells us this dyke passes underneath the magnesian limestone without dislocating its beds; and Mr. Forster says: "The beds of the magnesian limestone pass over the 90-fathom dyke, which has occasioned in them no confusion or dislocation, so that there can be little hazard in stating that the beds of the magnesian limestone belong to a more recent formation than those of the coal-field." We extract the following paragraph from Sir Charles Lyell's 'Elements of Geology': "The very different levels at which the separated parts of the same strata are found on the different sides of the fissure, in some faults, is truly astonishing. One of the most celebrated in England is that called the '90-fathom dyke,' in the coal-field of Newcastle. This name has been given to it because the same beds are 90 fathoms (540 feet) lower on the northern than they are on the southern side. The fissure has been filled by a body of sand, which is now in the state of sandstone, and is called the dyke, which is sometimes very narrow, but in other places more than 20 yards wide. The walls of the fissure are scored by grooves, such as would have been produced if the broken ends of the rock had been rubbed along the plane of the fault. In the Tynedale and Craven faults, in the north of England, the vertical displacement is still greater, and the fracture has extended in a horizontal direction for a distance of 30 miles or more."

We must not quit this subject without giving the following extract from Mr. Wallace: "After a careful examination of the district, no one can doubt that the millstone grit which caps the mountains must have existed in an unbroken sheet over the valleys of Alston Moor. There is, however, reason to suppose that upon these must have reposed the coal measures. Certainly, on the north side of the 90-fathom dyke, the Newcastle coal-field is found thrown down and lying opposite to the millstone grit on the upper part of the mountain limestone, which renders it conclusive that a portion of the former, at least, was superimposed upon the latter at the time of the formation of this great dyke."

Few districts in England offer more facilities to the geologist for the study of the deposition of minerals than does that of Alston Moor, where he may pursue his studies in the very workshop of nature. Veins of lead ore are to be met with in almost every part of the wild, heath-clad moorlands between the Tyne, Allen, Wear, and Tees. For ages it has been a busy mining district, and was probably known to the Romans, who had so many camps in the neighbourhood along the line of the great wall.

Comparatively few old mines exist, for the sides of adits in a long course of time become pressed near each other, so much so that old miners suppose that works made even in very hard rock slowly contract their dimensions. That mines have been wrought and produced lead ore at a very remote period is evidenced by the pigs of lead which have from time to time been found at different places in the country. A valuable collection of these antiquities is in the British Museum. From these we gather that, as early as the year 44, pigs of lead were manufactured; but the earliest evidence bearing on this district dates from the reign of the Roman Emperor Domitian, A.D. 81. In 1734, two pigs of lead were found on Hayshaw Moor, 8 miles N.W. of Ripley, in the West Riding of Yorkshire, on which is an inscription as above indicated. These pigs are supposed to have been made from ore raised at Greenhow Hill, in Yorkshire, not far from the spot where they were found. It is remarkable that the shape of pigs of lead has varied little in the last 1800 years. The earliest example was found in Somersetshire; its weight is 163 lb. (11 stones 9 lb.), and length 24 inches, and so with all others deposited in the British Museum, they vary between 20 and 24 inches in length, and from 9 to 16 stones in weight. How the mineral was extracted at these early periods can only be surmised. No doubt the ore was, at the outset, exclusively obtained by open workings, quarry fashion, on the backs of the veins; gradually this method would give way to shallow shafts and short adits, and these again would be succeeded by more extended workings, until we have the pits of the present day hundreds of fathoms in depth; adits several miles in length; and galleries, sumps, rises, and all the other varieties of mining operations now common to important mining fields. The old miners displayed considerable sagacity in opening out the veins, and choosing those which seemed to afford the best prospect of yielding the greatest profit. This the modern miner finds to his disadvantage, when he comes upon the "old man," the local term for ancient workings. The numerous shaft heaps that may be seen on the line of all old worked veins, and on the course of ancient adits, where the distance apart is not more than from 10 to 20 or 30 yards, is evidence of the great amount of labour which must have been expended in mining in earlier times before the invention of gunpowder. In examining the narrow adits and cross cuts of ancient times, rarely exceeding 2 feet in width, we see with what skill they have been projected, and with what careful exactness and neatness they have been cut through the solid rock by the aid of the pick alone.

No person can visit the mines of Alston Moor without having his mind directed to the question as to the origin of minerals They have been thought by some to have been pushed up from the molten interior of the earth, and others have supposed them to be due to sublimations from beneath, and to be found *only* in those places where the exhalations effected a free passage upwards; the causes or conditions being of a deep-seated character far removed from observation. These notions are fast giving way, and will no doubt soon be obsolete. Mr. Wallace, speaking of Alston Moor, says: " So far as this district is concerned there is nothing to support the theory that lead is due to exhalations from beneath, or to matter injected in a fluid state among the consolidated sedimentary rocks."

It is now beginning to be acknowledged that minerals have been formed from above by crystallization and the percolation of water, similar to stalagmites and stalactites of the limestone caverns of the present day; and no one can give the matter thorough attention without coming to that conclusion. Whether the particular rocks in which they are enclosed have to do with their deposition is an open question. The same kind of ores, lead for example, we find in almost all kinds of rock; limestone, slate, granite, basalt, sandstone, shale, &c.; and therefore it would appear as though we must look for their origin to some external source. In the same mine, also, there are often a variety of minerals, and near together in the same rock are veins of different ores. Also we find one district rich in one mineral, and another in another. Some are only in limited areas on the globe, and others seem to be tolerably equally distributed over every continent. Veins are found in every strata, whether on the tops of the highest mountains, or at the greatest depths to which man has ever penetrated.

All these apparent irregularities may no doubt be satisfactorily accounted for, and reduced to order and natural sequence, if we can once clear our minds of the prejudices resulting from the unnatural explanations of the past, and prepare ourselves to look at the subject on broad principles, and to apply the ordinary operations of nature which we see taking place around us at the present day. We must never overlook the fact that the present land, the mountains and valleys, are mere skeletons of what they were in former times. That almost every part of dry land has been covered by different kinds of strata, perhaps thousands of feet higher than at present, and that the whole of the land has also been many times covered by the ocean, the waters of which are found to contain almost every known mineral. Mr. Wallace, neglecting to take these facts into account, has unfortunately built on a false basis what would otherwise no doubt have been a correct theory as to the origin of minerals. He endeavours to prove that the circulation of waters near the surface is most favourable to ore deposits, and that these are materially influenced by the present configuration of the surface land. Consequently he is at a loss when he finds veins on the very summits of mountains and deep in the bowels of the earth. He says: " In such situations, nearly on the top of the hills, it is not easy to conceive from what other source the baryta can be derived than from the enclosing rock; and the presence of this and many other substances of an anomalous character is probably due to laws of chemical combination as yet unknown, but the action of which may be still in daily operation." Again: " In some mining districts various kinds of metallic ores are found plentifully in veins at a great depth below the sea level. It is stated in the last edition of the 'Encyclopædia Britannica,' on the authority of R. W. Fox, Esq., that Tresavean Mine has gradually attained to the extraordinary depth of 2112 feet below the surface, or about 1700 feet below the level of the sea. The Consolidated Mines and several others in Cornwall have also attained a very great depth below the sea level. Professor Phillips observes that there appears to be no limit either to height above or depth below the sea which defines the productiveness of veins, though in some countries the higher, and in others the lower, situations are most favourable. Instances of metallic substances being found at great depths below the sea level militate against the law of causation advocated in the preceding chapters. Certainly a free circulation cannot be effected under conditions of this kind. Sir C. Lyell supposes a twofold circulation of terrestrial waters,—one caused by solar heat, and the other by heat generated in the interior of the earth. It is to the former that the metallic deposits in the veins of Alston Moor are connected in causation. If the circulation from the interior of our planet could really be proved to exist, it might be inquired whether or not it may have affected the deposition of metallic substances in other districts and in rocks of more uniform hardness. As before observed, the hypothesis of the water's ascending from the interior of our planet appears unphilosophical, and except in the case of volcanic agency has not been satisfactorily proved."

Cracks, fissures, and caverns must necessarily occur in every kind of rock, but in some more than others, by water and carbonic and other acids acting mechanically and chemically on the strata, by the shrinking of land during consolidation or increased pressure from above, or by sinking into the hollows formed by water beneath, and many other causes too numerous to mention. Allowing that water will percolate into these hollows, charged with different substances brought from the rocks above, or from those immediately around, it must be admitted that they will deposit crystals of different substances which will gradually fill up those hollows, and as the rocks and their components are changed, being swept away and replaced during countless ages, the substances in the water will change, and form different minerals, sometimes a variety in one cavity, or sometimes fill the whole with one and sometimes with another mineral. To account for different mineral veins being in close companionship in the same kind of rock, we have only to suppose that the fissures are formed at different periods, and therefore filled when the water would filter through charged with different materials. That veins have been so filled from above is evident, for they often contain pebbles and other extraneous substances, and Westgarth Forster relates the remarkable circumstance that a piece of wood, rather convex on one side, and having the appearance of a chip or piece broken from a tree, 6 inches in length and about 4 in breadth, not in a fossil state, was found in a vein 50 fathoms below the surface. It was surrounded with galena (lead). Mr. Forster states that Mr. Wilson, when relating the circumstance, showed him the specimen.

From the same authority we learn, that in an old mine which had been closed for twenty years, white lead ore was found projecting from the sides of the vein to the length of 2 inches or upwards; from which it may be inferred that when circumstances are favourable minerals are being formed in the large laboratory of the earth at the present day the same as in the past. Mr. Wallace also remarks: " I see no reason why ores may not at the present time be in course of deposition wherever the conditions are favourable." Whether their growth is merely the result of certain chemical combinations, or whether they possess life like the vegetable kingdom, are questions which will naturally arise in the minds of those who view the beautiful and wonderful tree-like shapes which their crystals often assume. Coleridge truly observes: "The metal at its height of being seems a mute prophecy of the coming vegetation, into a mimic semblance of which it crystallizes." "The relation of vegetables and minerals," Mr. Wallace tells us, "may not consist in a mimic semblance only; it may be that the same kind of particles in different combinations enters into the composition of both. It is certain that in each case the substances of which they are composed are derived from the crude and heterogeneous masses of inorganic matter constituting the crust of the globe. It would appear, therefore, that their various properties or attributes, which enable us to become cognizant of their existence, are the result of the organization of a few simple substances according to chemical and in the case of vegetables to semi-vital laws regulating the formation and ascent of sap. Under some circumstances a certain analogy may be traced in the deposition and *crystallization* of *metallic* matter with the circulation of sap in vegetable growths, and of fluids or blood in animal forms. And although the mechanical circulation of fluids in veins certainly differs very essentially from the *vis à tergo* which impels the sap upwards to the terminal point of every branch, or in animals, from the *vital force* concerned in assimilation and secretion, which probably not only changes the nature, but also produces the movement in a stream of which the flow is development; still the circulation of fluids in veins may so far resemble that of sap in vegetables and blood in animals, as to promote certain chemical changes and combinations, to which not only the distribution, but also the origination of metallic substances in veins may be due. Minerals, like vegetables, are also subject to decay, water beneath the surface of the earth assisting in the decomposition of all kinds of rocks. At great depths its action appears to be not only detersive, but also reproductive, other substances being often brought by it to supply to some extent the place of those that have been removed." In this way in all likelihood will future geologists account for the metamorphism of rocks, and attribute to the action of water and chemical combination many effects now considered to be volcanic. Mr. Westgarth Forster, speaking of the similitude between the mineral and vegetable kingdoms, says: "The mineral substances produced *under the surface of the earth* differ, in this circumstance, from the subjects of the vegetable kingdom, to which, in other respects, they have some resemblance. Many venigerous fossils seem to grow nearly in the same manner as vegetables, the clefts, fissures, and veins in the strata, answering to the tubes in plants, and water is the vehicle of nutriment common to both. Fire, of the nature of which we still know so little, may perhaps be an auxiliary, equally necessary to all the three kingdoms of nature. On the other hand, we know with a kind of certainty that the mineral kingdom has existed before the other two, and, in part, furnished them with materials for their existence, although itself deprived of those wonderful and incomprehensible qualities of life, and the production of seeds, which are the distinguishing properties of the animal and vegetable kingdoms." By the aid of chemistry we shall, no doubt, ere long be able to solve the question as to the origin of minerals, and resolve those substances into simpler elements; and if they are the result, not of life, but of mere chemical combination, we anticipate that the day may come when the chemist will be able to combine those elements so as to copy the operations of nature.

MINERALOGY.

"Through dark retreats pursue the winding ore;
Search Nature's depths, and view her boundless store.
The secret cause in tuneful numbers sing,
How metals first were formed, and whence they spring;
Whether the active sun, with chymic flames,
Through porous earth transmits his genial beams,
With heat impregnating the womb of night,
The offspring shines with its paternal light ;—
Or whether, urged by subterraneous flames,
The earth ferments, and flows on liquid streams ;
Purged from their dross, the nobler parts refine,
Receive new forms, and with fresh beauties shine ;—
Or whether by Creation first they sprung,
When yet unpoised the world's great fabric hung :
Metals the basis of the earth were made,
The bars on which its fixed foundation's laid.
All second causes they disdain to own,
And from the Almighty's fiat sprung alone."

ALTHOUGH the central fire of this earth is hid from view, there can be no doubt that the whole globe was originally a purely incandescent mass, and that it is now, as it were, a sun crusted over and partially extinguished, the cooled surface of which forms the skin or crust which bears testimony of its former condition. This globe, formerly on fire, after countless ages, has cooled down, obeying the laws of the radiation of heat, and constituting this primitive crust, the study of which forms the science of Mineralogy. In no place can the laws which regulate the deposition of ores in veins or the arrangement of the earthy minerals be better studied than in the district of Alston Moor. Looking at the vast deposits here gathered, the question naturally arises: From whence spring the metals and minerals which form these formations? The only satisfactory answer is, from the interior of the earth, the seat of that intense heat which possesses power and force of expansion sufficient to affect the most distant part of its surface. These vast accumulations occur in the formation known commonly as the Yoredale series, or mountain limestone of Phillips, which seems to possess some peculiar condition in it which causes the accumulation of metallic ores in this locality, more particularly that of galena, the lead ore of commerce. Geologically, the Alston and Allendale districts consist of alternating beds of limestone, grit, shale, sandstone, and one layer of igneous rock, with a few and comparatively worthless seams of coal, the whole attaining a thickness of about 500 feet. This Yoredale series, although more fully developed in Yorkshire, can be best studied in the neighbourhoods of Alston and Weardale. These strata are pierced through by a considerable number of fissures, generally having a direction from the north of east to the south of west. Veins running north and south, usually called cross veins, also exist, but although yielding metalliferous ores to a certain extent, are not so productive as those which have a main direction of north of east to the south of west. In whatever direction, however, the veins run, the productive ones are found solely in the mountain limestone. It is in large cavities or holes encrusting the veins of solid ore that the minerals are discovered; and one of the most beautiful sights of nature, to a mineralogist, is to be observed on breaking into one of these, where the minerals encrusting the roof and walls throw back the light suddenly let in with a thousand reflected rays. The procuring of minerals of such a beautiful description as those found in this district cannot fail to be of the greatest pleasure to all persons inclined to study the works of nature through nature itself. The fluor-spars, so plentifully found round Alston Moor, are of such brilliant, delicate, and diverse colours as to really baffle description, and language would fail in attempting to do justice to the beauty of these specimens. From the lightest to the darkest green, from the lightest to the darkest pink and blue, all the varied tints are to be found, whilst many specimens have a base of green, surrounded by crystals of blue, or a base of pink by crystals of amber. In some specimens also two colours are observable in the one crystal: this occurs when viewed by transmitted and reflected light; the transmitted light producing a green shade, and the reflected a blue. Many of the crystals possessing these two colours contain air bubbles, and sometimes drops of fluid. It is a mineral calculated to excite the admiration of the most indifferent observer, in consequence of its beauty and variety of colours. Fluor-spar is a combination of lime with fluoric acid, being, consequently, a fluate of lime. Its primary form is that of an octahedron, but in this district it is found in the form of a cube. Its association is principally calcite; and when we speak of this mineral, also abundant at Alston Moor and Allendale, we are reminded what an important part it plays in the district. Calcite is carbonate of lime, or a mixture of lime with carbonic acid. Although not possessing the brilliant colours and tints of the fluor-spar, being principally white, ranging to a delicate flesh tint, how it surpasses that specimen in its countless crystallographic forms! This mineral alone is nearly the study of a lifetime, there being already more than five hundred secondary forms known, and it is possible to define the relations existing between any two of these. Even at the present day new modifications are being found. Two specimens from near Alston Moor have lately been procured by an American mineralogist (William S. Vaux, Esq.), both of which are completely new modifications of the rhombohedron. The faces of the angles are also peculiar, being striated, or exhibiting striæ transversely across the crystals, as if a file had been drawn across them. It will thus be seen that however countless forms of a particular mineral may occur, there is still room for discovery. This remark applies to nature in all its sections and branches.

Accompanying most of the lead veins at Alston Moor is the carbonate of barytes, a mineral of the greatest utility in the arts, being employed extensively in chemical works, and in the manufacture of plate-glass, porcelain, &c. In France, to which country it is largely exported, it is used in the manufacture of beet-root sugar. There is yet another earthy mineral which claims a word or two in passing. This is what is known under the name of gypsum, or, when occurring in a compact form, more generally that of alabaster. It is found near Carlisle; and also at Alston, associated with an earthy-red iron ore. It is used in the manufacture of glass and porcelain, but the rougher varieties more universally in agriculture, as a top-dressing for grass lands. Its formation is very remarkable, and may be accounted for in several ways: first, by the deposition from concentrated salt water, which may be of an oceanic or lacustrine origin; secondly, by minerals and rocks, whose constituent is lime, being acted upon by compounds of gaseous sulphur, either in a solution or free state; and, thirdly, by lime in most strata, being subjected to the chemical action of iron pyrites, the sulphide of iron. There are many other earthy minerals of the greatest use found in the district, but it would be impossible to enumerate them all severally and particularly here. All that occur, however, will be found in the descriptive list accompanying.

Leaving those minerals which are of "the earth, earthy," our attention is attracted to a few of the metalliferous products whose main characters are essentially different. Very few minerals or metals are found in a native state, but man has made himself acquainted with those operations necessary to reduce them to the condition which renders most of them in his hands of value to him in one degree or another, this degree depending upon the properties they may possess, and with the expensiveness of the processes necessary to render them available. Perhaps the metal of all others which has caused "hopes and fears" to arise in the breast of the explorer, is the iron pyrites, a mixture of iron and sulphur, as this species in outward appearance to the uninitiated most resembles the precious metal, gold. A very beginner, however, in mineralogy will soon detect in its fresh, glistening surfaces the difference from the rarer substance.

"Pirrites is a kinde of stone, yealow, like to the fire his flame, and in qualitie almost all one with the fire; for the which I suppose it tooke its name; it is soone kindled and set on fire. It also sparkleth, and being hardly holden and pressed in any man's hande burneth him sore or he perceiveth it. Whereupon the lapidare hath these two verses:

"The Pirrite must with easie hand
And marvellous soft enholden be;
For being prest and held to hard
Doth burne thy Flesh or ere thou see."

The old author of the above, John Maplet, although in error as to this mineral really burning our flesh before we are aware of it, was not altogether wrong, for this metal, being subjected to the action of water or the atmosphere, decomposes, during the process of which a considerable amount of heat is emitted. It occurs plentifully associated with barytes, pearl-spar, and quartz, in most of the metalliferous mines of Gilsland. Although not one of the ores from which iron is extracted, it is of great commercial value, by its producing sulphuric acid when artificially decomposed. It is also reduced for the procuring of sulphur, the iron that remains being the common well-known paint, red ochre. Galena is, however, the king of metals in this part of the country, both in a commercial and mineralogical light. It is the metal from which the lead ore of commerce is produced, and is a combination of lead with sulphur. There are no less than fifty-two mines working in Alston and the neighbourhood for this metal, nearly all of which are producing the most satisfactory results. It occurs in veins running generally north of east to the south of west. It contains silver in variable quantities, which is obtained from it by melting the lead, and as it begins to cool, "straining out the crystals with an iron strainer, the portion left behind containing nearly all the silver. This is repeated several times, each time the lead becoming richer. It is then cupelled." In former years the silver was not sought for, but as an ore containing only 3 oz. of silver to the ton (or but $\frac{1}{10000}$th part) may now be profitably worked, it is nearly always sought for. The crystallized, and what we may term mineralogical specimens, are found in the lodes of massive ore. Crystals of an enormous size have been discovered, some cubes measuring 7 to 8 inches across. Its associations are principally pearl-spar, calcite, fluor-spar, and witherite. A peculiar variety is termed Slickenside, from the fact of the surface being polished. Lately many hypotheses have been started as to how this has occurred, the former belief having been that the sides were polished by a slipping or rubbing motion similar to the effect that icebergs have produced upon the tops of some of the Cumberland mountains. It is now, however, more generally believed to be formed by electricity. When touched with a miner's pick, it is said to explode with dangerous violence. The polished surface looks like ordinary blacklead, whilst behind this coating a granular variety of limestone occurs, impregnated with galena.

The zinc ores are well represented, more particularly Blende, the sulphide of zinc, or, as the miners familiarly call it, "Black Jack." Its primary form is the rhombic-dodecahedron, but it is more generally found crystallized in tetrahedrons, or modifications of that form. It is black, and occurring often upon the pure white pearl-spar forms a beautiful contrast. It is also found associated with fluor-spar, quartz, and copper pyrites. In many mining districts it is called the "mother of lead," its presence being considered as a good omen; whilst in others, miners assert that where such blende occurs the deposition of galena is not great. In the Alston and Allendale districts it is generally looked upon as a most favourable sign.

The foregoing few minerals mentioned are the leading ones to be found in the country surrounding Gilsland; but there are others which, although perhaps not so important in the commercial world, are, in a strictly mineralogical light, of the greatest scientific importance. The following list contains *all* the minerals in the Gilsland district, and I am sure that those who devote a little time to the study of the science of mineralogy will not fail to be well repaid for their trouble, if they make the basis of their operations the country to which these few elementary remarks particularly apply.

NON-METALLIC MINERALS.

ORDER—CARBON.

COAL. Common coal. Black coal.

Structure compact, or slaty, often dividing with degree of regularity into columnar or rhombohedral fragments. Lustre, dull to brilliant. Colour, black, opaque. Fracture, uneven.

Hardness, 1·0 to 2·5. Specific gravity, 1·20 to 1·75.

Composition: principally consists of oxygenated hydrocarbons, or sometimes simple hydrocarbons, that is, containing no oxygen. Generally known as mineralized vegetable matter, animal contributing somewhat however to its composition. It is found at Alston Moor, generally in small veins. For list of collieries, see p. 263.

A variety, locally called *crow coal,* occurs plentifully on the ridge of Haska Fell. It is, however, very inferior to the ordinary, and is used chiefly for supplying the machinery of the mines.

ORDER—SULPHUR.

SULPHUR. *Phillips.* SCHWEFEL, *Mohs.* Synonyme, Brimstone.

Rhombic. Primary form a four-sided pyramid, with a rhombic base. Imperfect cleavage. Fracture, uneven. Disseminated. Lustre, resinous. Colour, sulphur yellow.

Hardness, 1·5 to 2·5. Specific gravity, 2·07.

Composition: sulphur, more or less pure.

It is found in disseminated masses, associated with gypsum, near the mines of Alston Moor. It is frequently met with also in small quantities in the metalliferous veins, especially those containing copper pyrites and galena. Sulphur, when combined with other elements, forms the class of substances known as sulphurets or sulphides. The sulphur of commerce is principally extracted from the iron and copper pyrites.

ORDER—FLUORIDE.

FLUORITE. Fluor-spar. Fluate of Lime. Fluoride of Calcium. Fluss-spath, *Naumann.*

Cubical. The primary form is the regular octahedron, but the solid angles in general are replaced by tangent planes, changing the figure into the usual cubical form. Fracture, conchoidal. Colourless, white, blue, green, violet, lilac, amber, yellow, and purple. Transparent, subtranslucent. Brittle. Streak, white. Phosphoresces when heated.

Hardness, 4·0. Specific gravity, 3·01 to 3·25.

Breithaupt obtained for a specimen from Alston Moor, 3·017.

Composition :

Fluorine	48·7
Calcium	57·3
	106·0

Fluor-spar is undoubtedly the most beautiful of all minerals, groups of the various colours ornamenting, without exception, all mineralogical collections. The Alston varieties are most remarkable for their brilliant colours and beauty, more than for their variety of forms and modifications. The crystals frequently contain drops of water, air bubbles, minute crystals of quartz, &c., particularly the small green specimens. Many specimens are of two distinct colours—green and blue; the one to be observed when viewed by transmitted light, and the other by reflected. Occurs plentifully of a deep blue, lilac, green, and amber colour in all the lead mines of the Weardale district, and in nearly all the mines of Alston Moor, including Brownley Hill (pale and deep amber), Nent Head (purple), Guttergill in great abundance (blue), Rodderup Fell (massive), and Crossfell (massive), in great abundance. The lilac and blue varieties are perhaps the commonest found in the district, and the bright green and dark amber the rarest. Curiously elongated cubes associated with the lenticular form of calcite and crystals of galena are met with of a deep violet colour.

Fluor-spar is used in considerable quantities as a flux in the reducing of copper and other ores, hence, probably, the name, from *fluo*, to flow.

Chlorophane is a massive variety of fluor-spar most convenient for showing phosphorescence by heat. By reducing the mineral to a powder, and placing it upon a shovel until nearly heated to redness, a bright blue glowing colour will appear upon the surface.

ORDER—CARBONATES.

ARRAGONITE. Arragonite, *Phillips, Hauy*. Needle Spar. Igloite.

Prismatic. Primary form a right rhombic prism of 116°10'.

Cleavage, distinct in one direction. Fracture, conchoidal or uneven. Lustre, vitreous. Transparent to translucent. Colourless, white, often yellowish white to wine yellow. Brittle. Dissolves with effervescence in muriatic acid. Hardness, 3·5 to 4·0. Specific gravity, 2·9 to 3·0. Composition of a fibrous variety.

Carbonate of lime	98·00
,, strontia	1·01
Hydrate red oxide of iron	0·14
Water	0·21
	99·36

Occurs in beautiful, delicate, transparent crystals in limestone, at the mines surrounding Alston Moor, associated with galena and quartz. Very fine specimens can also be procured from the spar iron "riders" of the lead veins at Nent Force. A blue azure sky colour is found at Hudgill Burn Mine.

Satin Spar is a fibrous or lamellar variety, containing 4·25 per cent. of carbonate of protoxide of manganese which sometimes communicates to it a rose tinge. It is found in a cliff of decomposing shale, near Alston. Having a satiny lustre (hence the name), and taking a good polish, it is employed in the manufacture of inlaid ornaments.

Flos-ferri (Flowers of Iron) is a stalactitical and coralloidal form of arragonite. It is pure white, resembling in appearance coral, the branches or stems being delicately interlaced and twisted in every fantastic direction. It is found in many of the mines in the neighbourhood of Alston.

CALCITE. Calcite, *Brooke* and *Miller*. Carbonate of Lime, *Phillips*. Kalkspath, *Naumann*. From the Latin *calx*, lime.

Rhombohedral. Cleavage easy, parallel with the faces of the fundamental rhombohedron. Fracture, conchoidal. Lustre, vitreous. Colourless, white, but often tinged brown, grey, green, yellow, and sometimes black. Streak, white. Brittle. Double refracting.
Hardness, 2·5 to 3·5. Specific gravity, 2·5 to 2·7.

Composition:

Carbonic acid	44·0
Lime	56·0
	100·0

This mineral in a massive form, under the name limestone, is abundantly scattered through the Gilsland district, most of the mountains being constituted of it.

Occurs in beautifully crystallized specimens at the following mines: Nent Head, associated with blende, iron and copper pyrites, and pearl-spar; at Brownley Hill, of a yellowish tinge, in hexagonal modified crystals. The variety commonly called nail head or lenticular, is one of the most beautiful, often being made up of aggregations of small crystals of this form highly modified and generally translucent; at Garrigill, in white modified crystals; at Ogill Burn, Old Haggs Mine, Blagill, Thorngill, Hudgill Burn, Holyfield, Guttergill, and nearly all the adjacent mines produce it more or less associated with galena and blende. Tyne Bottom Mine (Garrigill) has produced some very fine specimens in large transparent crystals, and others approaching the primitive form of the rhombohedron. Most magnificent and remarkable specimens were procured by the author from a mine in the parish of Alston, of a deep transparent honey colour. These were crystallized in elongated radiating transparent crystals, the base being built up of many small crystals of the same shape, all equally transparent, resembling in appearance a set of spires, forming the base, and a larger one protruding from the centre.

REICHITE. *Breithaupt.* (Berg und Hüttenmannische Zeitung, xxiv. 311.)

Under this name Breithaupt has described a pure calcite from the Alston Moor district. The measurements of the angles differ from the usual crystals, being according to Breithaupt's measurements 105° 20'. It is white in colour, and the specific gravity 2·666 to 2·677.

WITHERITE. Witherite, *Phillips.* Carbonate of Barytes. Barolite.

Prismatic. In modified rhombic prisms. Crystals,

generally compound. Cleavage, imperfect. Fracture, uneven. Translucent. Tasteless and poisonous. Very heavy.
Hardness, 3·0 to 3·75. Specific gravity, 4·29 to 4·35.
Composition:

$$\begin{array}{ll} \text{Baryta} & 77\cdot 6 \\ \text{Carbonic acid} & 22\cdot 4 \\ \hline & 100\cdot 0 \end{array}$$

This mineral is found in the lead veins of many mines traversing the coal formation at Alston Moor, associated with fluor-spar, calcite, and the various minerals characteristic of such veins. A variety coated with barytes is termed the sulphato-carbonate of barytes. It is of the greatest importance in the arts, being employed extensively in chemical works, in the manufacture of plate-glass, &c.

BARYTO-CALCITE. Baryto-calcite, *Brooke.*
Oblique. Primary form, an oblique rhombic prism. Cleavage, distinct. White, yellowish. Brittle.
Hardness, 4·0. Specific gravity, 3·6 to 3·7.
Composition:

$$\begin{array}{ll} \text{Carbonate of baryta} & 65\cdot 9 \\ \text{\quad ,, \quad lime} & 33\cdot 6 \\ \text{Silica} & \text{trace} \\ \hline & 99\cdot 5 \end{array}$$

This mineral, as will be seen, is an isomorphous mixture of the carbonates of baryta and lime. It is found plentifully in attached crystals, and massive in veins in mountain limestone, at Blagill, near Alston.

ALSTONITE. Alstonite, *Brooke* and *Miller.* Bromlite, *Johnston.*
Prismatic. Primary form, a right rhombic prism. Fracture, granular and uneven. Cleavage, distinct. Translucent.
Hardness, 4·0 to 4·5. Specific gravity, 3·68 to 3·70.

Composition:

Carbonate of baryta	..	62·16
,, lime	..	30·29
,, strontia	..	6·64
		99·09

Alstonite and baryto-calcite were formerly supposed to be identical, but such is not the case, the analyses being different, whilst the crystals of alstonite are prismatic, and those of baryto-calcite oblique.

Alstonite is found in small acute six-sided pyramids at Brownley Hill, near Alston Moor, in veins.

DOLOMITE. Dolomite, *Brooke* and *Miller*. Brown Spar. Pearl Spar.

Rhombohedral. Cleavage, perfect. Faces generally curved. Lustre, vitreous, more or less inclining to pearly in different varieties. White, but often yellowish. Brittle.

Hardness, 3·5 to 4·5. Specific gravity, 2·85 to 2·95.

Composition:

Carbonate of lime	.. ..	56·57
,, magnesia	..	43·43
,, iron	.. trace	..
		100·00

Found plentifully associated with calcite at the mines of Nent Head, Ogill Burn, Old Haggs, Garrigill, and Coal Cleugh, near Alston Moor. It is common at Alston Moor, also occurring in curved rhombs, the edges of which sometimes meet, associated with fluor-spar and galena. The variety *Brown Spar* occurs near Alston. The variety *Pearl Spar* occurs at Brownley Hill and Nent Head, associated with copper pyrites.

ORDER—ANHYDROUS SULPHATES.

BARYTES. Baryte, *Brooke* and *Miller*. Heavy Spar. Cawk.

Prismatic. Primary form, a right rhombic prism.

MINERALOGY.   253

Lustre, vitreous. Colourless, white, grey, brown, and yellow. Brittle.
Hardness, 3·0 to 3·5. Specific gravity, 4·3 to 4·7.
Composition: sulphate of barytes, 99·38, with traces of silica, sulphate of strontia, lime, and iron.
In nearly all the lead mines round Alston Moor associated with galena and calcite. A variety is called *Cockcomb Barytes* when formed by an aggregation of small opaque and greyish-white crystals.

GYPSUM. *Phillips.* Gyps, *Haidinger.* Selenite.
Oblique. Lustre, pearly. Flexible when in thin plates.
Streak, white. Sectile.
Hardness, 1·5 to 2·0. Specific gravity, 2·28 to 2·33.
Composition:

Sulphuric acid	46·31
Lime	32·90
Water	20·75
	99·96

Occurs in clear colourless crystals, with an earthy red iron ore, at Alston Moor.

ORDER—SILICA AND SILICATES.

QUARTZ. Quartz, *Phillips, Brooke* and *Miller.* Rock Crystal.
Rhombohedral. Colourless, and white the prevailing colour; also yellow, brown, pink, and black. Phosphorescent when two pieces are rubbed together.
Hardness, 7·0. Specific gravity, 2·5 to 2·8.
Composition, when pure:

Silicon	48·04
Oxygen	51·96
	100·00

Occurs associated with blende and fluor-spar at nearly all the mines of Weardale, Allens Head, and Alston Moor.

METALLIC MINERALS.

SIDERITE. Spathose Iron. Carbonate of Iron. Chalybite. Brown Spar.
Rhombohedral. Fracture, imperfect conchoidal. Yellowish brown, yellowish grey. Lustre, vitreous.
Hardness, 3·5 to 4·5. Specific gravity, 3·7 to 3·9.
Composition:

Protoxide of iron	54·57
" manganese	1·15
Lime	3·18
Carbonic acid	35·90
	94·80

Occurs occasionally, generally in a massive state, at Alston, Nent Head, Allendale, Teesdale.

PYRITES. Iron Pyrites, *Phillips.*
Cubical. Fracture, uneven or conchoidal. Brass yellow, inclining to gold yellow. Streak, brownish black, opaque. Emits sparks when struck with steel.
Hardness, 6·0 to 6·5. Specific gravity, 4·9 to 5·1.
Composition:

Iron	45·75
Sulphur	54·25
	100·00

It is an abundant mineral in the Gilsland district, being found in good specimens, associated with barytes, pearl spar, and quartz, at Ogill Burn, Old Haggs, Garrigill, Coal Cleugh, Rodderup Fells, and also in the mines at Alston. This mineral is extensively mined for the sulphur which is extracted from it.

MARCASITE. White Iron Pyrites.
Prismatic. Primary form, a right rhombic prism. Fracture, uneven. Brittle. Lustre, metallic. Greyish brass yellow.

Hardness, 6·0 to 6·5. Specific gravity, 4·65 to 4·88.
Composition:

Iron	45·75
Sulphur	54·25
	100·00

Occurs upon crystals of calcite, near Alston Moor.

ORDER—COBALT.

ERYTHRINE. *Beudant;* Cobalt Bloom. Arseniate of Cobalt.
Oblique. Colour, peach red; opaque, dull, earthy.
Hardness, 1·5 to 2·5. Specific gravity, 2·95.
Composition:

Arsenious acid	38·43
Oxide of cobalt	36·52
Protoxide of iron	1·01
Water	24·10
	100·06

Is found in a massive state only at the Tyne Bottom Mine, Alston.

ORDER—COPPER.

MALACHITE. Green Carbonate of Copper, *Phillips.* Malachit, *Haidinger.*
Oblique. Primary form, an oblique rhombic prism.
Fracture, uneven. Emerald green, verdigris green.
Hardness, 3·5 to 4·0. Specific gravity, 3·6 to 4·0.
Composition:

Oxide of copper	72·2
Carbonic acid	18·5
Water	9·3
	100·0

This mineral is said to have been found near Alston Moor, but although the author has several specimens from other parts of Cumberland, he has never been able to procure a specimen from this locality.

OLIVENITE. Right prismatic Arseniate of Copper, *Phillips*.

Prismatic. Primary form, a right rhombic prism. Cleavage, indistinct. Leek, olive, and blackish green. Brittle.

Hardness, 3·0. Specific gravity, 4·2 to 4·6.
Composition:

Oxide of copper	54·98
Arsenic acid	40·61
Water	4·41
	100·00

This mineral is to be found in small distinct crystals, with malachite on quartz, at Tyne Head Mine, near Alston.

CHALCOSINE. Redruthite, *Brooke* and *Miller*. Vitreous Copper, *Phillips*.

Prismatic Fracture, conchoidal to uneven. Very sectile. Blackish, lead grey. Lustre, metallic, dull. Streak, shining.

Hardness, 2·5 to 3·0. Specific gravity, 5·5 to 5·8.
Composition:

Copper	79·8
Sulphur	20·2
	100·0

Occurs at Tyne Head Mine, although very sparingly.

CHALCOPYRITE. Towanite, *Brooke* and *Miller*. Copper Pyrites, *Phillips*.

Pyramidal. Brass yellow, often gold yellow; very liable to tarnish; opaque. Lustre, metallic. Streak, greenish black.

Hardness, 3·5 to 4·0. Specific gravity, 4·1 to 4·3.

Composition :

Copper	30·15
Iron	32·37
Sulphur	35·34
	97·86

Is found, associated with other minerals, at Alston.

ORDER—LEAD.

Native Lead.
Found in small globules.
Hardness, 1·5. Specific gravity, 11·44.
Lustre, metallic. Colour, lead grey. Malleable and ductile.

Hitherto only found in minute globules in lava, and in the cavities of a meteoric iron.

This extremely rare mineral has been discovered, however, *in situ*, at Alston Moor, the only British locality, " in veins traversing limestone very near the surface, in small detached masses of galena bearing the aspect of torrefaction, and which are coated with oxide of lead.

" The metallic lead occurs in small globules dispersed over the surface.

" It is now known that the Romans worked the lead ore at this locality, and the way they worked was to smelt or roast the ore *in situ*, i. e. by digging away some of the earth on both sides of the metallic lode or vein, and putting in fuel and fire. In this way the galena must have been more or less roasted, thus accounting for the globules of pure lead." ('Manual of Mineralogy,' by Greg and Lettsom.)

Phillips, by Brooke and Miller, in their 'Mineralogy,' described native lead as occurring near Bristol, but it was afterwards discovered that the portions found and analyzed were simply portions of rifle bullets.

MINIUM. Native Oxide of Lead.
Fracture, earthy; even flat conchoidal. Opaque. Lustre, feeble. Colour, red. Streak, orange yellow.
Hardness, 2·5. Specific gravity, 4·6.

Composition :

Lead	90·60
Oxygen	9·34
	99·94

This very rare mineral occurs at Alston.

CERUSSITE. Cerussite, *Brooke* and *Miller*. Carbonate of Lead, *Phillips*.

Prismatic. Fracture, conchoidal. Transparent to translucent. Lustre, vitreous. Colourless, white grey, lead grey, and occasionally green, owing to an admixture of carbonate of oxide of copper, black. Streak, white.

Hardness, 3·0 to 3·5. Specific gravity, 6·4 to 6·6.

Composition :

Oxide of lead	82·0
Carbonic acid	16·0
	98·0

Occurs at Nent Head, and in small quantities at the principal lead mines of Gilsland district.

GALENA. Galena, *Brooke* and *Miller*, *Phillips*. Galenet, *Von Kobell*. Sulphuret of Lead.

Cubic. The prevailing forms are the cube and a combination of the cube and octahedron. Lustre, metallic. Opaque. Colour and streak, lead grey. Fracture, conchoidal, but difficult to obtain, owing to the readiness with which it cleaves. Often tarnished, especially on the faces of the octahedron. Rather sectile.

Hardness, 2·5. Specific gravity, 7·4 to 7·6.

Composition :

Lead	85·13
Iron	0·50
Sulphur	13·02
	98·65

Often the iron is omitted. Silver also enters largely into the composition of galena, from which it is extracted.

The lead ore of commerce. It occurs in the whole mountain limestone range of Cumberland, and is extensively worked. Crystallized specimens are abundantly met with in the Alston Moor mines, generally in the cubo-octahedron form or truncated octahedron.

Slickenside, or *specular* galena, is a smooth variety of galena, occurring in laminæ upon the mountain limestone. When struck with a miner's pick it explodes with dangerous violence. Various hypotheses have been started as to the cause of the surface being smooth and polished. Some believe this has taken place by a rubbing process, but it is now more generally believed to be caused by the action of electricity.

JOHNSTONITE. Supersulphuret of Lead.
Massive. Opaque. Colour, bluish. Lustre, metallic. Texture, fine granular.
Hardness, 3·0. Specific gravity, 6·7.
Composition, according to Johnston:

Galena	90·38
Sulphur	8·71
	99·09

Is found at Alston Moor, Cumberland.

ORDER—ZINC.

CALAMINE. Calamine, *Brooke* and *Müller*. Smithsonite, *Haidinger*.
Rhombohedral. Occurs reniform and botryoidal. Green and yellow. Lustre, vitreous. Streak, white. Brittle.
Hardness, 5·0. Specific gravity, 4·1 to 4·5.
Composition:

Oxide of zinc	64·81
Carbonic acid	35·19
	100·00

Occurs mammillated and in crusts, white, brown, and occasionally of a fine rich yellow, at Alston Moor; also at Farnberry Mine, Alston.

SMITHSONITE. Silicious Oxide of Zinc, *Phillips*.
Prismatic. Commonly with hemihedral terminations.
Colourless, white, green, and blue, but not very deep in
tint. Lustre, vitreous. Streak, white. Brittle.
Hardness, 5·0. Specific gravity, 4·1 to 4·2.
Composition:

Oxide of zinc	67·4
Silica	25·1
Water	7·5
	100·0

Occurs of a white colour, coating blende, at Alston.

BLENDE. Sulphuret or Sulphide of Zinc.
Cubic. Fracture, conchoidal. Transparent to opaque.
Lustre, adamantine. Colour, reddish brown, brown,
yellow, black, green. Brittle.
Hardness, 3·5 to 4·0. Specific gravity, 3·9 to 4·2.
Composition:

Zinc	67·03
Sulphur	32·97
	100·00

Usually contains also a small percentage of iron, and sometimes 2 or 3 per cent. of cadmium.

It is found at Nent Head, Ogill Burn, Old Haggs Mine, Garrigill, Coal Cleugh, and Rodderup Fell.

It is a very common mineral, occurring usually with galena, copper pyrites, and quartz. It is often termed by the miners "Mother of Lead," being looked upon as a good indication when searching for lead.

METALLIFEROUS MINES OF THE GILSLAND DISTRICT,

SITUATED AT OR AROUND ALSTON MOOR.

Lead, L.; Silver Lead, S-L.; Copper, C.; Zinc, Zn.; Barytes, B.

No.	Names.	Minerals raised.	Situation.
1	Bentyfield, E. End	S-L.	Alston Moor.
2	,, W. End	,,	,,
3	Black Syke	,,	Alston.
4	Blagill	,,	,,
5	Birchy Bank	,,	,,
6	Brown Gill	,,	,,
7	Brownley Hill	,,	,,
8	Bulman Hill	L.	Ousby.
9	Capel Cleugh	S-L.	Alston.
10	Carrs and Hanging Shaw	,,	,,
11	Carrs, west of Nent	,,	,,
12	Cashwell	,,	,,
13	Cowper Dyke Heads	L.	,,
14	Craig Green, N. Vein	S-L.	,,
15	Dowke Burn, E. End	,,	,,
16	,, ,, W. End	,,	,,
17	Dowgang Veins	,,	,,
18	Dowpot Syke	,,	,,
19	East Crossfell	,,	Kirkland.
20	Fletcheras	,,	Alston.
21	Farnberry	,,	,,
22	Flow Edge	,,	,,
23	Galligill Bents	,,	,,
24	Galligill Syke	,,	,,
25	Grassfield	,,	,,
26	Green Hurth	,,	,,
27	Guddamgill	,,	,,
28	,, E. End	,,	Alston Moor.
29	Holyfield	,,	,,
30	Hudgill Burn	,,	,,

METALLIFEROUS MINES—continued.

No.	Names.	Minerals raised.	Situation.
31	Lee House Well and	S.L.	Alston Moor.
32	Pasture Grove ..		
33	Long Cleugh ..	,,	,,
34	Long Cleugh, 2nd Sun Vein..	,,	,,
35	Middle Cleugh	,,	,,
36	Nattrass (Middle Vein)..	,,	,,
37	Nentsbury Green	,,	,,
38	Nentsbury Pasture ..	,,	,,
39	Park Grove Iron Vein ..	,,	,,
40	Peat Stack Hill	,,	,,
41	Priorsdale	,,	,,
42	Rampgill ..	,,	,,
43	Rodderup Fell	,,	,,
44	Scaleburn	,,	Alston.
45	Slaggy Burn ..	,,	,,
46	Small Cleugh ..	,,	,,
47	Smittergill Head	,,	,,
48	Sunnyside Vein	,,	,,
49	Thorngill, E. End ..	,,	,,
50	Thorngill Seit ..	,,	,,
51	,, W. End	,,	,,
52	Tyne Bottom ..	,,	,,
53	Windy Brow ..	,,	,,
54	Chesters *	L.	Haltwhistle.
55	Settleingstones *	S-L.	Haydon Bridge.
56	Stone Croft * ..	L. & B.	,,
57	Chesterwood *	S-L. B.	,,
58	Langley ..	S-L.	
59	Fallow Field *	,,	Hexham.

* The five mines marked (*) are to the north of the Tyne, and are being worked in the lower limestones and the whin. The range of country on the north side of the Tyne from Gilsland to Hexham is exciting a good deal of mining attention at present, and several tracts are being prosecuted with a good deal of enterprise. It will be very fortunate if this turn out to be a rich mining district, as the mines at Alston have been for some time very poor, and mining speculation has not been encouraged, so that a number of men have been obliged to leave the district. About a century ago from 8000 to 10,000 tons were raised, now there are only about 3000 tons.

COLLIERIES.

		Proprietors of Manors.
Coanwood Colliery	Haltwhistle	John Hope Wallace, Esq.
Blenkinsop ditto	Greenhead	J. B. Blenkinsop Coulson, Esq.
Hartleyburn Pit	Haltwhistle	H. L. Allgood, Esq.
Midgeholme ditto	Nawarth Collieries Brampton	Earl of Carlisle.
Roachburn ditto		
Bishophill ditto		
South Tyne Colliery	Haltwhistle	Messrs. C. & W. Adamson.
Melkridge and Henshaw Collieries	"	Sir Edward Blackett, Bart.
Rockhouse Colliery	"	Rev. Dixon Brown.
Fourstones ditto	Hexham	Greenwich Hospital.

BRYCE M. WRIGHT, F.B.Hist. S., &c.

BOTANY.

It is not our purpose in the present article to give an exposition of the Science of Botany : no one looks for such a thing in a guide-book. Our object is rather to secure for one of the most charming of recreative pursuits the attention of those who have not as yet devoted themselves to this delightful science, and to clear the path of certain obstacles that loom before the eye of the tyro, formidable and forbidding.

To the uninitiated no aspect of the study seems so deterring as that which sets before him the multiplicity of objects which form the subject-matter of the science. A terrible lion in the path is this thought of the infinite number and variety of vegetable forms. Trees, bushes, plants, ferns, mosses, grasses, sea-weeds! The tyro is appalled with the enumeration, and exclaims, "How is such a vast field to be traversed?" We can quite sympathize with the disheartened inquirer, all the more so that we remember putting the same question to ourselves— well, we shall not say how many years ago. Permit us then, good reader, to give you the benefit of our time-earned experience.

A look out upon the world of which we are a part shows us that it is made up of an infinity of individual things. Hopeless indeed would be the task of knowing, if everything were unique and unrelated to the whole. Our knowledge in such a case could only be of individuals, and meagre indeed would that knowledge be. But nothing is solitary, nothing unrelated; throughout the whole there run bold and clear lines of connection. These science lays hold of, and tracing them through earth and sea and sky, abridges for us the universe, and presents us with these splendid generalizations which are its own crowning glory. Amid such a multiplicity of vegetable forms, then, the science of botany comes to our aid. It discovers to us that there are certain distinct type-forms running through the whole; that these, comparatively speaking, are not by any means numerous; and that plants which to the eye seem widely unlike, may yet, on closer inspection, be found to have all the essential marks of a common structure. Here then is a science which perhaps more than any other ministers to that persistent desire of the inquiring intellect—to find the one in the midst of the many. Still more attractive does the study become when it is seen that even around our own homes—at our very door, we might say—we have familiar examples of the chief of these type-forms. Our own parish becomes a great botanical garden; our own familiar wildings an epitome of the flora of the world! To illustrate. Everyone knows that some plants bear flowers, while others do not. Here then, at the very outset, is a difference which parts the whole vegetable kingdom into two great divisions, and enables even the most unskilled to decide almost at sight to which division the plant before him belongs. Again, he must have noticed that among flowering plants, some, as the rose, have the leaves more or less rounded, with the veins forming a sort of network; in others, as the lily, the leaves are long and narrow, with the veins running in nearly parallel lines. The distinction is a vital one, and, being significant of others which invariably accompany it, is extremely valuable, from the ease with which it is recognized. Once more, the mutual relations of the parts that constitute the flower—calyx, corolla, stamens, and pistil—discover to us the type on which the plant in question has been formed. And here it is that we come upon the richest stores of mental gratification, in discovering the very models upon which Nature has proceeded in forming, with endless variety of size, colour, and proportion, the thronging multitudes of the vegetable kingdom. It is only thus that the study will disclose to the observant eye the world of wonders that lives and blooms around, beggaring all art, and defying all imitation.

But we have led our readers to believe that they may study the flora of the world at their own doors, or in such a charming retreat as the glens and shaws of Gilsland. How is it done? Everyone knows and loves the daisy. After the exquisite way in which Burns and Wordsworth have sung of it, it is almost sacrilege to take it to pieces for a botanical lesson. Examine it tenderly, then. The flower will be found to be, not one, but a whole head of flowers enclosed within a common circlet of tiny green leaves. It belongs to an order called from their structure Compositæ, an order which is estimated to contain no fewer than 10,000 species, or about $\frac{1}{12}$th of the total number of species of plants in the world. Wherever the foot of man has trod, members of the order have been found—in the Land of the Rising Sun no less than in the flower prairies of the West; on the dreary plains of Lapland as well as on the rank borders of the Congo. The same common structure belongs to all; the family likeness is well marked, and it is no ordinary acquisition which thus enables us to place in one grand collection, bound together by a common tie, and distinguished only by specific differences, such a large section of the entire body of plants. Pull a sprig of wallflower. The petals, or flower-leaves, will be found to be four in number, arranged in a cross-like fashion. This well-marked structure again serves to denominate the order, and we thus get the name of Cruciferæ (cross-bearers). When we make the acquaintance of any one member of the family, we have the happiness of being introduced to about 2500 others from all parts of the world. And so is it the case with the other great orders. We have their representatives springing around us in every woodland walk. Few indeed are the families one or more members of which are not to be found on every square mile of English ground. Thus it is that we gather up the many in the one, and thus it is that the science furnishes us with the pegs whereon memory may hang the vast and varied products of observation and reflection.

Few subjects in connection with plant-life are more curious and interesting to the intelligent botanist than that of distribution. The slightest observation shows that some plants are found everywhere, while others are restricted in their range. How do they come to be where they are? And why are others absent? The explanation is partly climatic, partly geological. Some plants grow in nearly all temperatures and soil, others require a definite amount of heat and moisture, and a soil of a particular composition. While, however, this may be stated as the general principle regulating the distribution of vegetable life, it must ever be borne in mind that there are special circumstances which frequently modify its application. Man himself is a disturbing element in the natural operation of the laws of growth and decay, and instances could easily be given where the most skilled geo-botanist would find it hard indeed to account for the presence or absence of a species in circumstances where everything pointed to a conclusion exactly the reverse of the facts. But flowers are often found growing far from what is known to be their original habitat. How are their seeds disseminated? The agents employed are various. Food-plants and plants employed in the arts and manufactures owe their distribution chiefly to the agency of man; the winds and the waters are ever bearing their minute freights over land and sea. Animals, too, have a share in the work of distribution; and, to aid the winds and the waters, some seeds have a balloon-like appendage to waft them afar over the earth, or are supplied with air cells to float them over the surface of the rivers and seas. Notwithstanding all we know of the dissemination of plant-seeds, there are certain phenomena which fairly puzzle the student of distribution. A piece of heath-clad common is taken in and limed: before long it is a rich pasture of clover and grass. None of the known agents at work in the meanwhile is sufficient to account for the change, nor, indeed, all of them together. Or a field, one sheet of yellow with the flowers of wild mustard, is ploughed and laid down in grass. It may be twenty years before it is again turned over, but no sooner is this done than there is the mustard again, as widespread and as luxuriant as ever. We are not to conclude then that because certain plants are not found in a locality they are not present in the soil. On the contrary, from what is known of the quiescent and tenacious vitality of wild seeds, it seems much nearer the truth to believe that the seeds are there, whether brought by oceanic currents ages ago, or by more recent means of which we know nothing, and that they are only waiting the stimulating influence of more favourable conditions of soil, heat, and moisture to make them germinate.

From certain indications in our experience, we more than suspect that not a few who would fain become botanists are actually frightened from making a commencement by the ponderous nomenclature of the science. And no wonder: it seems little short of barbarity to speak of the delicate denizens of the woods and dells by such uncouth names as Scolopendrium and Jungermannia. It is not at all a matter of necessity; most of our wildings have native names, and very suggestive they often are too; and while we readily grant that it is best to know both, we should recommend amateurs to abjure the use of the botanical name as savouring of pedantry. Our own English names are well worth notice. A whole volume of poetry, folk-lore, religion, and history, is locked up in them, and an additional charm of no ordinary kind is thrown round the pursuit when accompanied by an intelligent appreciation of the significance of names. In such examples as greenweed, yellowwort, and globeflower, we see our ancestors adopting the very readiest mode of naming; in daisy, and snowflake, and sundew, we have the play of elegant fancy; in Our Lady's mantle and St. John's wort their religious feelings find a place; while the shield and buckler ferns, and spearwort speak of times when the clang of mail was heard on many a listed field. Strong believers in pharmacy, they marked the medicinal virtues of lungwort and woundwort by their names; so, too, with the foe of that most English of diseases—the spleen. Their admiration would express itself in the queen of the meadow, or a more chastened flow of feeling in heart's-ease; or a conviction of a still subtler influence residing in the purple loosestrife. The harmonious colouring of nature, too, is well worth our closest attention, and a good deal might be said by way of commending it to the notice of our readers, but we write not so much for those who pursue botany as a study, as for those who feel that the wheels of life are clogging and must have a little rest, and that that rest must not be inactivity, but a change of pursuit. Food and exercise are never so beneficial as when the mind is pleasantly employed, so that the visitors to Gilsland who would enjoy all the physical advantages of a ramble must employ the mind. It has been held, and we believe there is a good deal of truth in it, that the love of flowers may be taken as a criterion of the health of the mind. Without doubt the love of flowers charms away much of the care and weariness of life, and weans the mind from the deadening jar of daily pursuits.

> "I love the flowers, the many flowers,
>   That in our lanes and meadows grow.
> Were you to ask, 'twould be a task
>   To tell you how I love them so.
>
> "I love the flowers, the woodland flowers,
>   For they to me are golden keys,
> Which ope the rusty gates of life,
>   And lead to sunny memories."
>
>   PETER BURN.

As the physical features of the district have been described in the historical and geological portions of this work, it is unnecessary in connection with botany to go over the same ground. The district for many miles around Gilsland may be described as a land of hill and dale, streams and tarns, wide-spreading wastes, and heathery fells, scraggy shaws, and umbrageous woods; Roman ruins and feudal remains; pleasant mansions and historical castles; and embosomed in all this wild and beautiful scenery is a rich and varied flora, rendering it specially attractive to the botanist. All that remains for us to do is to localize for our readers some of the most graceful and winning of our woodland beauties, and so to link in the remembrance of many, we trust, the "sunny memories" of rambles about Gilsland with the sweet and innocent lives of the wild flowers that blush, alas! too often unseen, among its shady dells. The golden saxifrage will be found luxuriating near a glossy green carpet of marchantia, watered by the spray of the Cromel Linn, while the beautiful white stars of the cross-leaved bedstraw will be seen peeping from the clefts of its rocky banks. The Baron House Bog, which has long been known as a rich botanical station, is now being drained, and many of the swamp plants that from time out of mind have had their home in its peaty bogs are rapidly disappearing; but the yellow loosestrife, mud-carex, and cranberry, seem loth to leave their old haunts, and may yet be found. The Northumberland lakes and the wide wastes amid which they are situated, at an elevation of from 700 to 800 feet above the level of the sea, are well known as rich botanizing grounds. The yellow water-lily, white water-lily, marsh-wort, water-starwort, skullcap, intermediate bladderwort, plantain, shoreweed, perfoliate pondweed, red pondweed, red mace, &c., may all be collected from the loughs, while on the wastes may be picked up the stone-bramble, crowberry, twayblade, small scabious, marsh bog-orchis, marsh cudweed, marsh andromeda, &c. Whether or not the Romans brought us any colonists we cannot say, but the whole course of the Wall, from Gilsland to Sewingshields, will be found most interesting botanizing ground. The spearmint, sage, chives, chamomile, &c., may all be collected. The woods of the district are all fine grounds for collecting wild flowers, and if we have not given them habitats in their shady recesses, it is simply because we wish tourists to cultivate habits of research and observation. The South Tyne, traversing the eastern range of the district for upwards of 30 miles, and rising from an elevation of 100 feet at Hexham to the heights of Crossfell, gives, with its numerous tributaries, wide ranges for botanizing. The lofty ridge of the Pennine range, from Tindale Fell to Crossfell, will be found a fertile field for Alpine plants, such as cloudberry, fine-leaved heath, and bog asphodel.

WILD FLOWERS.

Botanical Name.	Common Name.	Habitat.
RANUNCULACEÆ.		
Caltha palustris	Marsh marigold	Wet places.
Anemone nemorosa	Wood anemone	Woods.
Trollius Europæus	Globeflower	Rowfoot.
Ranunculus aquatilis	Buttercup	Ditches.
,, hederaceus	Ivy-leaved crowfoot	Watery wastes.
,, ficaria	Celandine	Coal Cleugh.
,, flammula	Lesser spearwort	Walltown Crags.
,, lingua	Spearwort	,,
,, auricomus	Wood crowfoot	Hedge banks.
,, acris	Upright meadow crowfoot	Meadows.
,, bulbosus	Bulbous crowfoot	Common.
,, arvensis	Corn ,,	Cultivated fields.
NYMPHIACEÆ.		
Nymphæa alba	White water-lily	Broomley Lough.
Nuphar lutea	Yellow ,,	Crag Lough.
PAPAVERACEÆ.		
Papaver dubium	Long smooth-headed poppy	Cultivated fields.
,, rhœas	Corn poppy	,,
CRUCIFERÆ.		
Thelaspi alpestre	Alpine penny-cress	South Tyne.
Capsella bursa pastoris	Shepherd's-purse	Common.
Draba incana	Twisted-podded whitlow-grass	Crossfell.
,, verna	Common whitlow grass	Limestones Scars.

Botanical Name.	Common Name.	Habitat.
CRUCIFERÆ—continued.		
Cardamine amara	Bitter lady's smock	Stream sides.
,, pratensis	Common meadow lady's smock	Damp ground.
,, hirsuta	Hairy lady's smock	,,
Turritus glabra	Long-podded tower mustard	Anick Grange.
Barbarea vulgaris	Bitter winter cress	Stream sides.
Nasturtium officinale	Common water-cress	Common.
Erysimum cheiranthoides	Garlic treacle mustard	Cultivated fields.
Raphanus raphanistrum	Wild radish	,,
RESEDACEÆ.		
Reseda luteola	Yellow weed	Road sides.
VIOLACEÆ.		
Viola palustris	Marsh violet	Damp ground.
,, odorata	Sweet violet	Tyneland.
,, lutea	Yellow pansy	Allendale.
DROSERACEÆ.		
Drosera rotundifolia	Sundew	Swampy heaths.
,, anglica	Great sundew	Muckle Moss.
CARYOPHYLLACEÆ.		
Saponaria officinalis	Common soapwort	Hexham Abbey.
Silene inflata	Bladder campion	South Tyne.
Lychnis floscuculi	Cuckoo flower	Meadows.
Stellaria nemorum	Wood stitchwort	Simon-burn.
,, holostea	Greater stitchwort	Hedge banks.
POLYGALACEÆ.		
Polygala vulgaris	Milkwort	Temon.
LINACEÆ.		
Linum catharticum	Purging flax	Common in pastures.
MALVACEÆ.		
Malva moschata	Marsh mallow	Tynedale.

Botanical Name.	Common Name.	Habitat.
HYPERICACEÆ.		
Hypericum perforatum	St. John's wort	North Tyne.
Hypericum hirsutum	Hairy St. John's wort	Woods.
GERANIACEÆ.		
Geranium sylvaticum	Wood crane's bill	Haydon Bridge.
„ pratense	Blue meadow crane's bill	Meadows.
„ pusillum	Small-flowered crane's bill	Hedge banks.
„ columbinum	Long-stalked crane's bill	Anick Grange.
„ lucidum	Shining crane's bill	Irthing.
„ Robertianum	Herb Robert	Naworth.
„ sanguineum	Bloody crane's bill	Edmond Castle.
LEGUMINOSÆ.		
Ulex nanus	Dwarf whin	Featherstone.
Genista tinctoria	Woad-waxen	Nunwick.
Ononis arvensis	Rest-harrow	Herdley Haugh.
Anthyllis vulneraria	Kidney-vetch, or lady's finger	Common.
Trifolium repens	White trefoil	Grassy grounds.
„ pratense	Purple „	„
„ medium	Zigzag „	Waste thickets.
„ procumbens	Hop „	Sandy soil.
Lotus corniculatus	Bird's-foot trefoil	Common.
Vicia sylvatica	Wood vetch	Ramshaw.
„ cracca	Tufted „	Meadows.
OXALIDACEÆ.		
Oxalis acetosella	Wood sorrel	Woods.
ROSACEÆ.		
Prunus spinosa	The sloe	Horse Close banks.
„ padus	Bird cherry	Featherstone Woods.
„ cerasus	Wild cherry	Softly Woods.
Pyrus aucuparia	Mountain ash	Naworth.
Spiræa ulmaria	Meadow sweet	Woods.
Geum urbanum	Herb bennet	„
„ rivale	Water avens	Damp woods.

Botanical Name.	Common Name.	Habitat.
ROSACEÆ—continued.		
Agrimonia eupatoria .	Agrimony	Staward Peel.
Potentilla argentea .	Hoary cinquefoil . .	Beaufront.
„ tormentilla	Tormentil	Black Sortie.
„ fragariastrum	Strawberry - leaved cinquefoil . . .	Grassy banks.
Comarum palustre .	Marsh cinquefoil . .	Swampy heaths.
Fragaria vesca . .	Wood strawberry . .	Hedge banks.
Rubus chamæmorus .	Cloudberry . . .	Thornhope Carrs.
„ saxatilis . .	Stone bramble . .	Gilsland.
„ Idæus . . .	Raspberry	Featherstone Woods.
„ suberectus .	Upright bramble . .	Staward Peel.
„ cordifolius .	Hazel-leaved bramble	Hedgcrows.
„ leucostachys .	Long-clustered bramble	Fourstones.
„ fruticosus . .	Common bramble . .	Allendale.
„ Koehleri . .	Koehler's bramble .	„
Rosa spinosissima .	Burnet-leaved rose .	Ashgill.
„ Sabina . . .	Sabine's rose . . .	Dilston.
„ tomentosa . .	Downy-leaved rose .	East Allendale.
„ inodora . . .	Slightly-scented briar	Hedge banks.
„ canina· . . .	Dog rose	Chesterholme.
Sanguisorba officinalis	Great burnet . . .	Frequent.
Alchemilla arvensis .	Lady's mantle. . .	Meadows.
Pyrus malus . . .	Crabtree	Blenkinsop.
ONAGRACEÆ.		
Epilobium angustifolium	Willow herb . . .	Knarsdale.
Epilobium hirsutum .	Great hairy willow herb	Lowlands.
„ palustre .	Marsh willow herb .	Swampy places.
Circæa lutetiana . .	Enchanter's nightshade	North Tyne.
HALORAGACEÆ.		
Myriophyllum verticillatum	Water milfoil . . .	Bellingham.
Callitriche verna . .	Water starwort . .	Ponds.
„ pedunculata	Peduncled starwort .	Ditches.
CUCURBITACEÆ.		
Bryonia dioica . .	Red-berried bryony .	Hexham.

T

Botanical Name.	Common Name.	Habitat.
GROSSULARIACEÆ.		
Ribes rubrum . . .	Red currant . . .	Warden.
CRASSULACEÆ.		
Sedum telephium . .	Orpine	Simon-burn.
„ villosum . .	Hairy stonecrop . .	Haltwhistle.
„ anglicum . .	White English stonecrop	Kirklinton.
„ album . . .	White stonecrop . .	Walls, Hexham.
„ acre . . .	Biting „	Rocks.
SAXIFRAGACEÆ.		
Saxifraga stellaris .	Starry saxifrage . .	Garrigill.
„ aizoides .	Yellow „ . .	Irthing, Gilsland.
„ granulata .	White „ . .	Ashgill.
Parnassia palustris .	Grass of Parnassus .	Haltwhistle.
ARALIACEÆ.		
Adoxa moschatellina .	Tuberous moschatell .	Bishop's Linn.
UMBELLIFERÆ.		
Hydrocotyle vulgaris .	Marsh pennywort .	Marshy places.
Sanicula Europæa .	Wood sanicle . . .	Woods.
Conium maculatum .	Hemlock	Waste ground.
Cicuta virosa . . .	Water hemlock . .	Nunwick.
Helosciadium nodiflorum . . .	Marsh wort . . .	Ditches.
Helosciadium inundatum	Least marsh wort . .	Swamps.
Bunium flexuosum .	Common earth nut .	Dry pastures.
Pimpinella saxifraga .	Burnet saxifrage . .	Tynedale.
„ magna .	Greater Burnet saxifrago	North Tyne.
Angelica sylvestris .	Wild angelica . . .	Moist woods.
Peucedanum ostruthium . . .	Masterwort . . .	Pastures.
Heracleum spondylium	Cow parsnip . . .	Haydon Bridge.

Botanical Name.	Common Name.	Habitat.
UMBELLIFERÆ—*continued*.		
Scandix pecten veneris	Venus' comb . . .	Cornfields.
Anthriscus cerefolium	Garden beaked parsley	Hexham.
,, sylvestris.	Wild beaked parsley .	Hedges.
Cherophyllum temulum	Rough chervil . .	Thickets.
CAPRIFOLIACEÆ.		
Sambucus nigra . .	Common elder . .	Woods.
,, ebulus . .	Dwarf elder . . .	Burnstones Bridge.
Viburnum opulus . .	Common guelder rose.	Thickets.
,, lantana .	Wayfaring tree . .	Chipchase Castle.
Lonicera periclymenum	Common honeysuckle	Woods.
RUBIACEÆ.		
Galium verum . .	Yellow bedstraw . .	Grassy banks.
,, palustre . .	White ,, . .	Gilsland.
,, mollugo . .	Hedge ,, . .	Staward Peel.
,, aparine . .	Cleavers	Slaggyford.
,, boreale . .	Cross-leaved bedstraw	Wardrew.
Asperula odorata . .	Sweet woodruff . .	Woods.
VALERIANACEÆ.		
Valeriana officinalis .	Great wild valerian .	Stream sides.
DIPSACACEÆ.		
Scabiosa succisa . .	Devilsbit scabious .	Grassy places.
,, columbaria .	Small ,, .	Wastes.
COMPOSITÆ.		
Apargia hispida . .	Rough hawkbit . .	Common.
,, autumnalis .	Autumnal hawkbit .	Welhope.
Hieracium pilosella .	Mouse-ear hawkweed .	,, Scars.
,, pallidum .	Hawkweed . . .	Gilsland.
,, prenanthoides	Rough-bordered hawkweed . . .	Ridley Hall.
,, umbellatum	Narrow-leaved hawkweed. . . .	Woods.
Lapsana communis .	Nipple wort . . .	Hedge banks.
Arctium lappa . .	Burdock	Staward Peel.

Botanical Name.	Common Name.	Habitat.

COMPOSITÆ—*continued*.

Carduus lanceolatus	Spear plume thistle	Kilhope Scars.
„ palustris	Marsh „	Damp fields.
„ heterophyllus	Plume thistle	Chesterholme.
Centaurea nigra	Black knapweed	Kilhope.
„ scabiosa	Greater „	Hexham.
Bidens cernua	Bur marigold	Crowhall Mill.
Gnaphalium uliginosum	Marsh cudweed	Hareshaw Moor.
Gnaphalium sylvaticum	Highland „	Allendale.
Tussilago farfara	Coltsfoot	West Allendale.
Petasites vulgaris	Butter burr	Bellister Path.
Erigeron acris	Blue fleabane	Rare.
Senecio jacobea	Common ragwort	Ashgill.
„ sylvaticus	Wood groundsel	Garrigill.
Chrysanthemum segetum	Corn marigold	Haltwhistle.
Chrysanthemum leucanthemum	White ox-eye	Allendale.
Pyrethrum parthenium	Common feverfew	South Tyne.
Pyrethrum inodorum	Corn „	Hexham.
Matricaria chamomilla	Chamomile	Roman Wall.
Achillea millefolium	Common yarrow	Ashgill.

CAMPANULACEÆ.

Campanula rotundifolia	Harebell	Lanes and heaths.
Campanula glomerata	Clustered bell-flower	Bellister Wood.
Jasione montana	Sheepsbit	Haltwhistle.

ERICACEÆ.

Erica tetralix	Cross-leaved heath	Kilhope.
„ cinerea	Fine-leaved „	Black Burn.
Calluna vulgaris	Heather	Tindale Fell.
Andromeda polifolia	Marsh andromeda	Muckle Moss.
Arbutus Uva Ursi	Red bearberry	Dipton Dene.
Vaccinium myrtillus	Bilberry	Softly Wood.
„ Vitis Idæa	Red whortleberry	Kilhope Law.
„ uliginosum	Great bilberry	Walltown Crags.
„ oxycoccos	Cranberry	Baron House Bog.

BOTANY. 277

Botanical Name.	Common Name.	Habitat.
GENTIANACEÆ.		
Gentiana verna . .	Spring gentian . .	Hills.
Chlora perfoliata . . .	Perfoliate yellow-wort	Chesterwood.
Menyanthes trifoliata	Buckbean	Peat bogs.
CONVOLVULACEÆ.		
Convolvulus arvensis.	Small bindweed . .	Hexham.
SCROPHULARIACEÆ.		
Verbascum thapsus .	Shepherd's club . .	Hall Bank Head.
Veronica arvensis. .	Wall speedwell . .	South Tyne.
Euphrasia officinalis .	Eye-bright . . .	Pastures and heaths.
Rhinanthus crista-galli	Yellow rattle . . .	Garrigill.
Digitalis purpurea .	Purple foxglove . .	Pynkinscleugh.
Linaria vulgaris . .	Yellow toadflax . .	Haydon Bridge.
Scrophularia vernalis.	,, figwort . .	Otterburn.
OROBANCHACEÆ.		
Lathræa squamaria .	Toothwort	Hazel woods.
LABIATÆ.		
Salvia verbenaca . .	Sage	Walltown Crags.
Mentha viridis . .	Spearmint	Mint Hill.
,, hirsuta . .	Hairy mint . . .	River sides.
,, arvensis . .	Corn mint	Cornfields.
Thymus serpyllum .	Wild thyme . . .	Heathy banks.
Origanum vulgare .	Marjoram	North Tyne.
Ajuga reptans . .	Blue bugle . . .	Featherstone.
Lamium album . .	White dead-nettle .	Waste ground.
,, purpureum .	Red dead-nettle . .	,,
Galeopsis ladanum .	Red hemp-nettle . .	Haydon Bridge.
Stachys palustris . .	Marsh woundwort .	Allendale.
,, ambigua . .	Ambiguous woundwort	Lipwood.
Glechoma hederacea .	Ground ivy . . .	Hedge banks.
Nepeta cataria . .	Cat mint	Hexham.
Marrubium vulgare .	White horehound .	Tyne, Hexham.
Prunella vulgaris . .	Selfheel	Grassy places.
Scutellaria galericulata	Skullcap	Crag Lough.

278 BOTANY.

Botanical Name.	Common Name.	Habitat.
BORAGINACEÆ.		
Myosotis palustris	Forget-me-not.	Common.
,, cæspitosa	Water scorpion grass.	Watery places.
,, sylvatica	Wood ,,	Woods.
,, arvensis	Field ,,	Hedge banks.
,, versicolor	Yellow and blue scorpion grass	,,
Borago officinalis	Borage	Knarsdale.
LENTIBULARIACEÆ.		
Utricular intermedia.	Intermediate bladderwort	Crag Lough.
,, minor	Lesser bladderwort	Plenmeller Fell.
PRIMULACEÆ.		
Primula vulgaris	Primrose	Featherstone.
,, veris	Cowslip	Blenkinshope.
Trientalis Europæa	European chickweed	Roman Wall.
Lysimachia vulgaris	Yellow loosestrife	Poltross Burn.
,, nemorum	Yellow pimpernel	Ashgill.
PLUMBAGINACEÆ.		
Armeria maritima	Seapink	Herdly Haugh.
PLANTAGINACEÆ.		
Plantago major	Plantain	Road sides.
,, media	Hoary plantain	,,
,, maritima	Sea-side plantain	Unthank Moor.
Littorella lacustris	Plantain shoreweed	Greenly Lough.
POLYGONACEÆ.		
Polygonium bistorta	Snakeweed	Banks of Tyne.
,, viviparum	Alpine bistort	Gilderdale.
Rumex crispus	Curled dock	Stream sides.
,, aquaticus	Water ,,	Allen Heads.
,, acetosa	Common sorrel	Grassy ground.
,, acetosella	Sheep's ,,	Sandy heaths.
EMPETRACEÆ.		
Empetrum nigrum	Crowberry	Heaths.

BOTANY.   279

| Botanical Name. | Common Name. | Habitat. |

EUPHORBIACEÆ.

| Mercurialis perennis | Dog's mercury | Woods. |

URTICACEÆ.

| Humulus lapulus | Hop | Low Ash Holme. |

AMENTIFERÆ.

Myrica gale	Bog myrtle	Beacon Hill Wood.
Salix pentanebra	Sweet bay-leaved willow	Allendale.
„ ambigua	Ambiguous willow	Hexham.

CONIFERÆ.

| Taxus baccata | Yew | Allen Cliffs. |
| Juniperus communis | Juniper | Park Bents. |

ORCHIDACEÆ.

Neottia Nidus avis	Bird's-nest	Wardrew.
Listeria cordata	Heart-leaved tway-blade	Sewingshields.
Epipactis latifolia	Broad-leaved helleborine	Langley Castle.
„ palustris	Marsh helleborine	South Tyne.
Orchis pyramidalis	Pyramidal orchis	Haltwhistle.
„ mascula	Early purple „	Woods.
„ latifolia	Marsh „	Meadows.
„ maculata	Spotted „	Heaths.
Habenaria albida	Small white „	Heathy pastures.
„ bifolia	Butterfly „	Horse Close.
Malaxis paludosa	Marsh bog „	Muckle Moss.

IRIDACEÆ.

| Iris Pseudacorus | Yellow water-iris. | Blenkinsop Castle. |

AMARYLLIDACEÆ.

| Narcissus pseudo-narcissus | Daffodil | Nether Hall. |
| Galanthus nivalis | Snowdrop | Bishop's Linn. |

Botanical Name.	Common Name.	Habitat.
LILIACEÆ.		
Allium schenoprasum	Chives	Walltown Crags.
„ ursinum . .	Ramsons	Woods.
Gagea lutea . . .	Yellow gagea . . .	Whinitly Burn.
Hyacinthus non-scriptus	Wild hyacinth . .	Bellister Woods.
TRILLIACEÆ.		
Paris quadrifolia . .	Herb paris. . . .	Woods.
HYDROCHARIDACEÆ.		
*Anacharis alsinastrum.	Water thyme . .	Talkin Tarn.
FLUVIALES.		
Potamageton perfoliatus	Perfoliate pondweed .	Crag Lough
Potamageton lucens .	Shining „ .	„
„ heterophyllus	Various leaved „ .	Walltown.
„ rufescens .	Red „ .	Greenly Lough.
ARACEÆ.		
Lemna minor . . .	Lesser duckweed . .	Ponds and ditches.
Typha latifolia . .	Reed mace . . .	Crag Lough.
JUNCACEÆ.		
Juncus effesus. . .	Softrush	Cromel Linn.
„ lamprocarpus.	Fruited jointed rush .	Lipwood Moss.
„ squarrosus .	Heathrush. . . .	Damp moors.
Luzula pilosa . . .	Hairy woodrush . .	Woods.
Narthecium ossifragum	Bog asphodel . . .	Moors.
Juncus filiformis . .	Threadrush . . .	Tindale Tarn.
Luzula sylvatica . .	Great hairy woodrush	Woods.
„ spicata . .	Spiked mountain rush	Bew castle.

* Probably introduced from America. Male flower unknown in England. As this alien water pest has considerably detracted from the beauty of this fine sheet of water, and excited a good deal of interest a few years ago by stopping for a time the annual boat-races, we give a description of the plant that its appearance in any sheet of water may be at once detected. "Stem long, branching; whorls of leaves many, close together; flower, very small, but with a very long slender tube, often 2 or 3 inches long; sepal tinged with green and pink, externally, incurved, hooded." A local gentleman, well versed in botany, kindly writes, "How it got into the Tarn I cannot say, for I saw it there many years before it was publicly noticed. I have seen it in many places. It is like mint, and grows by slips." It has been established nine or ten years in Farding's Lake, near Marsden, and also in the Aln.

BOTANY.

Botanical Name.	Common Name.	Habitat.

CYPERACEÆ.

Scripus sylvaticus	Wood clubrush	Bellingham.
„ palustris	Spike „	Otterburn.
Carex pauciflora	Flowered sedge	Twice Brewed.
„ flava	Yellow „	Kilhope Law.
„ lævigata	Beaked „	Bellingham.
„ limosa	Mud „	Baron House Bog.
„ pendula	Pendulous „	Park Crags.

EQUISETACEÆ.

Equisetum arvense	Corn horsetail.	Cornfields.
„ variegatum	Variegated horsetail	Irthing Wardrew.
„ sylvaticum	Wood „	
„ hyemale	Rough „	Tippalt."

FERNS.

All the hills and dales, the woods and picturesque ruins, of this highly interesting and romantic district, are the natural haunts and habitat of ferns, which add attraction and beauty to every spot where they are found. The study of these graceful plants has become popular and fashionable, and not without just cause, for it has an expanding and refining influence on the mind, and is one of the few out-of-door pursuits peculiarly adapted to the gentler sex. There are few lovelier sights, or choicer companions for a ramble, than that of a blooming maiden, suitably attired, and with trowel and collecting case, busily botanizing in the most lovely corners of the land.

Those who are ignorant of ferns may, without previous study, quickly begin to recognize them. They are plants that have no richly coloured flowers, but leaves of graceful elegance, which have the under surface covered with regularly arranged dustlike patches of minute seeds; and once having begun to note carefully these seed patches, the student has entered the royal road to the knowledge of the different species of ferns.

The tract of country embraced in this book is rich in the different species, and nearly all of them may be found within a limited area: spleenwort and the royal fern excepted.

The lady fern, that feminine Narcissus of the woods and glens, is widely distributed over all the district, and for its exquisite grace and form is unequalled by any other British species. It is found in the shady bowers of Unthank, the cosy nooks of Blenkinsop, the charming glens of Featherstone, the rich expanses of Naworth, the woody dells of Edmond Castle; and it grows on every bank of the Irthing.

> "Where the copsewood is the greenest,
> Where the fountain glistens sheenest,
> Where the morning dew lies longest,
> There the lady fern grows strongest."
>
> SCOTT.

The common polypody, though of humble look, possesses much of interest and beauty. It is evergreen in many situations, and its rich orange-coloured spores catch the eye like a gleam of golden sunshine. It is in almost every hedge, on decaying oaks, and moss-covered walls; giving a charm to every spot where it is found.

The beautiful beech fern nestles in great luxuriance beneath the waterfall in Glen Dhu, and few cascades will be visited without meeting with it.

The parsley fern is found on many of the hills in the northern counties, but as it generally grows in miniature caverns formed by the scattered masses of rocks high on the hill sides, it is rarely met with except by the hardy and persevering collector. It also finds a home on many of the heights crowned by the ruins of the great Roman wall.

The shieldferns are plentiful, and few surpass them in beauty. They will be found in hedges and the shady clefts of rocks.

The rigid buckler fern delights in the weathered limestone rock; the common buckler fern seems to court the society of man, and creeps into the sheltered nooks near cultivation; while the mountain buckler fern is fond of the solitary den, or the rifted mountain.

The holly fern is, as we might expect, scarce, for it courts the withering blast on the barest peaks.

Alternate spleenwort is a rare fern in the north, but a

specimen was found on the Kyloe Rock, near Belford, a few years ago.

Ruta muraria delights in the crumbling mortar of bridges and ruins, and is found on the Roman wall, as well as on many of the old castles.

Green spleenwort luxuriates in the fissured rock of the wild dell, and is so tiny that it is only beautiful to the cultivated mind and the eye of taste. It is to be found near Wardrew, Gilsland. A search for it in the Croglin Water will repay the tourist collector, who will also, while in the locality, do well to ascend the Croglin heights, and thus obtain one of the best views in the north of England. The Trichomanes spleenwort, an exquisite little beauty, may be found on any kind of rock, as it creeps in the crevices of bridges, ruins, and churches. Sea spleenwort luxuriates in the dark caverns of sea cliffs.

The hart's tongue is very ornamental—the variety crispum particularly so—and being decidedly different from any other British species it is easily recognized.

The scaly fern is a charming "wee thing," and clings with pertinacity to an old ruin or a crumbling rock. It is a very close fissure indeed that its wiry roots cannot penetrate.

The common hard fern often ornaments craggy precipices on the hills, but its favourite ground is damp clay or spongy gravel.

The bracken is a favourite with all, poets included, and in the summer and autumn it gives a rich and varied colouring to most of our wildest heathlands. In the natural woods of the district it often attains to a height of 6 or 8 feet, festooning the hazel, birch, and rowan, and giving great beauty to our woodlands.

Both varieties of the British bladder fern possess elegance, and are found in most rocks, and the crumbling relics of the Roman wall.

Osmunda regalis is the most stately of all our British ferns, and is generally found in marshy grounds and sheltered situations.

Moonworts are tiny ferns which give an interest, if not ornament, to the gelt. The dens in Naworth will, in all probability, yield a rich harvest of them.

The adder's tongue is found in many of the moist meadows of the north, and has, on examination, a kind of out-of-the-way prettiness.

The crisp-edged hay-scented fern has an elegant drooping habit, and is valuable as a pot plant from its evergreen character. It is found on many of the weathered rocks on the beautiful banks of the Irthing.

Our object in this brief commentary has not been so much to draw attention to these beautiful plants or to give the localities, as to indicate in a very summary way the kind of spots where the different kinds are likely to be found. We do not believe in going direct to a given place to *find* a fern, but in exploring the likeliest places in a locality and *finding* for ourselves. We have rambled through every glen in the district in search of ferns, recreation, and health, and can confidently, from experience, advise every visitor to Gilsland to take a glen and fell tonic along with the spa water, and, if perseverance be brought to bear, we will guarantee as the result a happy and healthy mind, as well as a healthy and vigorous frame.

Botanical Name.	Common Name.	Habitat.
Polypodium vulgare	Common polypody fern	Witches' Glen, Featherstone
„ phegopteris	Beech fern, or mountain polypody	Glen Dhu, Knarsdale.
„ dryopteris	Oak fern, or smooth three-branched polypody	Gilsland.
Allosorus crispus	Rockbrake, or mountain parsley fern	Sewingshields.
Polystichum aculeatum	Common prickly shieldfern	Scar, near Alston.
„ angulare	Soft „ „	Unthank Hall Woods.
„ lobatum	Common „ „	Black Cleugh.
„ lonchitis	Alpine shield, or holly fern	Glen Dhu Waterfall.
Listrea oreopteris	Mountain buckler fern	Black Burn, Tindale Fell.
„ Felixmas	Common buckler, or male fern	Whinltly Wood.
„ rigida	Rigid buckler fern	Knar Burn.
„ dilatata	Broad „ „	Grindon, Bardon Mill.
„ recurva	Hay-scented, or triangular buckler fern	Banks of the Irthing.
Athyrium Felix fœmina	Common lady fern	„ „
„ de pauperatum		Morley Wood.
Asplenium germanicum	Alternate spleenwort fern	Kyloe Rock; rare.
„ Ruta muraria	Rne-leaved spleenwort, or wall rue	Gilsland.
„ viride	Green spleenwort fern	Cramel Linn.
„ Trichomanes	Common maidenhair spleenwort fern	Gilsland.
„ adiantum nigrum	Black maidenhair spleenwort fern	Coombe Crag.
„ ceterach	Scaly spleenwort fern	Denton Hall.
„ marinum	Sea spleenwort fern	St. Bee's Head, and Whitehaven.

Botanical Name.	Common Name.	Habitat.
Scolopendrium vulgare.	Common hart's tongue fern	Whinitly Wood.
,, crispum	,, ,, fern	Gelt, Castle Carrock.
,, lobatum	,, ,, ,,	Gelt Burn.
Blecknum spicant	Common hard fern	Wood Hall Hills.
Pteris aquilina	Common brake fern	Woods and fells.
Cystopteris fragilis	Brittle bladder fern	Knar Burn Bridge.
,, dentata	,, ,,	Moss Kennel.
Osmunda regalis	Royal flowering fern	Wigton, Dubmill, and Wreay.
Botrychium lunaria.	Common moonwort fern	Gelt Burn, Brampton.
Ophioglossum vulgatum	Common adder's tongue fern	Rose Hill and Bolton.

INDIGENOUS GRASSES.

Many of the grasses growing by the waysides and in the woods, pastures, and meadows of the north of England are eminently graceful and beautiful, and are only neglected because they are common. Surely the class of plants that compose the bright gay mantle of our hills, valleys, and woodlands should interest us above all others. The vesture is nature's handiwork and of nature's colouring, and however brilliant, is never glaring, but always refreshing and attractive. Some of the grasses when in flower have a simple grace and beauty peculiarly their own, and when we have seen bouquets of foreign varieties decorating drawing-rooms we have often been surprised that some attempt had not been made to popularize the study and collection of our own native beauties. The creeping bent grass, water hair grass, and tufted hair grass are very beautiful, and make pretty decorative bouquets, especially the gracefully spiked panicle of the tufted hair grass, which is often of a silvery grey colour. The reed meadow grass if collected immediately before it is in full flower retains its rich purple colour for months, and its massive plumes when nicely arranged make handsome bouquets. The common quaking grass, from its pleasing associations, is often collected. The cotton grass, so abundant over all the peaty moors in the district, is very pretty when carefully gathered. On Hartley Burn Moor it is very abundant. Some of the grasses are very fragrant, especially when dried. It would be out of place here to write about the nature and value of the different grasses. This list must not be accepted as exhaustive, but simply a beginning, as an incentive to tourists and naturalists.

Botanical Name.	Common Name.	Height.	Time of Flowering.
		ft. in.	
Anthoxanthum odoratum	Sweet-scented spring grass	1 0	May.
Phleum pratense	Common cat's-tall, or Timothy grass	3 0	August.
Alopecurus pratensis	Meadow fox-tail grass	2 0	"
„ geniculatus	Jointed fox-tail grass	1 2	July, Oct.
Agrostis vulgaris	Fine bent grass	1 1	July, Aug.
„ stolonifera	Creeping bent grass	1 4	"
Aira aquatica	Water hair grass	1 0	June to Aug.
„ cæspitosa	Tufted hair grass	3 0	June, July.
„ flexuosa	Zigzag mountain hair grass	0 10	June to Aug.
„ caryophyllea	Silvery hair grass	0 8	June.
Holcus lanatus	Meadow soft or Yorkshire grass	2 0	July, Aug.
„ mollis	Creeping soft grass	1 3	August.
„ avenaceus	Cat-like soft grass	4 6	June to Aug.
Sesleria cærulea	Blue moor grass	1 0	May.
Poa aquatica	Reed meadow grass	5 0	July, Aug.
„ fluitans	Flote meadow grass	3 0	July to Sept.
„ compressa	Flat-stalked meadow grass	1 2	June, July.
„ trivialis	Rough-stalked „	1 8	June to Sept.
„ pratensis	Smooth-stalked „	1 2	May, June.
„ annua	Annual meadow „	0 9	April to Oct.
Briza media	Common quaking grass	1 4	May, June.
Dactylis glomerata	Rough cock's-foot grass	2 2	July to Sept.
Cynosurus cristatus	Crested dog's-tail grass	1 9	July, Aug.
Festuca ovina	Sheep's fescue grass	0 10	June.
„ duriuscula	Hard „	2 0	June, July.
„ gigantea	Giant „	3 6	July to Sept.
„ pratensis	Meadow „	2 0	June to Aug.
„ elatior	Tall „	4 0	"
Bromus mollis	Soft brome grass	2 0	June to Sept.
Avena pubescens	Downy oat grass	1 6	June.
„ flavescens	Yellow „	1 8	June to Aug.
Arundo colorata	Canary reed grass	4 6	June.
Triticum repens	Creeping wheat grass	2 to 5 ft.	June to Sept.
Eriophorum pubescens	Cotton grass	1 0	May to July.
Arundo arenaria	Sea reed grass	2 0	June.

LYCOPODIUM (CLUB-MOSSES).

Those ancient giants now so dwarfed are intermediate plants between the ferns and true mosses. The common club-moss or stag's horn is widely distributed over the hills in the district, and is a particularly handsome plant. We have found it on Plenmellor Fell several yards in length. It is said to make a beautiful object when cultivated, and suspended from the side wall of a greenhouse. The savin-leaved club-moss is a pretty plant, and may be found at Crag Lough.

The liverworts will be found spreading their coats of

BOTANY. 287

green over the rocks in nearly every cascade in the locality. The jungermannia are a most interesting genus, and are distributed widely over the district.

LYCOPODIUM, OR CLUB-MOSSES.

Botanical Names.	English Names.	Habitat.	Season of Fruiting.
Lycopodium clavatum	Common club-moss	Mountain pastures.	Summer.
,, alpinum	Savin-leaved club-moss	,, ,,	,,
,, selago	Fir club-moss	Peat soil, on mountains	,,
,, selaginoides	Lesser alpine club-moss	Moist places, on mountains	,,

HEPATICÆ, MARCHANTIA, OR LIVERWORTS.

Botanical Names.	English Names.	Habitat.	Season of Fruiting.
Marchantia polymorpha	Polymorphous marchantia	Shady banks, common.	Summer.
,, hemisphærica	Hemispherical	Watercourses, shady banks	Spring.
,, conica	Conical	Mountain streams, &c.	,,

JUNGERMANNIA.

Botanical Names.	English Names.	Habitat.	Season of Fruiting.
Jungermannia asplenioides	Spleenwort jungermannia	Shady banks, rocks, and woods	Spring.
,, bicuspidata	Forked	On trees, hedge banks, &c.	,,
,, albicans	Whitish	Moist banks, &c., &c.	,,
,, complanata	Flat	Trunks of trees.	,,
,, reptans	Creeping	In woods and on rocks	,,
,, platyphylla	Flat-leaved	On walls, rocks, and trees	,,
,, tomentella	Spongy	Moist places, common.	,,
,, serpyllifolia	Thyme-leaved	Trees and rocks, subalpine	,,
,, multifida	Many-lobed	Damp heaths, sides of drains	,,
,, dilatata	Dilated	On trees, common.	,,
,, furcata	Forked	Trees, moors, rocks, common	,,

MOSSES.

"One tiny tuft of moss alone,
Mantling with freshest green a stone,
Fixed his delighted gaze."

Mosses, insignificant as they appear to be, have a high claim on our attention and admiration, because they play an important part in natural history as one of the primal agents in beautifying the bald spots of the landscape, and in clothing the sterile nakedness of nature. The first vegetation that appears on the bare rock, to prepare by its accretive growth and decay for plants of a higher order, is the moss, and it has been computed, by a high authority in moscology, that mosses form the fourth part of the vegetable covering of Great Britain. And are we not greatly indebted to mosses for the comfort of our own firesides, and the wealth we enjoy, and position we occupy as a nation? for our coal fields are only a vast aggregation of submerged, compressed, and mineralized club-mosses, tree ferns, horsetails, &c.; and is it not possible, nay highly probable, that the morasses formed by the growth and decay of mosses, which we now consider so worthless, may be engulphed, compressed, and mineralized in order to store fuel for future ages? Linnæus, in his Flora of Lapland, gives the following interesting particulars as to the use of moss in the nursery economy of the Laps: "The Lapland matrons are well acquainted with the moss. They dry and lay it in their children's cradles to supply the place of bed, bolster, and every covering, and being changed night and morning it keeps the infant remarkably clean, dry, and warm, and makes a most delicate nest for the new-born babes." But we have not space to treat of their economy in nature, but must rest content with briefly directing attention to their elegant structure and beauty.

"The tiny moss, whose silken verdure clothes
The time-worn rock, and whose bright capsules rise
Like fiery urns on stalks of golden sheen,
Demand our admiration and our praise
As much as cedar kissing the blue sky."

The district of Gilsland is rich in mosses, and a quiet saunter up any of the shady glens will gratify the most enthusiastic votary. This, too, is the border land of historical mosses (or boggy lands formed by the growth and decay of sphagnums, &c.), so notorious in traditionary song, story, and history, over which the roving Scotchmen "trooped" to harry their southern neighbours, and from the mosses over which they rode they received the appropriate name of mosstroopers.

> "A stark moss-trooping Scot was he
> As e'er couched Border lance by knee,
> Through Solway sands and Tarras moss
> Blindfold he knew the paths to cross;
> Steady of heart and stout of hand
> As ever drove prey from Cumberland."—SCOTT.

The habitat of mosses is wherever there is a naked spot to clothe, be it on the barren moor, dripping rock, sterile sand, or spreading tree, and to add to their beauty and picturesque effect they are of all hues and shades of colour. Those who have not bestowed close attention on these minute cryptogamous plants will on examining them closely be greatly surprised at their simple elegance and beauty. They are not merely textureless carpets of the lowest organisms, but plants of elegant structure, graceful foliage, and rich colouring. In the rage for new designs we have often been surprised that the elegant forms of mosses have not been caught up by manufacturers. On a river bank in early spring, when the meadows are brown, what is more refreshing to the eye than the bright green cushions of Bryum crudum, fringed as they often are with cushioned selvedges of purple Bryum alpinum. The sphagnums given will all be found in the boggy places on the wastes of the locality, their spongy foliage and white colour contrasting prettily with the dark-coloured heath around them.

A wide field is open for investigation in this fascinating pursuit, and as the tufts are easily carried, and moisture soon makes them reassume all their original form, no class of plants can be investigated with greater facility. Farmers reading this article will, we fancy, exclaim, bother the mosses! they destroy the half of our grass lands. We would remind them that mosses are nursed in the lap of poverty, and only take possession of the soil after it has been too much impoverished to grow anything else. Enrich the soil and mosses will disappear. Instead of describing particular mosses and the localities where they are to be found, we have briefly, under habitat, described the materials on which they generally grow, in order to excite and cultivate attention. A ramble is never so healthy and pleasing as when it is one entirely of discovery.

290 BOTANY.

MOSSES (*Musci*).

Botanical Name.	Common Name.	Habitat.	Season of Fruiting.
Andreœa alpina.	Alpine split moss	Alpine and subalpine rocks; rare	Spring.
,, rupestris	Rock split moss	,, ,, not rare	,,
,, Rothii	Black falcate split moss.	,, ,, rare	,,
Phascum serratum	Serrated earth moss	Very minute, on the ground, in damp places	
,, alternifolium.	Alternate-leaved earth moss	Moist banks; fruit rare	Winter.
,, crispum	Curly-leaved earth moss	Banks and fields	Spring.
,, subulatum	Awl-leaved earth moss	Dry banks, fields, and heaths	,,
,, cuspidatum.	Cuspidate earth moss	Banks, fields, and gardens	,,
Sphagnum obtusifolium	Blunt-leaved bog moss	Bogs, and still pools, common	,,
,, squarrosum	Spreading-leaved bog moss.	Bogs, common	Summer.
,, acutifolium.	Slender bog moss.	Wet bogs	Spring.
,, cuspidatum.	Long-leaved floating bog moss.	,, ,, fruit rare	,,
Gymnostomum ovatum.	Minute-tufted beardless moss	Banks and wall tops	Winter.
,, truncatulum	Little blunt-fruited beardless moss		
Heimii.	Long-stalked beardless moss	Banks, fields, and garden grounds	Summer.
Anœctangium ciliatum.	Hoary-branched beardless moss	Pastures, near the sea generally	Spring.
Diphyscium foliosum	Leafy diphyscium	Rocks and stones	Summer.
Splachnum sphæricum.	Globe-fruited splachnum	Banks, &c., in alpine situations	,,
,, minioides	Brown tapering ,,	Decayed dung of animals in alpine places	,,
		On the ground on the mountains	

BOTANY.   291

Eucalypta vulgaris	Common extinguisher moss	Banks and wall tops	Spring.
,, ciliata	Fringed ,,	On the ground, and rock on the mountains	Summer.
Weissia cirrata	Curly-leaved weissia	On posts and trees, &c.	Spring.
,, curvirostra	Curved-beaked weissia	Banks, walls, and rocks	Autumn.
,, contraversa	Green-cushioned weissia	Banks and wall tops	Spring.
,, acuta	Sharp-pointed weissia	Moist alpine rocks	Summer.
Grimmia apocarpa	Sessile grimmia	Rocks, walls, and trees	Spring.
,, pulvinata	Grey-cushioned grimmia	Rocks and walls	,,
,, ovata	Ovate grimmia	Rocks in mountainous districts	Summer.
Didymodon purpureus	Purple didymodon	On turf-topped walls, &c., common	Spring.
,, capillaceus	Fine-leaved didymodon	Banks and rocks, in the mountains	,,
,, heteromallus	Curved-leaved grimmia	Banks and wall tops, common	Summer.
Trichostomum aciculare	Dark mountain fringe moss	Wet rocks and stones	Spring.
,, polyphyllum	Many-leaved fringe moss	Walls, rocks, and stones	,,
,, lanuginosum	Woolly fringe moss	Stony ground, on the mountains	Winter.
Dicranum bryoides	Lesser pinnate-leaved fork moss	Moist banks, &c.; abundant	Spring.
,, adiantoides	Adiantum-like fork moss	Moist dripping rocks and banks	Autumn.
,, scoparium	Broom fork moss	In woods, copses, &c.; common	Winter.
,, varium	Variable fork moss, minute	Damp, bare, clayey ground, &c.	,,
,, heteromallum	Silky-leaved fork moss	Shady banks, rocks, &c.	Autumn.
Tortula rigida	Aloe-leaved screw moss	Clay banks, &c.; rare	Spring.
,, muralis	Wall screw moss	Walls, everywhere; common	,,
,, ruralis	Great hairy screw moss	Walls, thatched roofs, trees, &c.	Winter.
,, unguiculata	Bird's claw screw moss	Hedge banks and sandy fields	Summer.
,, fallax	Fallacious screw moss	On walls and in fields; common	Spring.
Cinclidotus fontinaloides	Fountain lattice moss	Calcareous streams, on rocks, stones, and wool	Winter.
Polytrichum undulatum	Undulated hair moss	Banks and woods, in shady places	

u 2

292 BOTANY.

Botanical Name.	Common Name.	Habitat.	Season of Fruiting.
Polytrichum piliferum	Bristle-pointed hair moss	Heaths, moors, and turfed walls	Spring.
,, commune	Common hair moss	Woods, heaths; very common	Summer.
,, aloides	Dwarf long-headed hair moss	Moist sandy banks, &c.	Autumn.
,, nanum	Dwarf round-headed hair moss.	,, ,,	Winter.
Funaria hygrometrica	Hygrometric cord moss	On ground where wood has been burned, &c.	Spring.
Orthotrichum anomalum	Anomalus bristle moss	Rocks and walls, &c.	,,
,, affine	Pale straight-leaved bristle moss	On trees, pales, &c.	Autumn.
,, striatum	Common bristle moss	,, ,,	Summer.
,, crispum	Curled bristle moss	On trees in woods	Autumn.
,, pulchellum	Elegant bristle moss	On trunks of trees; rare	Summer.
Bryum palustre	Marsh thread moss	Bogs; common fruit, rare	,,
,, julaceum	Slender-branched thread moss	Near streams and waterfalls	Autumn.
,, argenteum	Silvery thread moss	Wall tops, thatched roofs	Spring.
,, pyriforme	Pear-fruited thread moss	Sandy soil, and on sandstone rocks	Summer.
,, capillare	Greater matted thread moss	Rocks, walls, &c.	,,
,, caespititium	Lesser matted thread moss	Wall tops, roofs of houses, &c.	Spring.
,, nutans	Silky pendulous thread moss	On peat soil, &c.	Summer.
,, alpinum	Alpine thread moss	Moist rocks and stones	,,
,, hornum	Swan's-neck thyme thread moss	Shady woods	Spring.
,, roseum	Rosaceous thyme thread moss	Grassy banks and heaths	Autumn.
,, ligulatum	Long-leaved thyme thread moss	Woods and moist banks; fruit rare	Spring.
,, punctatum	Dotted thyme-leaved thread moss	Margins of streams, near tree roots	,,
,, cuspidatum	Pointed-leaved thread moss	Woods, at the roots of trees	,,
,, Toseri	Minute diaphanous thread moss	River sides: rare, by South Tyne	,,

BOTANY. 293

Bryum marginatum	Thick-edged-leaved thyme thread moss	On ground in woods, moist, stony places	Summer.
Bartramia pomiformis	Common apple-fruited moss	On rocks and dry banks	Spring.
,, ithyphylla	Straight-leaved apple moss	Subalpine, on dry banks, &c.	,,
,, fontana	Fountain apple moss	By springs, in turfy soil	Summer.
,, arcuata	Curved-stalked apple moss	Subalpine, on moist rocks; fruit rare	Winter.
Neckera crispa	Curled neckera	Trees and rocks; beautiful moss	Spring.
Daltonia heteromalla	Lateral-leaved daltonia	Trunks of trees	Summer.
Fontinalis antipyretica	Greater water moss	Growing in rivers, streams	Spring.
Hookeria lucens	Shining hookeria	Moist banks, in woods; a rare moss	,,
Hypnum trichomanoides	Blunt fern-like feather moss	Base of trunks of trees, near streams	,,
,, complanatum	Flat feather moss	,, ,, in moist places	,,
,, riparium	Short-beaked water feather moss	Banks of streams, on stones, &c.	Summer.
,, undulatum	Waved-leaved feather moss	In shady woods, &c.	Winter.
,, denticulatum	Sharp fern-like feather moss	Shady moist places; common	Autumn.
,, tenellum	Tender awl-leaved feather moss	Old walls and rocks	Summer.
,, populeum	Matted feather moss	Stones in shady places	Spring.
,, stramineum	Straw-like feather moss	Banks and wet bogs; fruit rare	,,
,, murale	Wall feather moss	Walls and moist stones	,,
,, purum	Neat meadow feather moss	On banks and under trees; fruit rare	,,
,, piliferum	Hair-pointed feather moss	,, ,, shady woods	Autumn.
,, schreberi	Schreberian feather moss	In woods, among trees and bushes	,,
,, plumosum	Rusty feather moss	Moist banks, rocks and stones	,,
,, pulchellum	Elegant feather moss	Alpine places, among rocks	Spring.
,, sericeum	Silky feather moss	On trees and rocks, &c.	,,
,, lutescens	Rough-stalked feather moss	Stems of trees, and on moist banks	,,
,, alopecurum	Fox-tail feather moss	Woods, shady banks, stones, &c.	Winter.
,, dendroides	Tree-like feather moss	Woods and meadows, &c.; fruit rare	,,
,, curvatum	Curved feather moss	Trees and rocks	Spring.

294 BOTANY.

MOSSES—continued.

Botanical Name.	Common Name.	Habitat.	Season of Fruiting.
Hypnum myosuroides	Mouse-tail feather moss	On trees	Autumn.
,, splendens	Glittering feather moss	Woods, heaths, &c.	Spring.
,, proliferum	Proliferous feather moss	,, ,, and banks	,,
,, prælongum	Very long feather moss	Moist shady banks, dead trees	Winter.
,, rutabulum	Rough-stalked feather moss	On the ground, dead ferns, stones	,,
,, velutinum	Velvet feather moss	Woods and hedge banks	Spring.
,, ruscifolium	Long-beaked water feather moss	Stones, wood, and rocks, in streams	Winter.
,, striatum	Common striated feather moss	Shady woods	Spring.
,, cuspidatum	Pointed bog feather moss	Bogs and marshy ground	Summer.
,, loreum	Rambling mountain feather moss	In woods, among bushes, on moors	Winter.
,, triquetrum	Triquetrous feather moss	In dry woods, &c.	,,
,, brevirostre	Short-beaked feather moss	In shady woods	Spring.
,, squarrosum	Drooping-leaved feather moss	Abundant in pastures; fruit rare	Winter.
,, filicinum	Lesser golden fern feather moss	Marshy ground, near streams	Spring.
,, palustre	Marsh feather moss	On marshy springy ground	,,
,, anduncum	Claw-leaved feather moss	Marshes and streamlets	Summer.
,, uncinatum	Sickle-leaved feather moss	Moist banks, &c.	Spring.
,, rugulosum	Wrinkled-leaved feather moss	Heathy ground; fruit rare	,,
,, commutatum	Calcareous fern feather moss	Calcareous dripping rocks	,,
,, scorpioides	Scorpion feather moss	Turfy bogs, &c.; fruit rare	,,
,, cupressiforme	Cypress-leaved feather moss	Banks, trees, and stones; abundant	,,
,, crista castrensis	Ostrich plume feather moss	Beautiful in fir woods; rare	Summer.
,, moluscum	Plumy-crested feather moss	Calcareous rocks and stones	Winter.

MUSHROOMS AND POISONOUS FUNGI.

We make no apology for introducing such a well-known esculent as the mushroom into a guide-book. Excursionists are always fond of gathering them, and as they can be eaten either fresh or stewed they add an agreeable variety to their table. The only edible mushrooms are those grown in open pastures, *Agaricus campestris*, and the fairy-ring mushroom, *Agaricus arcades*. The true edible mushroom when in the first or middle stage of growth is easily distinguished by its fine pink or flesh-coloured gills and pleasant smell, and has been used from time immemorial in China, India, and Africa, and long held in high esteem in this country. It springs up in old open pastures, and should only be gathered in such places, while the poisonous generally grow in woods, or on their margin. Mushrooms at all times should be used with caution, for when grown in certain places they have bad effects. Thorough mastication is at all times necessary, but when accidents do happen an emetic should be immediately administered, and then either vinegar or lemon-juice given. If any doubts exist, soak in vinegar before using. Authorities are agreed that if a silver spoon, a silver coin, or onion be dipped into a vessel of seething mushrooms, it will be stained a dark colour if they are poisonous, and remain quite unstained if they are good. The beautiful colouring of some of the poisonous fungi is very striking—rose-coloured pink, scarlet, orange, olive, red, with an endless variety of shades and tints, but space prevents us doing more than drawing attention to these gorgeous coloured objects. Lichens are common everywhere, and will be found adhering to rocks, trunks of trees, and the most barren soil. They are curious objects, and well worth the study of tourists. All the fungi tribe are nature's scavengers.

> " The Roman wall, with lichens hoar,
> Time-battered, grim and stern ;
> And knarled oaks thick bearded o'er
> With lichen, moss, and fern."

LICHENS.

Botanical Name.	Common Name.	Habitat.	Season of Fruiting.
Opegrapha atrata	Black opegrapha	Frequent on trees	
Lepraria flava	Bright yellow lepraria	On trees and rocks; common	
Lecidea atrata	Inky-fruited lecidea	On rocks	
,, confluens	Confluent-shielded lecidea	Rocks and walls; common	
,, geographica	Map lecidea	Plentiful on primitive rocks	At all seasons.
Lecanora subfusca	Brown-shielded lecanora	Rocks and trees; common	
Parmelia conspersa	Chestnut-shielded parmelia	Walls and rocks	
,, olivacea	Olive-coloured parmelia	Walls, rocks, and trees	
Sticta sylvatica	Pitted wood sticta	Rocks and trees in woods	
Cetraria glauca	Glaucous cetraria	Trunks and branches of trees	
,, islandica	Iceland moss	On the ground on the hills	
Usnea barbata	Jointed usnea	On trees in woods	
Cladonia rangiferina	Reindeer moss	Moors and heaths	

FUNGI, OR MUSHROOMS.

Botanical Name.	Common Name.	Habitat.	Season of Fruiting.
Agaricus campestris	Common mushroom	Pastures and woods	
,, orcades	Fairy-ring mushroom	Meadows and pastures	
,, muscarius	Fly amanit	In fir woods; beautiful	
,, tonarius	Toned mushroom	In woods, &c.	Summer and Autumn.
Polyporus squamosus		In woods on trees	
,, velutinus			
Boletus Grevillei		Common in woods	
Pesiza cupularis	Cuped pesiza	On rotten wood and sticks	
,, pulchella	Elegant pesiza	,,	
Lycoperdon gemmatum		Sandy pastures, ,,	
Uredo segetum		On cereal plants, oats, barley, &c., too common	
,, rosæ	Rose rust	On roses, too common	

J. C.

(297)

MOTHS, BUTTERFLIES, AND BIRDS.

BUTTERFLIES.

The transformations of a butterfly from the egg to the beautiful creature on the wing is so marvellous that it attracts the attention of men of the most refined minds. Butterflies flitting from flower to flower are such lovely objects in nature that they not only attract admiration, but they often tempt the most mature and sedate to give chase with all the abandon of youth. In our rambles we have often been tempted to capture these gaudy insects, and being comparatively unversed in their nomenclature, and without a local list, we have had great difficulty in puzzling out their names. The following incomplete list, gathered from various local authorities, will, we trust, to some extent supply this desideratum, and prove a nucleus to one more complete. We will only add, that butterfly hunting, while inspiriting to the young, may with advantage be indulged in as a recreative amusement by all. A list of the moths found in the district has also been given.

MOTHS.

Entomological Name.	Common Name.
Acherontia antropos	Death's-head moth.
Anthrocera filipendulæ	Six-spot Burnet moth.
Smerenthus ocellatus	Eyed hawk-moth.
,, populi	Poplar hawk-moth.
Sphinx convolvuli	Hawk moth.
Macroglossa stellatarum	Humming-bird moth.
Sesia fuciformis	Broad-bordered hawk-moth.
Trochilium apiforme	Hornet moth.
Spichia bembeciformis	Lunar hornet-moth.
Trochilium tipuliforme	Currant clearwing moth.
,, vespiforme	Gnat clearwing moth.

BUTTERFLIES.

Entomological Name.	Common Name.	Habitat.	Month of Appearing.
Pieris brassicæ	Garden white butterfly	Kitchen gardens	June to August.
" rapæ	Small garden white butterfly	Gardens and fields	May to July.
" napi	Green biennial white butterfly	Damp fields and marshy places	May to August.
Cardamines	The orange-tip butterfly	Wood sides and lanes	May.
Lasiommata egeria	speckled wood butterfly	Woods	April and May.
" megera	wall butterfly	Dry lands and walls	May to September.
Hipparchia semele	grayling butterfly	Rocky and gravelly banks	July to September.
" janira	meadow brown butterfly	Abundant in grassy places	June to August.
" tithonus	large heath butterfly	Dry fields and lanes	July and August.
" hyperanthus	ringlet butterfly	Woods and hedgerows	June and July.
Cœnonympha davus	March ringlet butterfly	Wet mossy bogs	June to August.
" pamphilus	small heath butterfly	Grassy heaths and fields	June to September.
Venessa atalanta	red admiral butterfly	Gardens and highways	Aug. and September.
" Io	peacock butterfly	Fields and gardens	"
" urticæ	small tortoiseshell butterfly	Waste grounds and roadsides	June to October.
Grapta C. album	comma butterfly	Gardens and meadows	July and August.
Argynnidi paphia	silver-washed fritillary butterfly	Fields and bramble sprays	" "
" algala	dark-green fritillary butterfly	Heaths and woods	" "
" euphrosyne	pearl-bordered fritillary butterfly	Woods and hedgerows	May to August.
" selene	small pearl-bordered fritillary butterfly	"	"
Melitia artemis	greasy or marsh fritillary butterfly	Marshy meadows and woods	June and July.
Thecla quercus	purple hairstreak butterfly	Oak and lime trees	July and August.
Chrysophanus phlœas	small copper butterfly	Shady vales and pastures	April to August.
Polyommatus argiolus	azure blue butterfly	Woods and holly hedges	May to August.
" alsus	Bedford, or little blue butterfly	Dry, grassy places	May and June.
" alexis	common blue butterfly	Fields and grassy lanes	May to September.
Thanaos lages	dingy skipper butterfly	Hill sides and dry banks	May to August.
Pamphila sylvanus	large skipper butterfly	Grassy places, near woods	May to July.

BIRDS.

We have only space to give our readers a mere list of the birds observed in the district treated of in this Guide.

In a catalogue, compiled by Mr. John Hancock, of the Tyneside Naturalists' Field Club, there are no less than 265 different species mentioned as having been observed in Northumberland and Durham, being more than two-thirds of the whole British species. This ornithic richness is chiefly owing to the diversity of physical features, which is admirably suited to the feathered tribe. Our list is a long way short of 265, but very casual visitors, of which there is a large number, and sea-coast birds, have been omitted as not coming within our range.

Classification we have ignored, merely giving the common name, and dividing them into residents and visitors.

RESIDENTS.

Merlin.	Linnet.	Red grouse.
Sparrowhawk.	Mountain linnet.	Blackcock.
Kestrel.	Lesser redpole.	Partridge.
Brown owl.	Common bunting.	Pheasant.
Barn owl.	Yellowhammer.	Golden plover.
Long-eared owl.	Skylark.	Peewit.
Kingfisher.	Titlark.	Curlew.
Creeper.	Pied wagtail.	Common snipe.
Carrion crow.	Water ouzel.	Waterhen.
Rook.	Blackbird.	Coot.
Jackdaw.	Song thrush.	Heron.
Magpie.	Redbreast.	Black-headed gull.
Jay.	Wren.	Black-backed gull.
Starling.	Great titmouse.	Wild duck.
House sparrow.	Blue titmouse.	Teal.
Greenfinch.	Wood pigeon.	Little grebe.
Chaffinch.		

VISITORS.

Buzzard.	Willow wren.	Stone curlew
Cuckoo.	Swallow.	Woodcock.
Ring ouzel.	Sand martin.	Common sandpiper.
Fieldfare.	Swift.	Corncrake.
Redwing.	Nightjar.	Wild goose.
Redstart.		

J. M. C.

INDEX.

ALLENDALE TOWN, 152, 158.
Allen River, 141, 158, 160.
Alston, 152, 195
Andrew-de-Harcla, 14, 49.
Armathwaite, 51.
Ashgill Force, 156.
Askerton Castle, 105.
Ayle Burn, 158.

BANKS HEAD, 87, 88, 199.
Barcombe, 140.
Bardon Mill, 135, 138, 141, 159, 160.
Beardie Grey, 127.
Beaumont, 192.
Bede, 10, 163.
Bellister Castle, 119, 122.
Belted Will, 98.
Beltingham, 160.
Benwell, 211.
Bewcastle, 104, 106, 204.
Birdoswald, 80, 86, 199.
Bishop Ridley, 141.
Black Burn, 116.
——— Dike, 206.
Blenkinsop Castle, 119, 129.
Borcovicus, 135, 203.
Boustead Hill, 191.
Bowness, 173, 186.
Brampton, 52.
Broom Lee Lough, 135.
Brown Dikes, 207
Burgh-by-Sands, 189, 191.
Busygap, 206.
Byker Hill, 212.

CADWALLO, 210.
Caldew, 3.
Cambeck, 197.

Carlisle, 1, 193.
——— Castle, 25.
——— Cathedral, 19.
Carrowburgh, 207.
Carville Hall, 212.
Carvoran, 118, 134, 177, 201.
Castlesteads, 197.
Catton Road, 159.
Cauldron Snout, 157.
Cawfield Mile Castle, 136, 201.
Chesterholm, 135, 138.
Chesters, 201, 208.
Chineley Burn, 139.
Chinese Wall, 184, 202.
Chipchase Castle, 208.
Chollerford, 199, 208.
Christenbury Crag, 113, 114.
Cilurnum, 208.
Coal Cleugh, 158.
Common House, 133, 136.
Coome Crags, 80, 84, 86, 199.
Craggle Hill, 198.
Crag Lough, 135.
Cramel Linn Fall, 72.
Croglin, 52.

DALSTON HALL, 31.
Dean House, 211.
Denton Burn, 211.
——— Fell, 116, 133.
——— Hall, 103.
Devil's Wall, 183.
Dilston Castle, 167.
Drawdykes Castle, 194.
Drumburgh, 185, 188.
Dykesfield, 191.

EAST ALLEN, 159.
Easton, 191.
Eden, 3, 47.

INDEX.

Edward I., 13, 25, 29, 91, 189.
Ellenborough, 204.

FEATHERSTONE CASTLE, 119, 123.
Fisher's Cross, 185.

GARRIGILL, 154, 195.
Gelt, 54, 56.
Gilsland, 59, 200.
—— Church, 63.
—— Chalybeate Well, 70.
—— Sulphur Well, 65.
Glen Dhu, 132.
Glen Whelt, 118, 133.
Graham's Dyke, 183.
Great Chesters, 136, 177, 201.
Greenhead, 126, 129, 130, 133, 200.
Green Lee Lough, 134, 136.
Gretna Green, 40.
Grinsdale, 193.

HALTON CHESTERS, 211.
Haltwhistle, 119, 135.
—— Burn, 136.
Hare Hill, 198.
Harlow Hill, 211.
Harribee Hill, 9.
Hartley Burn, 116, 133.
Hartside, 154.
Haydon Bridge, 138, 145.
Heddon-on-the-Wall, 211.
Hellbeck, 55.
Hexham, 159, 161.
—— Church, 163.
—— Priory, 166.
—— Moot Hall, 167.
High Force, 156.
Highhead Castle, 15, 31.
Holme Cultram Abbey, 33.
Housesteads, 133, 135, 138, 178, 203.
Hyssop Holm Well, 193, 194.

IRTHING, 54, 59, 65, 68, 72, 82, 84, 199.

KING ARTHUR'S HALL, 205.
Kinmont Willie, 17.

Kirk Andrews, 45, 192, 193.
Kirksteads, 193.

LAMBLEY, 116, 132.
Lanercost Priory, 86.
Langley Castle, 151.
Linstock Castle, 32, 195.
Lonning Head, 195.
Lord Lucy, 14.
Lyulph, 12.

MAIDEN WAY, 201.
Mare and Foal, 134.
Martin, John, 146.
Mary, Queen of Scots, 16, 26.
Michael Scot, 37.
Mohope Burn, 158.
Mumps Hall, 75.

NAWORTH CASTLE, 86, 102.
Ned Coulson, 150.
Nent Force, 153.
Nenthead, 153, 154.
Netherby, 43.
Newcastle, 211.
Newtown of Irthington, 197.
Nine Banks, 159.
Nine Nicks of Thirlwall, 136, 201.
North Tyne, 208, 209.
Northumberland Lakes, 133.
Notitia, Imperii, the, 9, 175.
Notterish Hill, 129.
Nunnery, 51.

OLD CARLISLE, 10.
Orchard House, 61.
Oswald, 210.
Over Denton, 64.

PEEL CRAG, 202.
Petrifying Well, 78.
Petteril, 3.
Plankey Mill, 161.
Poltross Burn, 63, 79, 200.
Popping Stone, the, 68.
Port Carlisle, 185.
Procolitia, 207.

RADCLIFFES, THE, 168.
Ridley Hall, 141, 160.
Roman Milestone, 139.
Roman Wall, 79, 136, 172.
Rose Castle, 29.
Runic Cross, 12, 107.
Rutchester, 211.

ST. CONSTANTINE'S CAVES, 47.
St. Cuthbert, 10, 163.
St. Wilfrid, 161.
Saxon Crypt, 166.
Scaleby Castle, 196.
Scotch Dyke, 45.
See of Carlisle, 29, 31.
Sewingshields, 204.
Silloth, 186.
Sir Walter Scott, 68, 75.
Skinburness, 37.
Sockey's Leap, 114.
Solway Moss, 46.
South Tyne, 141, 154.
Stanwix, 193, 194.
Staward-le-Peel, 160.
Stephenson, Robert, 211.
Swinburne Castle, 208.

TALKIN TARN, 54.
Tarraby, 194.
Temple Heap, 74.
Thirlwall Castle, 117, 119, 130, 200.
Tindale Fell, 116.

Tipalt, 200.
Tipper Moor, 207.
Triermain Castle, 104, 105.
Tutman Hole, 153.
Twice Brewed, 133, 134.
Tynemouth, 175, 212.

UNTHANK, 145.
Upper Denton Church, 75.

VALLUM, THE, 179.

WADE, GENERAL, 19.
Walton, 197.
Waltown, 138.
Wallsend, 173, 212.
Walwick, 208.
Wardrew House, 61.
Watling Street, 211.
West Allen, 158.
Wetheral Priory, 46.
—— Village, 50.
White Flat, 197.
Whitfield Hall, 159.
Whitley Castle, 158.
Willimontswyke Castle, 158.
Willowford, 199.
Winshields, 202.
Witch's Cot, 126.
Wolstey Castle, 36, 38.
Written Crag, 56, 197.
Wylie Syke, 74.

LONDON: PRINTED BY EDWARD STANFORD, 55, CHARING CROSS, S.W.

www.ingramcontent.com/pod-product-compliance
Lightning Source LLC
Chambersburg PA
CBHW022052230426
43672CB00008B/1151